MAKING COMMERCIAL
CONTRACTS

MAKING COMMERCIAL CONTRACTS

John Parris

LLB(Hons), PhD

BSP PROFESSIONAL BOOKS

OXFORD LONDON EDINBURGH

BOSTON PALO ALTO MELBOURNE

First published 1988

British Library
Cataloguing in Publication Data
Parris, John
    Making commercial contracts.
    1. Contracts—Great Britain
    I. Title
    344.106′2   KD1554

ISBN 0-632-01862-3

BSP Professional Books
A division of Blackwell Scientific
    Publications Ltd
Editorial Offices:
Osney Mead, Oxford OX2 0EL
    (Orders: Tel. 0865 240201)
8 John Street, London WC1N 2ES
23 Ainslie Place, Edinburgh EH3 6AJ
52 Beacon Street, Boston
    Massachusetts 02108, USA
667 Lytton Avenue, Palo Alto
    California 94301, USA
107 Barry Street, Carlton
    Victoria 3053, Australia

Set by DP Photosetting, Aylesbury, Bucks
Printed and bound in Great Britain by
Billing & Sons, Worcester

Contents

the loss and not merely have been the occasion for it, before damages can be awarded – Damages only for breach of contractual obligation – The duty to mitigate – The duty to mitigate only arises when there has been a breach of contract – Remoteness of damage – Damages for late payment of monies due – Damages fixed by the terms of the contract – How to distinguish liquidated damages from penalties – Specific performance will only be ordered where damages are an inadequate remedy – But specific performance will never be ordered in some cases – Specific performance may be refused in some cases – Injunctions: prohibitive and mandatory.

Restrictive covenants in contracts of employment – Vendors of
businesses – Solus agreements – Horizontal agreements – Agreements to oust the jurisdiction of the courts – Agreements contrary
to the interests of justice – Agreements for trading with an enemy
– Agreements for the procurement of honours – Gaming and
wagering contracts – Agreements induced by duress – Agreements
induced by undue influence – Inequality of bargaining power –
'Economic duress' – The English doctrine of consideration – Past
consideration is no consideration – Consideration need not be
adequate – Forbearance to sue is consideration – Consideration
and the performance of existing duties – Consideration and
existing legal duties – Consideration and obligations to third
parties – Existing contractual obligations – Consideration and the
release of debts – Release of debts at common law – Promissory or
equitable estoppel – Consideration must move from the promisee
– Mistake and its effects on contractual obligations – Mistake as to
the nature of the transaction – Mistake as to the subject matter of
the contract – Mistake as to existing goods (*error in substantia*) –
Mistake as to the ownership of property (*res sua*) – Impossibility at
the time of making the contract – False contractual assumptions –
Mistake as to the identity of the other contracting party.

Preface

There are several good books on the English law of contracts and a host of derivative and bad books. Both categories fail to deal adequately with the real problems experienced by businessmen who enter into contracts. All too often, because of a failure to understand the principles underlying the English law of contract, they find themselves with problems and by the time they have consulted their lawyers, they have all too often prejudiced their position.

This is a book written primarily for businessmen and their advisers in the hope that it will invite them to ask themselves the right questions before they commit their companies to contractual obligations.

Very often, businessmen do not realise they are entering into contractual obligations when they do deals. Even more often, they are careless about the exact status of the other contracting party. The sorry story of the International Tin Council and the shameful repudiation of its obligations by Her Majesty's Government and all the other governments concerned, is a vivid example of this.

Sometimes they enter into obligations which are outside the powers of their companies; and all too often, they make agreements which will not be enforced by the courts. It is hoped that this book will afford some guidance.

It is also hoped that this book will also be useful to law and accountancy students and even to solicitors in practice and in commerce.

John Parris
1987

Chapter 1

The Nature of a Contract

1.01 How contracts can be made

Ask the ordinary man in the street what a contract is and he will probably say 'a piece of paper signed by two persons'. In fact in English law, very few contracts have to be in writing to be enforceable. Those that have to be are dealt with in [2.17].

Binding contracts can be made

(a) *orally*, that is by word of mouth. This is a more accurate expression than the usual term 'verbally'. 'Verbally' means by the use of words; and 'orally' means by spoken words.

(b) *by conduct*. Suppose a man gets on a bus. There is, undoubtedly, a contract between the bus company and the passenger. When and how the contract is made is still a matter of uncertainty in English law. If he gets on a bus going in the wrong direction, does he have to pay the fare? [1.08]. Another familiar example of a contract made by conduct is when goods are taken from a supermarket shelf and are taken to the check-out point.

There may also be contracts in effect made by estoppel [1.11] where the parties are held to contractual obligations because they have behaved in such a way that an objective observer would conclude they had assumed contractual obligations one to the other. This may apply even if one or both deny they had accepted contractual obligations. (Examples are given subsequently [1.11].)

(c) *In writing*, either:
   (i) by exchange of letters, which may incorporate by reference some standard form document;
   (ii) partly by some written document and partly orally, as where a tender is submitted and it is accepted on the telephone;
   (iii) partly by some written document and partly by conduct, as

where a tender is submitted and goods are delivered and
accepted;
(iv) by a formal written contract;
(v) by an even more formal document termed a Deed [1.05].

1.02   What is a contract?

The present writer's great uncle, Sir Frederick Pollock, more than a
century ago, attempted to define a contract as 'a promise ... that the law
will enforce'. Another writer, Anson, defined it as 'a legally binding
agreement made between two or more persons'. A later edition of the book
which still bears Anson's name said 'it is better to eschew the idea of
defining a contract altogether'.

The reason, although Anson's book does not mention it, is that there is
really no such thing as a 'contract'. That is, there is nothing which has a
separate and independent existence apart from the obligations imposed by
the law on persons. It is therefore not strictly correct to speak of 'a
contract' at all, and it is correct only to refer to 'contractual obligations'.
Grammatically, the word 'contract' should be used only as an adjective to
describe a type of obligation imposed by law – never as a noun. Naturally,
it is impossible to define accurately the non-existent, but it is perfectly
possible to describe with accuracy the circumstances in which the law will
impose obligations of the class called 'contractual' on persons.

However, though it may not strictly be semantically correct to speak of
a 'contract', it is a convenient piece of shorthand, and it is now too late,
after judges and lawyers have been referring to 'contracts' for centuries to
seek to establish purity of language. The present author will, therefore,
like all those before him, make use of this familiar but inaccurate
expression, even as he pedantically insists there is no such thing.

To understand this situation correctly it is necessary to go back to the
origins of the matter since, as a leader writer in *The Times* correctly stated,
'the English legal system is medieval with Victorian trimmings'.

Contractual obligations, like all other obligations, are those imposed by
the courts.

1.03   The royal courts and merchants' courts

For many hundreds of years, following the Norman Conquest there were
three sets of courts in England; the feudal ones, held by the feudal lords;
the courts of merchants; and the king's courts. There were a multitude of
these courts such as those of universities, the church, and the Cinque

Ports but these are not relevant to the present topic. The first ones disappeared with the feudal system and have contributed little to the English law of obligations.

Some of the courts of merchants have persisted until recent times. The court of 'Pie Poudre' ('the dusty feet') of Bristol, for example, was only abolished in 1981 and the present author once had a correspondence with its registrar to try to find out to which court an appeal would lie from a decision of the Bristol court of Pie Poudre. The Registrar did not know and nobody else did.

The enforcement of contractual obligations by the King's Court came only late in English legal history. Nearly two thousand years ago the Romans had a highly sophisticated system of contract law, but the author of the book we know as 'Glanvill' could write around AD 1187:

> 'Private agreements are not usually enforced by the Courts of our Lord
> the King ...'

A promise made in solemn form under the seal of the man who made it (usually in relation to the holding of land) might be enforced against him in the King's Court by the Writ of Covenant; but other promises were not. But in the Court of the City of London, a covenant not under seal could be enforced. A merchant therefore could be held to a promise without his seal – but not by an action in the King's Court; not, that is, at common law. Similarly, it was actionable in the City of London Court to call a woman 'whore', but not in the King's Courts.

1.04 What are contractual obligations?

At a time when the inhabitants of the British Isles were painted savages, the Romans had a detailed law of contracts. To them, a contract was a personal legal obligation which came into existence because the parties to it had agreed to accept certain responsibilities or had entered into situations where the law imposed obligations on them. They contrasted obligations of this nature with those which the law imposed on citizens irrespective of their wishes.

That is true of contracts in English law today. They are obligations which are assumed voluntarily, as opposed to those obligations which the law imposes on everybody. Each one of us has a duty not to injure another. It is a duty imposed by law and about that we have no option. If we neglect that obligation the law will enforce it by ordering us to pay compensation (called 'damages') and in cases of deliberate or wanton injury, by punishing us by criminal process.

Nobody is liable on a contract, however, unless he has agreed to accept the obligation, or he has led the other party to believe that he has, or if a reasonable man would conclude that he has accepted it.

The Romans prided themselves that, unlike the Greeks, contracts which were not put in writing but were only oral would be enforced by their law. But in England, for many centuries, no contract was enforceable by the King's Court (though it might be by a local merchants' court) unless it was not only in writing but was also sealed with the seal of the man who had accepted it as a legal obligation. Such a document was (and still is) called a *deed*.

The superstitious reverence which still attaches to deeds – that is, documents under seal – dates back to the days when not even the monarchs could read and write, and the only ones who could were the clergy. In fact, English law for centuries presumed that anybody who could read was ordained. Hence the 'neck verse', Psalm 51, verse 1:

'Have mercy upon me, O God; according to thy loving kindness; according to the multitude of thy tender mercies blot out my transgressions.'

If a man could recite that in Latin, it could save his life, if he were convicted of a capital crime, of which there were no less than 975 in the eighteenth century. He was deemed to be 'entitled to the benefit of clergy' and the King's Courts did not execute the clergy. Women, of course, since they could not possibly be clerics, were not afforded the same privilege. They were hanged.

1.05 Deeds

Deeds were, and are, of two sorts, *indentures* and *deeds poll*. In an indenture, there are at least two parties and the substance of the agreement was written out twice on the same piece of parchment or paper and an irregular line was then cut between the two copies. Each party kept one copy and only these two copies could match up to the line cut between them. That was because our ancestors in these islands, especially the priests, were accomplished forgers. Even a man's seal was no assurance that he had assented to the document; in the days of Elizabeth I there was a shop in Fleet Street which specialised in providing forged seals, including – for fifteen shillings – the Great Seal of England, a seal so sacred that the Lord Chancellor never parted with it, and slept with it under his pillow at night.

A deed poll, by contrast, was executed by one party only and so called because it was 'polled', that is, cut with a straight edge. They were used for recording in a solemn form such things as change of name, so as to provide a permanent record of it; and also for a promise to pay money to somebody else without anything in return for it.

Although the terms are still in use, for all practical purposes the distinction between the two was abolished in 1846 and an indenture may now be a single document executed by all the parties to it.

Building contracts originally were all in the form of indentures and there are many still extant from medieval times written in (bad) Latin or Norman French. We have the very contract for the erection of the tomb of Richard II in Westminster Abbey. It is dated 1394 (though, incidentally, he did not occupy the tomb until 1400).

Here is the beginning of an even earlier one, of 1239, for the building of a wharf on the Thames:

HAEC INDENTURA FACTA INTER DECANUM ET CAPITA-
LUM ECCLESIAE SANCTI PAULI LONDON EX PARTE UNA
ET RICHARDUM COTEREL CARPENTARIUM EX PARTE
ALTERA TESTATUR ...

Translated into English, it is very similar to a deed of today:

THIS INDENTURE MADE BETWEEN THE DEAN AND
CHAPTER OF ST PAUL'S CHURCH, LONDON, OF THE ONE
PART, AND RICHARD COTEREL, CARPENTER, OF THE
OTHER PART, WITNESSETH THAT ...

Many similar contracts – with masons, carpenters, plumbers etc. – still exist, including those for Catterick Bridge (1427), the tower of Walber-wick Church in Suffolk, Eton College Chapel and King's College Chapel, Cambridge. All the great cathedrals were built by similar contracts in the form of indentures.

Often builders had to provide security for due performance in the form of a bond by some third party to pay a fixed sum on default, but in one case for work in the construction of York Minster, the masons contracted to finish the work within the time specified 'on pain of excommunication' – a penalty unlikely to act as much of a deterrent to a modern building contractor.

The covenants, that is, the obligations under those deeds were enforceable by a Writ of Covenant in the King's Court of Common Pleas.

1.06   The action of *assumpsit*

The royal courts would only enforce contract evidenced by deeds. But, as
time passed, three separate royal courts came into existence, the Court of
Exchequer, the King's Bench Court and the Court of Common Pleas.

In those days, and indeed up to the nineteenth century, the judges were
paid by fees and were in brisk competition to attract litigation to their
courts.

The Writ of Covenant had a great number of defects. For one thing, the
only barristers who could appear in the court of Common Pleas were the
Serjeants, who hung around the pillars of the Old St Paul's Cathedral
looking for work, and who were deemed 'brothers' of the judges in the
Court of Common Pleas. They were horrendously expensive.

Secondly, trial in the Common Pleas was subject to the process called
'compurgation' whereby if the defendant could produce eleven persons
who would swear before Almighty God that they believed the defendant on
his oath, he could be exonerated. Needless to say, there were, hanging
around Westminster Hall in which the Court of Common Pleas sat, a host
of compugators, who, for money, were prepared to perjure their immortal
souls.

There were other defects in the Writ of Covenant and in the sixteenth
century the judges of the King's or Queen's Bench Court moved in to pick
up remunerative business from actions about contracts.

Originally concerned with what we would today term 'criminal offences'
the court moved first into the civil business by extending the criminal
offence of 'breach of the King's peace' into trespass to land and trespass to
the person. From that, they went into a whole range of causes of actions by
inventing 'actions on the case'. That is where the injury resulted in damages
which were not direct, as in trespass, but consequential.

From this, the judges developed *'assumpsit'* – a tort action whereby the
plaintiff complained that the defendant had undertaken to do something
but had failed to do it.

To start with, the action could only be where a person had promised to
do something but had done it so badly that he had caused loss to the other
party – what the lawyers to this day call misfeasance. But by the middle of
the sixteenth century, it extended to what lawyers term non-feasance, i.e.
non-performance of the contract.

To succeed, the plaintiff had to prove:

(i)   that the defendant undertook to do something (or, for that matter, not
to do something);

(ii) that the defendant had failed to do it (or had done what he promised
not to do); and

(iii) that he, the plaintiff, had suffered loss in consequence.

It will be observed that the promises were independent of each other so that a separate action and not a counterclaim had to be brought in respect of each alleged breach of an undertaking. To some extent, this was remedied in the eighteenth century as a matter of procedure by two statutes of 'set-off'. A 'set-off' is a right by a defendant to deduct from a sum claimed by a plaintiff money due to the defendant. But although there are references in modern cases by judges to the 'common law right of set-off', the common law never did and never has to this day, given a right to a defendant to set off claims against a plaintiff against claims made by the plaintiff. Judges who talk about the 'common law right of set-off' do not know law still less their legal history.

Even in the eighteenth century, contractual obligations were not regarded as important part of English law, and Blackstone, writing in 1756, devoted only twenty-eight pages to them in his vast work (in contrast to three hundred and eighty pages on the subject of property) and then only to contracts as a means of transferring the ownership of property.

1.07 The *consensus ad idem* theory

English ideas about contractual obligations were therefore in a very uncrystallised state when, in 1805, there was translated into English a massive and comprehensive 'Treatise on the Law of Obligations' written more than forty years earlier in French by Pothier (1699–1772). Few books have had greater influence and it is to be regretted that all reference to this author has disappeared from the latest edition of the Encyclopaedia Britannica.

The English law of contract without Pothier is like Hamlet without the ghost; without him the tortuous evolutions and convolutions of the nineteenth century are barely explicable, but without him, too, there might well have been no play at all.

Unwisely, English theorists and judges accepted many of Pothier's ideas and tried to incorporate them into the English common law; and that in spite of the fact that Pothier had not been writing about the common law at all, but about the type of adapted Roman law that applied in France before the French Revolution. Only in the last decade has our law on contractual obligations begun to free itself from these imported ideas and revert to earlier native concepts.

From Pothier stems the idea that there is no contractual obligation unless the parties had arrived at *consensus ad idem*, once defined as 'a concurrence of intention of two parties, one of whom promises something to the other, who on his part accepts the promise'.

Hence, sentences appear in earlier textbooks to suggest that consensus is essential to a valid contract, e.g.

'if there is no true agreement between the parties ... if the parties are not *ad idem*, there is no contract'.

This concept, however, is now widely recognised as erroneous and obsolete. As Harriman pointed out years ago:

'This consensual theory is insufficient to explain the law of contract. It derives its chief force from the vigour with which two leading English writers have endorsed the theories of continental jurists.'

He referred, of course, to Pollock and Anson. In the vast majority of cases where contractual obligations are assumed in real life, there is nothing remotely like *consensus ad idem*, at least in the sense of complete identity of the minds of the parties on all material terms.

1.08   Are offer and acceptance essential to a contract?

The doctrine of consensus is, however, still not without influence when the effect of mistake on a contract is under consideration. Even here, however, it has been superseded to a large extent by the court looking to see whether it would be fair and equitable to hold a party to obligations he has assumed when he was under a serious mistake at the time when he undertook them.

Linked to the consensus theory is the idea that the agreement is arrived at by a process called 'offer' and 'acceptance' and that these are essential. Unhappily for this theory, there are numerous cases where the courts have held that contractual obligations existed, even though it was impossible specifically to identify anything which could be called an 'offer' or anything which would be called 'acceptance'.

In many other cases, the so-called 'offer' is an entirely artificial concept. What logic is there in the law that when an intending passenger asks at a railway booking office for a ticket to Victoria, that does not constitute an offer but when the railway clerk pushes a piece of pasteboard towards him, that does? As Lord Denning has said:

'In those cases the issue of the ticket was regarded as an offer by the company. If the customer took it and retained it without objection, his act was regarded as acceptance of the offer . . . These cases were based on the theory that the customer, on being handed the ticket, could refuse it and decline to enter into a contract on those terms. He could ask for his money back. That theory was, of course, a fiction. No customer ever reads the conditions. If he had stopped to do so, he would have missed the train or boat.'

In other similarly familiar circumstances, no court has yet said what constitutes the offer in the case of buses. When a bus carries a passenger there can be no doubt that both the bus owners and the passenger have assumed contractual obligations, but the courts have yet to decide exactly when and how.

In a case in 1947, the then Master of the Rolls, Lord Greene, discussed this topic and suggested that the contract was made either when the passenger got himself onto the platform or, perhaps, when he got inside the bus: *Wilkie* v. *L.P. Transport Board* (1947). But this raises interesting and so far unresolved questions as to whether there can be a concluded contract when a passenger gets on a bus believing it is going to Liverpool Street when in fact it is travelling in the opposite way. If he travels two miles in the wrong direction, is he liable to pay the fare?

It is sufficient at the moment to observe that contractual obligations can exist when there is no *consensus ad idem* and nothing that can be specifically identified as an 'offer' and 'acceptance'. Neither can therefore be fairly described, as they are in most elementary text books, as 'essential to a valid contract'.

See also on this topic [6.13].

1.09 Express promises

When Sir William Blackstone, the first Professor of English common law, came to write his masterly treatise in the eighteenth century, before dealing with the action of *assumpsit*, he first described the Writ of Covenant available for promises contained in a document under seal, and then went on:

'A promise is in the nature of a verbal covenant and wants nothing but the solemnity of writing and sealing to make it absolutely the same. If, therefore, it be to do any explicit act, it is an express contract, as much as any Covenant and the breach of it an equal injury.'

The first ground on which contractual obligations are imposed on a person by law is where he has made an express promise.

But not every express promise is enforceable as a contractual obligation and there are numerous promises which the law will not enforce for a variety of reasons, including:

(i)   *Uncertainty* – where the promises were not sufficiently specific to enable a court to enforce them [7.03].

(ii)   *No contractual intention* – where there was no intention to enter into a contractual obligation [7.02].

(iii)   *Without consideration* – because the promise was not made under seal and the man who made it got nothing in return for it. In other words, it was what lawyers term 'a parol promise without consideration' [7.25].

(iv)   *Without contractual capacity* – because there was a want of contractual capacity on the part of the person who made the promise (for example, if he were under 18, and therefore in law a minor, and if the promise were one which the courts will not enforce against minors [4.02].

(v)   *For want of form* – because the promise was one which the law requires to be in a special form, e.g. in writing, and it was not.

(vi)   *For illegality* – because the promise was to do something illegal. No-one would expect the courts to enforce a promise by bank robbers to share the proceeds of their crime equally; though long ago an enterprising highwayman did once try to collect his share of the proceeds through the courts by suing on an unspecified 'agreement' [7.08].

(vii)   *Misrepresentation* – because the promise has been induced by the false statements of the person to whom it has been given [7.37].

(viii) *Mistake* – the courts may in some circumstances also release a person from the obligations of his promise, if it was given because of an important mistake [7.42].

These exceptions are all considered in more detail later.

It must also be pointed out that whereas in common speech, 'a promise' normally means an undertaking to do something in the future, in law there can also be a promise about the condition of a thing or its quality or as to the existence of a present set of facts.

1.10   Implied promises

Blackstone also went on to say that in addition to express contracts (where the promisor has in fact given a promise in words) there were also implied contracts. That is where the party had not in fact made a promise but where the law would impute or ascribe one to him 'such as reason and justice dictate'.

He gave two instances, of which the first was *quantum meruit* (literally, 'as much as he deserves'):

'If I employ a person to transact any business for me or perform any work, the law implies that I undertook to pay him so much as his labour deserves.'

So, if a motorist takes his car into a garage and asks them to mend a puncture, even though he does not expressly say 'I will pay you a reasonable price for your services' the law attributes such a promise to him. Garage owners, like other people, do not work for nothing and there is an implied understanding that they shall be paid for what they do and that this shall be at a reasonable rate – whatever is fair in those circumstances. If, however, a young lady were to suffer a puncture by her roadside and a young man were to appear and mend it for her, there would be no implied promise. The law would not, in those circumstances, impute a promise to her to pay anything, since 'according to the common usages of mankind' as the old books charmingly describe it, such services are normally rendered for nothing, or for such rewards as gratitude alone may suggest.

Similar to this is what Blackstone termed *quantum valebant* (literally,'as much as they were worth').

'There is also an implied *assumpsit* in a *quantum valebant* very similar to the former; being only where one takes up goods or wares of a tradesman without expressly agreeing the price.'

This common law principle has in part now become statutory: section 8 of the Sale of Goods Act 1979 reads:

(i) The price in a contract of sale may be fixed by the contract or may be left to be fixed in a manner thereby agreed, or may be determined by the course of dealing between the parties.
(ii) Where the price is not determined in accordance with the foregoing provision the buyer must pay a reasonable price. What is a reasonable price is a question of fact dependant on the circumstances of each particular case.'

It follows that if two people agree, the one to buy, and the other to sell, a particular article ('a chattel') without naming a price, binding obligations have been assumed on both sides.

But it is otherwise where the purchase and sale is of land or a house, for each piece of land has a unique quality and there is therefore no 'reasonable price' that can be implied. Hence there is no contract, since an essential term – namely, the price – has not been determined [7.08].

1.11   Contracts by estoppel

In modern times the law has imposed contractual obligations where there has been no express promise, in situations where one could not be implied in the way contemplated by Blackstone, and in circumstances where there certainly has been no agreement or anything approaching consensus between the parties.

Serjeant A. M. Sullivan KC (the last of the old Common Pleas serjeants [1.05] was interested in buying a yacht called *The Ailsa*. The owner, a Mr Constable, was selling the yacht 'as she lies', which was well understood in yachting circles to mean that he was making no promises and giving no warranty as to her condition. The buyer had to take her as he found her. But Mr Constable did tell the Serjeant orally that she was ' . . . sound and good . . . and makes no water'. When the Serjeant agreed to buy he sent a cheque to the owner's agents with a letter which read: 'I want to be sure that he (Mr Constable) understands that . . . I rely upon his word and not upon inspection or survey'. The cheque was cashed without comment. The hull of *The Ailsa* turned out to be crumbling from dry rot and Serjeant Sullivan sued Constable and obtained damages for breach of a contract containing a term that the yacht was sound: *Sullivan* v. *Constable* (1932).

Clearly, Constable never intended as a term of the contract of sale to give a promise that the yacht was sound. In fact, he thought he was doing the exact opposite and had made it plain that he intended to sell the boat 'as she lies'. Yet he was held by the court to have assumed a contractual obligation.

The principle of law upon which this decision was arrived is known as 'estoppel'. A person is not allowed to deny the truth of a statement formerly made by him or the existence of facts he has by words or conduct induced another to believe in. It is of much wider application than contract law, but in this sphere, the principle was set out early in the last century by Baron Parke in *Freeman* v. *Cooke* (1848). A man is not allowed to deny the fact (which is what 'estoppel' means) that he had given a promise if he makes a representation which 'he means to be acted upon and it is acted upon accordingly'.

Strictly speaking, the principle of estoppel only applies where four conditions are fulfilled. A man is prevented (or stopped or estopped) from denying the truth of something he has previously asserted if:

(i)   it was an assertion of present existing fact and not of future performance. There cannot therefore strictly be such a thing as estoppel by a promise to do something in the future (although there is now the modern doctrine of 'equitable' or 'promissory estoppel').

(ii) the assertion of fact was intended to be acted upon by the other party to whom it was made.

(iii) it was in fact acted upon by that party.

(iv) that party suffered detriment in consequence of the falseness of the assertion.

Those are the rules of estoppel and a few judges have therefore found technical difficulties in applying the term to the position where a man has behaved in such a fashion as to lead the other party to believe he was giving a promise. They therefore fall back on saying that he is 'precluded by his conduct from denying' that he gave such a promise – as Mr Constable was:

> 'The vendor and his agent, having kept that cheque without comment, the vendor could not be allowed to say that there was no such term in the contract.'

This all comes to the same thing really – a contract by estoppel.

1.12 The objective test for contractual obligations

The question in contracts by estoppel is a subjective one; did one party make a statement which he intended the other to rely upon, and did the other in fact rely on it? More favoured nowadays is a test for contractual obligations which might fairly be termed the 'objective test'.

As an alternative to the situation above, where a man makes a representation he means to be acted on, in *Freeman* v. *Cooke* (1848) Baron Parke also considered a further situation:

> 'If, whatever a man's real intention may be, he so conducts himself that a reasonable man would take the representation to be true and believe that it was meant that he should act upon it and he did act upon it as true.'

Here the test is an external one; what would a reasonable man have concluded? If a reasonable man would conclude that the parties have accepted certain contractual obligations, then the law imposes such obligations on them – whatever their real state of mind:

> 'The law is content with the outward manifestation of agreement and is not concerned whether the parties are really agreed.'

A firm of boilermakers were asked by the defendants to machine certain parts of a malting drum, and, not really wishing to undertake the work, they quoted a very high price of '30 shillings a cwt'. This offer was accepted under the impression that it was '30 shillings a ton'. The defendants, when sued by the boilmakers, contended that there was no express contract since one had meant 30 shillings a cwt, and the other 30 shillings a ton, and therefore there was no agreement and no *consensus ad idem* between them; hence, the defendants' only liability was to pay a reasonable sum – *a quantum meruit* – on the basis of an implied obligation. This argument was rejected by the courts. The plaintiffs, the boilermakers, were entitled to be paid 30 shillings a cwt: *Ewing and Lawson* v. *Hanbury & Co.* (1900). Clearly there was the outward manifestation of agreement and it was immaterial that there was no real consensus. As an earlier edition of *Cheshire and Fifoot on Contract* put it:

> 'The parties are to be judged not by what is in their minds, but by what they have said or written or done.'

Or, as Lord Denning put it:

> 'Once the two parties, whatever their inmost states of mind, have to all outward appearances agreed with sufficient certainty in the same terms on the same subject matter, then the contract is good.'

What he really meant was that the law will allow neither party in those circumstances to deny that they have assumed those contractual obligations.

1.13   A definition of contractual obligations

It is now possible to summarise the nature of contractual obligations and, perhaps, with great hesitation, to put forward a definition of a contract.

Situations where contractual obligations have been found by the court to exist include:

(i)   where there is an express promise intended to have legal consequence;
(ii) implied promise: where there is no express promise but the law will imply such a one as justice requires;
(iii) no promise but estoppel, where a person is precluded from denying that he has given a promise;
(iv) where a reasonable man would conclude a promise had been given

and, again, where a person is precluded from denying that he has given a promise;

(v) where the law, as a matter of business convenience, imposes the obligation – as, for example, in the contracts by post situation.

A fair definition, therefore, would perhaps be to adopt the somewhat satirical words used by the American Judge Learned Hand in *Hotchkiss* v. *National City Bank* (1937):

'A contract is an obligation which the law will attach to certain acts or words of the parties which ordinarily are considered to have a contractual intent.'

And if it be suggested that such a definition is circuitous, it is no more so than any of the other definitions quoted above [1.02].

1.14 The difference between contractual obligations and trusts

In most cases, contractual obligations are imposed by law upon persons as a result of their voluntary words or acts. There are, however, other obligations of a different character which people commonly assume by their voluntary acts or words. These are known as trusts. A trust has been defined as 'an equitable obligation binding a person (called 'the trustee') to deal with property over which he has control ('the trust property') for the benefit of a person or persons ('the beneficiaries') . . . any one of whom may enforce the obligation.'

One of the principles applicable to contractual obligations is that a person who is a stranger to a contract – that is, one to whom the promises were not given – can neither sue on the contract nor be made subject to the obligations of it. That is so even though the contract is made expressly for the benefit of the stranger. For example, Tom and George promise one another to pay £100 each to John. John cannot sue either if they fail to pay him.

But where there is a trust, the person for whose benefit the trust has been created, the 'beneficiary' can sue the persons who have undertaken the obligation of the trust. That is, if Tom and George set up a fund and make themselves trustees of £200, £100 of which each has contributed, for the benefit of John, he can sue them for the money.

The dividing line between contract and trust until recently was disturbingly vague and even now the position is not absolutely clear. However, in general terms, the following may serve to distinguish the two:

(i) There is no trust except where the parties have indicated that it was their intention to create one.

> 'It is not legitimate to import into the contract the idea of a trust when the parties have given no indication that such was their intention': Sir Wilfred Greene, Master of the Rolls in *re Schebsman* (1943).

(ii) There must be a fund or property which is subject to the trust and there is no trust unless the donor acknowledges formally that he holds property in trust or the property has been validly transferred to trustees. Even a valid contract to create a trust does not give a right of action to the person intended to benefit; he can only sue when property has become subject to the trust.

(iii) If there is a trust, the parties who have created it cannot later vary it by agreement between themselves, whereas in all contractual situations the parties can alter the terms by agreement whenever they wish, and even cancel the obligations or rescind the contract if they so desire.

There is also a further class of obligations from which it is important to distinguish contractual ones. Confusingly, these are called 'quasi-contractual' obligations.

1.15   Quasi-contractual obligations

The term 'quasi-contractual' obligations derives from the Roman law expression *obligatio quasi ex contractu*. But, as often happens when a Latin expression is adopted into English law, a completely different meaning is attached to it. In Roman law, if a storm blew off the roof of your neighbour's house while he was away from home and you, uninvited but as an act of charity, spent money in putting a tarpaulin over it thus protecting his property, you could recover your expenses from him *quasi ex contractu*. English law, however, apparently thinks nothing of charitable acts, and in similar circumstances no such expense could be recovered from your neighbour – not even if he promised later to reimburse you [7.26].

The English so-called 'quasi-contractual obligation' is quite different, and the only possible justification for the use of the term is that one theory of the origin of these obligations, current as late as 1914, was that they rested on a notional promise. This theory, for which there was some historical foundation, is not now generally accepted and it would be more appropriate to refer to this class as 'the equitable obligation of restitution and recompense'.

For example, if I owe Harry some money and by mistake pay it to his twin brother Tom, there is no contractual obligation on Tom to repay me; yet it is obviously unfair that he should be allowed to retain it. It is an 'unjust enrichment' for which equity will impose on Tom an obligation to restore. As Lord Mansfield said in 1760:

' ... It lies for money paid by mistake; or upon a consideration which happens to fail; or for money got through imposition (express or implied) or extortion; or oppression; or an undue advantage taken of the plaintiff's situation, contrary to the laws made for the protection of persons under those circumstances.'

In other words, the gist of this kind of action is that the defendant, upon the circumstances of the case, is obliged by the ties of natural justice and equity to refund the money.

A rather startling extension of this doctrine was made by the Court of Appeal when it held that a man who, believing himself to be the owner of a damaged car which, in fact, had been stolen, spent £226 repairing it, was entitled to recover this sum from the true owner before the car was returned to him: *Greenwood* v. *Bennet* (1972).

There are also what are termed 'fiduciary obligations' which may arise where there is no formal trust but equity will impose obligations similar to those of a trust. Directors of a company are under such an obligation to the company.

1.16 The difference between contracts and torts

The distinction between a tort and a contract lies in the fact that:

(i) in contract, the obligation is imposed by law only as the result of an act or words by the persons concerned, whereas in tort the obligation is imposed by law on everybody, even though liability may only be incurred when some act is done or some words uttered; and

(ii) in contract, the duty lies only to a specific person or persons, whereas in tort it lies towards everybody.

Often in practice it is difficult to distinguish between the two, and indeed the same act may be both a tort and a breach of contract [5.01]. For example, a fare-paying passenger may be able to sue for an act of negligence which is a breach of the general duty to take care (i.e. a tort), which act is also a breach of the obligation to take care assumed contractually.

The distinction between contract and tort, however, is of practical importance for the following reasons:

(i)   The measure of damages recoverable for tort (at least for a deliberate one) is greater than for a breach of contract.

(ii) The right to an action starts in contract when the breach takes place, not when the loss is suffered; whereas in tort (apart from trespass) the cause of action arises when damage results, not when the wrongful act was done. So that although the Limitation Act of 1980 provides for the same period of limitation of right of action, namely six years, for 'actions founded on simple contract or tort', those six years may expire earlier in a claim based on breach of contract than for a claim based on tort. Under the Latent Damages Act 1986, whenever the cause of action arises, the plaintiff has three years from the date when he knew he had a cause of action or could with reasonable diligence have discovered one, to bring the action before it is statute-barred. The action also imposed a 'long-stop' period of fifteen years from the wrongful act of default.

(iii) A claim for damages arising out of a breach of contract can be proved for in a bankruptcy, whereas a claim arising out of tort usually cannot be. This means that for a breach of contract a dividend may be recovered, whereas in tort it may not be.

(iv) A contractual right, including a right of action arising out of a breach of contract, can usually be assigned to another person, whereas a right of action arising out of a tort cannot be.

(v)   A person under 18 ('a minor') may be liable at almost any age for his torts, whereas he is not liable on contracts except in special circumstances.

There are also important differences in procedure in actions in the courts.

Chapter 2

Types of Contracts

2.01 Unilateral and synallagmatic contracts

Basically all contractual obligations may be divided into two kinds: unilateral and bilateral. The latter is sometimes termed 'synallagmatic', since there may well be more than two parties to a contract.

If the reader does not know the word 'synallagmatic', can't find it in the dictionary and considers it 'gratuitous philological exhibitionism', he will not be alone. The word was but recently imported into the English language by Lord Diplock from the French Civil Code. A synallagmatic contract is a contract of mutual obligation – a situation, in fact, where all the parties are subject to contractual obligations.

A unilateral contract, on the other hand, is the situation where only the man making the promise is under a contractual obligation. If I promise £1,000 to you should you swim the Irish Channel, that creates no contractual obligation on you to do so – not even if you express to me your intention of performing the feat. But should you do so, I am obliged by law to pay to you the £1,000.

'Under contracts which are only unilateral (the "if" contracts) ... the promisor undertakes to do or to refrain from doing something on his part if another party ("the promisee") does or refrains from doing something. But the promisee does not himself undertake to do or refrain from doing that thing. The commonest contracts of this kind in English law are options for good consideration to buy or to sell or to grant or take a lease, competitions for prizes ...'

'In its more complex and more usual form, as in an option, the promisor's undertaking may be to enter into a synallagmatic contract with the promisee ...'

'It never gives rise to any obligation on the promisee to bring about the event by doing or refraining from doing that particular thing': Lord Diplock in *United Dominions Trust* v. *Eagle Aviation* (1968).

In the synallagmatic contract which, of course, is the more common variety, and the one in which the fact of agreement may well be a material factor, all the parties are under contractual obligations.

'Each party undertakes to the other party to do or refrain from doing something and in the event of failure to perform his undertaking, the law provides the other party with a remedy': Lord Diplock.

2.02 A practical example of a unilateral contract

As has been seen [1.14], in English law if two parties enter into contractual obligation to one another to confer a benefit on a third party, that third party cannot sue to get that benefit. In *Scruttons Ltd* v. *Midland Silicones Ltd* (1962) a drum of chemicals was shipped from New York to London on a bill of lading, that is a contract between the shipper and the carrier. That contract limited liability by the carrier to the sum of US$500. The carriers had a separate contract with stevedores for the discharge of their vessel and that contract had a similar limitation clause. Damage was done of £593 and the shippers, who were of course in no contractual relationship with the stevedores, sued them in negligence for this sum. The House of Lords held that they could recover.

In exactly the same situation in the Privy Council case of *The Eurymedon* (1975), the bill of lading contained the words that

'it is hereby expressly agreed that no servant or agent of the Carrier (including every independent contractor from time to time employed by the Carrier) shall in any circumstances whatsoever be under any liability whatsoever to Shipper, Consignee or Owner ... and every exemption ... herein contained ... shall also be available and shall extend to protect every such servant or agent ... and for the purpose ... of this clause the Carrier is or shall be deemed to be acting as agent or trustee for the benefit of all persons who are or might be his agents from time to time (including independent contractors).'

This clause has come to be known as *The Himalaya* clause since it originated as a result of a passenger's action for injuries suffered on board the P & O cruise ship of that name.

This time, the Privy Council upheld the protection afforded by the bill of lading to stevedores, on the ground that the bill of lading contained a promise to the world at large that if stevedores should discharge the cargo described in the bill they would be relieved of all liability. That is, there came into existence a contract between the shipper and the stevedore.

Lord Wilberforce said:

'The Bill of Lading brought into existence a bargain initially unilateral but capable of becoming mutual between the shippers and the stevedores ... This became a full contract when the stevedore performed services by discharging the Goods ...'

He quoted Lord Justice Bowen in *Carlill* v. *Carbolic Smoke Ball Co.* (1893):

'Why should not an offer be made to all the world which is to ripen into a contract with anybody who comes forward and performs the conditions?'

This case was decided only by a majority of three to two and on the basis of this very specious argument by Lord Wilberforce. There was no evidence before the court that the stevedore knew of the terms of the bills of lading and if there were a direct unilateral contract between the shipper and the stevedores made thereby, why did the carriers have to contract as 'agents and trustees'? And what if it is the consignee or subsequent owner of the goods who sues the stevedores in negligence? He cannot surely be held to have made an offer to the world at large? (See also [2.04].)

There was a very powerful dissenting opinion delivered by Lord Simon who agreed with the New Zealand Court of Appeal that there had never been an offer to the world at large. He said there were two sorts of unilateral contracts:

'A says to B "If you will dig over my kitchen garden next Tuesday, I will give you £2". B replies "Agreed. If I dig over your kitchen garden next Tuesday I will get £2 from you".

'In the second type A may say to B "If you dig over my kitchen garden next Tuesday, I will pay you £2". B does not verbally communicate his acceptance of the offer but does dig over A's kitchen garden.'

The other dissendent in the Privy Council was the late Lord Dilhorne (formerly Mr David Maxwell-Fyffe). On this occasion he was both brief and to the point.

'The clause does not ... either expressly or impliedly contain an offer by the shippers to the carriers to enter into one agreement whereby if the appellants performed services in relation to the goods, the shippers would give them the benefit of every exemption from and limitation of liability (clause) contained in the Bill of Lading.'

In *The New York Star* (1980), the Privy Council departed from the unilateral contract argument and Lord Wilberforce simply said:

'In the normal situation involving employment of stevedores by carriers, accepted principles enable and require the stevedore to enjoy the benefit of contractual provisions in the Bills of Lading.'

2.03 Problems with unilateral contracts

The nature of unilateral contracts has been discussed earlier [2.01]. There are various problems about them which now fall for discussion. The solutions to such problems are not helped by the persistent tendency of textbook writers, following the nineteenth century judges, to treat the promise in a unilateral contract as the same thing as 'the offer' of a synallagmatic one.

Logically they are quite different. If a man says to a girl 'I will give you £10 if you dye your hair blonde by Thursday' that means: 'I here and now accept a contractual obligation to pay £10, subject to your doing the thing I require'. There is no obligation on the promisee, of course, to dye her hair.

If, on the other hand, he makes a proposal in the form of an offer of a synallagmatic contract, he is saying: 'I will accept contractual obligation, if you will also accept a contractual obligation'. His offer is strictly conditional on an acceptance by the other, and the assumption of contractual obligations lies in the future. In the first case, there is an immediately binding obligation on the promisor; in the second case there is no binding obligation on the offeror unless and until his offer is accepted. A promise and the offer of a promise are two different things.

So, if the man says 'If you will promise to dye your hair blonde by Thursday I will give you £10', he is making an offer of a synallagmatic contract which only becomes binding if the offeree promises to do the thing asked.

The distinction between the two sorts of contracts may be a fine one, but it is fundamental. For one thing, damages can never be awarded against the promise of a unilateral contract for the simple reason that since he assumes no contractual obligations, he can never be in breach of them: *United Dominions Trust* v. *Eagle Aviation* (1968).

The application of this distinction is of vital importance in other respects. In the first case, that of the unilateral contract where the only obligation is on the promisor, the promisee does not have to communicate in any way with the promisor to obtain the promised sum. All she has to do is to dye her hair or whatever is asked for.

In the second case, that of the synallagmatic contract, there is no contractual obligation on the offeror until not only has his offer been accepted by the other party, but that acceptance has been communicated to the offeror. Then, and only then, does his offer of a promise become a promise.

Most of the problems that have arisen about unilateral contracts can be resolved if this distinction is borne in mind.

2.04 Must the promisee know?

The problems are:

(1) Can the promisee recover the sum promised if he did the act required before the promise was made?
(2) Can the promisee recover the sum promised if he did the act required in ignorance of the promise?

These two problems are closely related. If the promise of a unilateral contract is equated to the offer of a synallagmatic contract, obviously a man cannot accept an offer which has not been communicated to him. And it would appear to be essential that the act must be done at the request of the promisor and therefore after the promise has been made.

It is for this reason that the decision in the case of *Gibbons* v. *Proctor* (1891) has been so hotly assailed over the years. The defendant, a parson, had printed a handbill offering a reward for information leading to the criminal prosecution of a person who had committed a crime. The plaintiff, before he had seen this handbill and, apparently, before he knew that a reward was offered, provided information which led to the conviction of the person who had committed the crime. It was argued on behalf of the defendant that the plaintiff was in no way influenced by the offer of the reward as he did not even know of it. In spite of that fact, he succeeded in being awarded the reward. The same principle is also to be found in the earlier case of *Smith* v. *Moore* (1845) and has been followed in several United States cases; so much so that a leading textbook in that country sees no obstacle to the creation of a principle that 'where an offer has been published, that act empowers others to create contractual relations by doing the act requested even though without knowledge of the request': *Corbin on Contracts*, Vol. 1. Sec. 59, p. 245.

If you substitute the word 'promise' for the word 'offer', that is an acceptable proposition in view of the present author. There is nothing in law, morality or justice that requires that a man should know of a promise before he can recover for doing the very thing the promisor required. Indeed, the exact opposite is true. If the promisor was prepared to pay for information, and gets what he wanted, why should he be allowed to escape from his contractual obligation on a technicality?

However, one thing is clear. A unilateral contract must require some act by the promisee. If it is money to be paid on the happening of a certain event only, it is a conditional gift and not a unilateral contract. 'I will give you £10 if there is an earthquake tomorrow' is not a contract at all, but a promise without consideration, a conditional gift, because it requires no action from the promisee. So the promisee cannot recover the £10, even if there is an earthquake because he has done nothing to procure it. But, of course, the same promise in a synallagmatic contract, such as an insurance contract where the promisee has provided consideration for the promise would be enforceable.

2.05   Can the promisor withdraw?

A much more difficult problem is whether the promisor can withdraw his promise before the promisee has completed his performance. And related to that is yet another problem: does the promisor impliedly promise that he will do nothing to prevent the promisee performing the act the promisor requests?

I promise you £100 if you walk from London to York. Am I entitled, as you approach the walls of York, to dash up and say 'I withdraw my promise?' Am I entitled to have every road to York barricaded to prevent you from earning your £100?

If the promise is the same as an offer it is axiomatic that an offer can be withdrawn at any time before it is accepted. But, as we have seen, it is not really that at all. The rational and sensible solution would be to say that in unilateral contracts, there are implied promises by the promisor that he will not withdraw his promise once the promisee has started on the performance of the act required, and that he will do nothing to prevent the promisee performing the act.

For that sensible suggestion there is some authority. As long ago as 1864 Mr Justice Willes said in *Inchbold* v. *Western Coffee*:

'I apprehend that wherever money is to be paid by one man to another upon a given event, the party on whom is cast the obligation to pay is liable to the party who is to receive the money if he does any act which prevents or makes it less probable that he should receive it.'

And, more recently, Lord Denning said in *Ward* v. *Byham* (1956), where a father had promised to pay £1 a week towards the maintenance of an illegitimate child:

'I regard the father's promise in this case as what is sometimes called a unilateral contract, a promise in return for the mother's looking after the child. Once the mother embarked in the task of looking after the child there was a binding contract.'

Earlier the same judge had said the same thing in *Errington* v. *Errington and Woods* (1952). The plaintiff in that case brought an action for recovery of a house. The father-in-law of the defendant had promised her that a house that he owned would be hers if she and her husband paid the mortgage instalments. His Lordship said:

'The father's promise was a unilateral contract, a promise of the house in return for their act of paying the instalments. It could not be revoked by him once the couple entered on the performance of the act ... The father expressly promised the couple that the property should belong to them as soon as the mortgage was paid and impliedly promised that so long as they paid the instalments to the building society they should be allowed to remain in possession. They were not purchasers because they never bound themselves to pay the instalments, but nevertheless they were in a position analogous to purchasers. They have acted on the promise and neither the father nor his widow, his successor in title can eject them in disregard of it.'

Unhappily against these sensible observations, there is the express authority of the House of Lords. In *Luxor (Eastbourne) Ltd* v. *Cooper* (1941), two companies each promised an estate agent £5,000 if he should introduce a person who would buy two cinemas they owned. The estate agent found such a person but, instead of buying the cinemas, the transaction was effected by the purchaser buying the shares in the two companies which owned the cinema. The House of Lords held that the estate agent was not able to recover anything.

'Contracts by which owners of property, desiring to dispose of it, put it in the hands of agents on commission terms, are not (in default of specific provisions) contracts of employment ... No obligation is imposed on the agent to do anything.'

In other words it was a purely unilateral contract.

'Implied terms as we know can only be justified under the compulsion of some necessity. No such compulsion or necessity exists in the case under consideration. The agent is promised a commission if he introduces a purchaser at a specific price ... The agent takes the risk in the hope of substantial remuneration for comparatively small exertion ... A sum of £10,000 (the equivalent of the remuneration of a year's work by a Lord Chancellor) for work done within a period of eight or nine days is no mean reward and is one well worth the risk.'

Most estate agents' contracts, however, are not now unilateral contracts, but synallagmatic ones, for the agent expressly promises amongst other things, to use his best endeavours to sell the property. However, despite this binding authority, which was quoted to him, Lord Justice Goff in *Daulia Ltd* v. *Four Milbank Nominees* (1978) said:

'There must be an implied obligation on the part of the offeror not to prevent the condition becoming satisfied, which obligation ... must arise as soon as the offeree starts to perform. Until then, the offeror can revoke the whole thing, but once the offeree has embarked on performance, it is too late for the offeror to revoke the offer...'

His judgment is likely to be followed by other courts.

2.06 Offer and acceptance

In some contracts of mutual obligation, it is possible to identify an offer by one party and an acceptance by the other which leads to obligations on both. But anybody who has had to read the often voluminous correspondence and minutes of negotiations leading to a contract of the ordinary commercial type will know that frequently it is impossible to isolate any particular moment when one side makes an offer and the other accepts it.

In very simple situations it may, however, be possible. For this purpose, therefore, an offer may be defined as a conditional promise to accept certain contractual obligations provided the other party signifies that he also is willing to do so. And the general rule of law is that, in circumstances where this is applicable, the offer must be communicated to the offeree and there are no obligations on either party until the offeree has communicated his acceptance of the offeror.

'Suppose, for instance,' said Lord Denning in one case, 'that I shout an offer to a man across a river but I do not hear his reply because it is drowned by aircraft flying overhead. There is no contract at that moment. If he wishes to make a contract, he must wait till the aircraft is gone and then shout back his acceptance so that I can hear what he says.'

2.07   Contracts created by inactivity

The idea that there could be an offer by one party's silence and an acceptance by inactivity by the other party, would have been laughed to scorn a few years ago. But this is what the courts have now held in the case of references to arbitration. Very many arbitrations, particularly maritime ones arising out of cargo claims or for demurrage of chartered ships, are started but not followed up.

The law, as stated by Lord Diplock in *Bremer Vulkan Schiffbau etc.* v. *South India Shipping* (1981) and reaffirmed in *Paal Wilson & Co* v. *Partenreederei Hannah Blumenthal* (1983) is that the parties to the arbitration are under a mutual obligation to each other to join in applying to the arbitrator for appropriate directions to end any delay.

However, in *Andre et Cie* v. *Marine Transocean* (1981), the Court of Appeal held that silence and delay in pursuing the arbitration on the part of the claimant constituted an offer to abandon the arbitration, and inactivity on the part of the respondent constituted acceptance of the offer so as to constitute a binding contractual obligation to abandon the arbitration.

This extraordinary proposition appears to have been accepted by the House of Lords in the *Hannah Blumenthal* case (*supra*).

In *The Golden Bear* case (1986), Mr Justice Staughton said

'A contract created by simple inactivity is an odd creature in English law ... but I am bound by the authorities to hold that a contract to abandon an arbitration can be thus made.'

On the facts of that case, he held that the shipowner's conduct over an eight year period had been such as to enable charterers to assume they were offering to abandon the reference to arbitration.

If the respondent knew or believed that was not the case, no acceptance could be inferred. His Lordship said:

'But in cases where the respondent has reasonably not given any thought at all as to whether such an offer was being made, but if he had done, he would have assumed that the claimant was offering to abandon the arbitration, such acceptance can be inferred.'

2.08 Acceptance of offers by post

There is, however, one unusual situation where the law imposes contractual obligations against the will of one of the parties and with neither real nor apparent agreement nor estoppel of any kind to justify it. This is where the offer is made by post and the offeree is expressly invited to reply by post or might be said impliedly to be invited to reply by post. Hence, the contract is completed when the letter of acceptance is posted, not when it reaches the offeror; indeed, the contract is binding even if the letter of acceptance never reaches the offeror. The contractual obligations become binding on both parties even though the offeror may in the meantime have withdrawn his offer.

A Mr Fraser, on 7 July, made an offer to Mr Henthorn to sell him certain houses in these terms: 'I give you the refusal of the Flamank Street property at £750 for fourteen days'.

The very next day, Fraser posted a letter at 1 pm revoking this offer, as he was entitled to do in spite of the promise to keep it open for fourteen days. At 3.50 pm the same day Henthorn posted a letter accepting the offer, and at 5 pm the same day Fraser's letter of revocation was delivered to him. It was held there was a binding contract for the sale of the property, made at 3.50 pm on 8 July when Henthorn posted his letter of acceptance: *Henthorn* v. *Fraser* (1892).

Poor Mr Fraser was therefore saddled by law with a contractual obligation to sell his house, an obligation that he did not want and from which he had expressly withdrawn. The reason for this extraordinary situation is explained in the case of *Household Fire Insurance* v. *Grant* (1879) where the letter of acceptance (a letter of allotment of shares) was never delivered at all but where the unfortunate intended recipient was held liable to pay for shares he didn't then want. Lord Justice Thesiger said:

'The contract ... is usually made when the letter (of acceptance) is posted ... There is no doubt that the implication of a complete, final and absolutely binding contract being formed, as soon as the acceptance of an offer is posted, may in some cases lead to inconvenience and hardship. But such there must be at times in every view of the law ... At the same time I am not prepared to admit that the implication in question will lead to any great or general inconvenience. An offeror may, if he chooses, always make the formation of the contract he proposes dependent on the actual communication to himself of the acceptance. If he trusts to the post he trusts to a means of communication which, as a rule, does not fail ...'

The Post Office in Lord Justice Thesiger's day and in 1892 when Mr Fraser was able to post a letter in Liverpool at 1 pm which was delivered to Birkenhead at 5 pm the same day must have been a very different thing from the Post Office of today. It has been suggested that the theory behind this legal doctrine is that the offeror has expressly or impliedly made the Post Office his agent to receive acceptance on his behalf. It would be interesting to have Mr Grant's views on that subject, as he paid the full price for shares which were then worthless bits of paper.

The only real justification advanced for this doctrine is that it is said to be a matter of business convenience, that is, expediency. It is by no means clear that this will always be the position in English law. Lord Justice Lawton said in a case in 1974:

'the rule does not apply if ... the negotiating parties cannot have intended that there should be a binding agreement until the party accepting the offer ... had in fact communicated the acceptance ... to the other side.'

2.09   Contracts made by telex

In respect of contracts made by telex, two questions arise:

(a) where is the contract made, and
(b) when is the contract made?

In *Entores Ltd* v. *Miles Far East Corporation* (1955), it was held that there was no binding contract until notice of acceptance was received by the person who had made the offer, and that the place when the acceptance was received was the place where the contract was made. This decision was approved by the House of Lords in *Brinkibon* v. *Stahay Stahl* (1983).

2.10   Oral acceptances of written quotations

If a party places an oral order on a written quotation of a supplier, he is bound by all the conditions which the supplier has included in his quotation.

In September 1977, Zambia Steel and Building Supplies Ltd approached James Clarke and Eaton Ltd, regarding the supply of a quantity of glass. They received a quotation on a document which contained in print on the face of it: 'Quotations are made on our terms of business printed overleaf'. Overleaf the terms of business included:

'Disputes on this contract to be settled by arbitration in England, according to English law'.

Zambia Steel sent a purchase order, but continued negotiations about quantities and price. Later, on 2 May 1977, a new quotation was prepared on the same form, and after further discussions, it was orally accepted. The goods were shipped, but were, it was claimed, damaged in transit. A writ for breach of contract was issued by Zambia Steel against James Clarke and Eastern Ltd on 26 August 1983. On 17 October 1984, the defendants moved to stay the proceedings on the ground that there was a valid arbitration agreement.

The Arbitration Act 1975 is mandatory in that where one of the parties to an arbitration agreement is non-domestic, the courts must stay any litigation. Section 7 of the Act, however, provides that: 'Arbitration agreement means an agreement in writing ... to submit to arbitration'.

The Court of Appeal held that the terms of business of James Clarke and Eaton Ltd were terms of the contract and that there was therefore an arbitration agreement in writing. The litigation commenced by Zambia Steel, had to be stayed, pending an arbitration which, in effect, meant that the writ would never be heard.

Therefore, readers should remember that if there is a written quotation, with a multiplicity of conditions, and this is accepted orally, so are all the conditions.

2.11   Agreements 'subject to contract'

Until very recently in England it was established law that if the parties made an agreement 'subject to contract' that was not a binding contract because they had clearly evinced an intention not to be bound until a formal contract had been executed. Particularly was this true in relation to agreements regarding the acquisition of property.

> 'It is everyday practice for intending purchasers of property who are making an offer to make their offer in the form of "subject to contract" with the result that they are not at that time bound and have a *locus poenitentiae* until the formal contracts are exchanged,'

said Lord Justice Mangham in *George Trollope and Sons* v. *Martyn Bros* (1934). (*Locus poenitentiae* means, literally, 'a place for repentance' but is better translated as 'an opportunity for changing the mind'.)

So, it was generally held for many years that if the magic words 'subject to contract' were included in an offer, the parties had clearly intended that there was to be no binding contractual obligations until written contracts were exchanged.

Within recent years, however, it has been held that if the parties in fact agreed all the essential elements in their contract, and then include the magic words 'subject to contract' these words can be meaningless.

It was so held in *Michael Richards Properties* v. *Wardens of St. Saviour's Parish, Southwark* (1975). There the plaintiffs' offer to purchase property was accepted subject to the 'approval of the Charity Commissioners, and subject to contract'. The Charity Commissioners gave their consent, but the purchasers then declined to buy, denying that there was a binding contract. It was held that there was complete agreement between the parties, subject to the consent of the Charity Commissioners, and therefore the words 'subject to contract' were meaningless and could be ignored.

It is impossible to reconcile that decision with *Dutton's Brewery Ltd* v. *Leeds City Council* (1982), a Court of Appeal decision. However, in *Alpenstow Ltd* v. *Regalian Properties Plc* (1985), Mr Justice Nourse interpreted a contract including the words 'subject to contract' as being contractually binding. His argument was that since those words were not used at the start of the negotiations, but from four or five months later, the vendors were bound to supply a draft contract which the purchasers were bound to approve, subject to reasonable amendments. More logical minds might have come to exactly the opposite conclusions. While the parties were negotiating, and proposals and counter-proposals were flying backwards and forwards, there clearly was no agreement. But when an agreement came in sight, four or five months later, there was the time for one of the parties to say 'I agree – subject to contract'.

In *Cohen* v. *Nessdale Ltd* (1981), upheld on appeal (1982), Mr Justice Kilner Brown put forward a more sensible idea. If negotiations started under the 'umbrella' of 'subject to contract' and proceeded to agreement without 'subject to contract' being restated, the umbrella was still over them and there was no binding contract. In that he followed *Tevenan* v. *Norman Brett (Builders) Ltd* (1972).

However, in view of the uncertainty created by the decision of Mr Justice Nourse, and the decision of the Court of Appeal in *Law* v. *Jones* (1973) (although disapproved of by a subsequent Court of Appeal in *Tiverton Estates* v. *Wearwell* (1974)) it is desirable that some more emphatic words should be used to make it clear that there is to be no binding contractual obligation until formal contracts are exchanged.

A good precedent can be found in the Irish case of *Joseph Kelly* v. *Irish Nursery and Landscape Co. Ltd* (1981), where the purchasers' solicitors had written:

'It must be understood that no agreement enforceable at law is made or intended to be created until the exchange of contracts has taken place.'

And, five months later:

'We reiterate that no agreement enforceable at law is made or intended until contracts have been exchanged.'

This was necessary because the previous year, the Irish High Court had held that the inclusion of the words 'subject to contract' by a solicitor constituted an unauthorised addition to the terms agreed by the parties and could be ignored.

Currently, the law in England on this subject is in such a mess, that any businessman who does not want to be bound by an agreement until it is incorporated in a written agreement, should make this abundantly plain, by using words with a similar meaning to those used in the *Irish Nursery* case (*supra*).

2.12   Written contracts

'We just do not need to have a written agreement. We are old friends, we have done business together for years; what do we need to put it in writing for?' was the view of the Vice-president (Marketing) in the Australian case of *Hospital Products Ltd* v. *United States Surgical Corporation* (1984). It was, needless to say, an expensive belief. It has led to a long and expensive action in the Supreme Court of New South Wales, followed by an even longer and more expensive hearing in the NSW Court of Appeal, followed by a vastly longer and more expensive hearing in the Federal High Court of Australia, which, in spite of its name, is the final Court of Appeal in Australia. If appeals to the Judicial Committee of the Privy Council from Australia had not been abolished, it would still be on its way there.

The judges in the High Court were divided five to three and their judgments contain more words than the whole of this book – and they are not so easy to read. The facts of the case are set out, briefly, in [5.04]. Here it may be noted that but for a concession by counsel in the pleadings that there was a contract made partly orally, partly in writing and partly by terms to be implied, the hearings could have been even more prolonged.

All this was on top of other proceedings commenced in August 1980, in the Federal Court of Australia in which USSC, after an appeal by Hospital Products to the High Court of Australia, lost on the grounds that the Federal Court lacked jurisdiction to entertain all the causes of action (see 55 ALJR 120).

Meanwhile, legal proceedings for conspiracy are proceeding at the instance of USSC in New York and there are actions in Connecticut and Texas, including proceedings for infringement of patent.

'What do you need to put it in writing for? We're old friends', must by now have cost USSC many millions of dollars.

2.13   Unwritten agreements

There are practical difficulties in enforcing oral contracts, so much so that many laymen think they cannot be enforced by the courts.

If a judge has no contemporary correspondence or minutes of conversation which enables him to determine who is telling the truth, he is usually astute to determine who is really telling the truth after cross-examination of the parties. An interesting illustration of this is *Harris* v. *Bernard Sunley Ltd* (1986). Mr Harris contended before the High Court that the defendants had agreed to buy his family's minority shareholding in Sunley Leisure Ltd for £500,000. This took place in a telephone conversation between the plaintiff and a Mr Ray Elston, a director of Bernard Sunley Ltd. Mr Justice Whitford held that a binding agreement had been made on the telephone between the plaintiff and Bernard Sunley Ltd, represented by Mr Elston on 16 April 1985.

He described Mr Elston as 'unreliable a witness as I have ever heard ... His attitude was plainly that he would dance to any tune, his chairman, Mr John Sunley, and the Managing Director, Mr John Fryer, were prepared to play.' For reasons of their own, they had decided not to go ahead with the deal.

A nephew of the plaintiff commented after the case: 'Mr Harris has done building work all over Yorkshire for years and has always done business on a handshake. This shows the difference between the northern and southern way. A Yorkshireman's word is his bond.'

Prudent businessmen will conclude that the southern way of doing business is now current in the United Kingdom – and take precautions accordingly. It is wise, therefore, to record in a diary the substance of a conversation at the time and even more prudent to write and confirm all discussions.

2.14 Signed standard contracts

The general rule of law is that a person is bound by a written or printed contract which he has signed whether or not he read it, understood it, or accepted it.

Miss L'Estrange bought a cigarette vending machine from Graucob Ltd under a 'Sales Agreement' which she signed without reading. The agreement was printed on brown paper and in 'regrettably small print' and one term excluded all liability for the condition of the machine. It never did work, but the Divisional Court held that the suppliers were protected by the clause in small print. As Lord Justice Scrutton put it:

'When a document containing contractual terms is signed ... the party signing it is bound and it is wholly immaterial whether he has read the document or not.'

So much for the necessity of consensus, offer and acceptance etc.: *L'Estrange* v. *F. Graucob Ltd* (1934).

If a person signs a document, a reasonable man would conclude that he had, so far as the other contracting party is concerned, accepted all the terms of it.

'The law is clear, without any recourse to the doctrine of estoppel, that a signature to a contract is conclusive',

Lord Devlin has said.

A defendant can say that the terms are unfair and unreasonable, that he never voluntarily agreed to them, that it was impossible to understand or even read them and that if he had tried to negotiate any change the other party would not have listened to him. In vain. He has signed the contract, and a reasonable man would conclude that he had accepted the terms, whether he knew them or not, and the law therefore imposes those contractual obligations on him.

2.15 Contracts of adhesion

The full operation of the principle can be seen in what are today the most common forms of contracts – those where one party, usually a member of the public, has no opportunity of negotiating the terms but must accept or reject those offered by the other party. If you want to buy a new motor car, it is highly probable that you will be allowed to do so only on the terms dictated by the manufacturers. If you want to hire-purchase it, you must most certainly accept the terms offered by the finance companies – or go without. If you want to take a package holiday, go on a cruise or cross the Channel with your car, all you can do is to accept the terms imposed by the other contracting party, often by a piece of paper which, as Lord Devlin aptly put it, is 'the sort of document ... not meant to be read, still less understood'.

Such contracts are sometimes termed contracts of adhesion (from the French, who first recognised them as *contrats d'adhesion*), because one party can only adhere to them or reject them completely. Sometimes they are called 'Standard Form Contracts'.

Often the terms of such contracts are, to put it bluntly, iniquitous. One famous holiday camp will only accept guests on terms that the person who makes a reservation for his family or party undertake to recompense them if it, the camp, has to pay compensation to any member of his family or party injured by its negligence. And a certain car ferry firm only carries cars on terms that the owner is entirely responsible for any damage or injury caused by that car, even if caused by their negligence. And their parent company only carries passengers on cruises under a condition which purports to exclude all liability for all negligence by the company or any of its servants; so that, on the face of it, if a drunken ship's doctor castrates you instead of removing your appendix, you can sue neither him nor the company.

The courts have shown a regrettable lack of courage in dealing with such contracts, on the ground, as Lord Reid put it, that

'the general principle of English law [is] that the parties are free to contract as they may think fit'.

In that, they did not follow the Elizabethan and seventeenth century Court of Chancery which did not hesitate to set aside contracts, such as commodity loans, on the grounds that the terms were unfair. Right up to the middle of the last century cases are to be found in which Equity would grant relief for 'unconscionable bargains'.

However, within recent years the courts have invented a variety of specious excuses for everyday exemption clauses, where an injured party had the financial resources and determination enough to sue.

Several Acts of Parliament have dealt severely with exemption clauses contained in contracts of adhesion. For example, the Transport Act 1962, section 43, provides that so far as the British Railways Board, London Transport Board, British Transport Dock Board and British Waterways Board are concerned, all terms or conditions which purport to exclude or limit the liability to passengers for death or bodily injury shall be 'void and of no effect'.

The Unfair Contract Terms Act 1977 applies the same principles to all contracts which purport to exclude liability for death or personal injuries. It also upholds other limitation of liability clauses where one party enters into a contract on the other's standard form only to the extent that they are 'reasonable'.

Apart from that, the legal position is clear; contracts of adhesion are binding, irrespective of whether both parties accept all the terms or not; but there is some difference between those documents which are signed and those 'common form' documents, such as railway tickets, which are not.

2.16   Unsigned common form documents

With unsigned documents the law is slightly different. Here, the law states that a man must be given reasonable notice that there are conditions annexed to the issue of the document. He need, however, be given no notice as to what the conditions are; apparently, it is enough if he is told there are terms and, if he takes the ticket with that knowledge, he is then bound by those terms.

> 'If in the course of making a contract one party delivers to another a paper containing writing, and the party receiving the paper knows that the paper contains conditions which the party delivering intends to constitute the contract, I have no doubt that the party receiving the paper does, by receiving and keeping it, assent to the conditions contained in it, although he does not read them and does not know what they are.'

In the distant and happier days when issues of fact were decided by a jury, a Mr Parker left a bag in the left luggage office of the South Eastern Railway. For that privilege he paid 2d and received a ticket on the face of which were the words: 'The company will not be responsible for any package exceeding the value of £10'. The bag was lost and Mr Parker claimed its value of £24.10s. The Court of Appeal held that the jury should be directed to answer three questions:

(i)   Did the plaintiff know there was writing on the ticket?
(ii) If he knew there was writing did he know the writing contained conditions?
(iii) Even if he did not know the writing contained conditions, was, in the opinion of the jury, reasonable notice given him that the writing contained conditions? (*Parker* v. *S.E. Railways* (1877).

If the answer to (i) was 'Yes' and either (ii) or (iii) were answered affirmatively, the railway company was protected by the limitation clause.

From being an issue of fact for the jury to decide, over the years the question whether there was reasonable notice or not turned into a question of law, so that by 1923 Mr Justice Swift could say:

'I am of the opinion that the proper method of considering such a matter is to proceed upon the assumption that where a contract is made by the delivery, by one of the contracting parties to the other, of a document in a common form stating the terms upon which the person delivering it will enter into the proposed contract ... if the form is accepted without objection by the person to whom it is tendered this person as a general rule is bound by its contents ... whether he reads the document or not.'

In law and practice, the question has now resolved itself into the simple formula: as far as contractual documents are concerned does the document on the face of it bear the words 'For conditions see back'? If it does, it would appear that reasonable notice has been given that there are conditions and that is sufficient to make them part of the contract.

The effect can be seen in a case of importance. A Mrs Thompson, who could not read, gave her niece the money to buy an excursion ticket from Manchester to Darwen. On the face of the ticket appeared the words 'For conditions see back', and on the back were the words: 'Issued subject to the conditions and regulations in the company's timetables and notices and excursion and other bills'. Mrs Thompson was injured through negligence of the railway company's servants. One condition amongst that multifarious crowd of documents excluded liability to the ticket-holder for injury, however caused.

The jury at the trial found that reasonable notice of the conditions had not been given to Mrs Thompson, but the Court of Appeal reversed this verdict, holding that the fact that a considerable search had to be made before the conditions could be discovered was immaterial:

'The mere circuity which has to be followed to find the actual condition does not prevent a passenger having notice that there was a condition': *Thompson* v. *L.M.S.* (1929).

No attempt has been made in any of the long line of judgments to justify this position on the basis of principle and the only grounds on which these decisions can be upheld is that a reasonable man would conclude that a person who accepts such a ticket must be taken to indicate to the other that he accepts all the conditions whether he knows of them or not, and is therefore precluded from denying it. Apparently, according to Chitty, the leading textbook on contract law:

> 'It is immaterial that the party receiving the document is under some personal, but non-legal disability such as blindness, illiteracy, or an inability to read our language.'

But what if that disability was in fact known to the other contracting party? On this point there is as yet no decision of the courts and it is one of the debating points that examiners at degree level delight in asking students.

And what if the conditions annexed by reference are totally unreasonable? What if, for example, the condition in Parker's case had included a term that if he left his bag in the left luggage office for more than twenty-four hours, he should have to pay the railway company £10,000. One of the judges in the Court of Appeal in Parker's case was prepared to hold that such a condition would not be binding, on the ground that there was an unexpressed and unwritten term that none of the unknown conditions would be unreasonable. But in none of dozens of the 'ticket-cases' as they are called, has any condition been held void because it was unreasonable. And, surely, for a cruise company or a railway company to exclude all liability for their own negligence might well be considered by some people as utterly unreasonable: as would a motor car manufacturer who disowned all liability in law for a vehicle he had just manufactured and allowed an innocent purchaser to put on the road. Yet both are the sort of exemption clauses which have repeatedly been held binding.

In 1956, Lord Justice Denning, as he was then, was prepared to hold that the more unreasonable the condition, the greater notice must be given of its existence.

> 'Some clauses which I have seen would need to be printed in red ink on the face of the document with a red hand pointing to it before the notice could be held to be sufficient.'

And in 1970, as Master of the Rolls, he seems to have been able to persuade a Court of Appeal to agree that what is necessary before a term can be part of the contract is not merely reasonable notice that there are conditions, but reasonable notice of the condition exempting from liability. As Lord Justice Megaw said:

> 'The question here is of the particular condition on which the defendants seek to reply and not of the conditions in general.'

This is a recent trend and a radical departure, which of course undermines the force of the decision in *Thompson* v. *L.M.S.* and if reasonable notice must, in fact, be given of the exempting clauses, it would appear that the blind and those who do not speak our language may well not be bound by notices they cannot read.

It may, however, be doubted whether these observations by Lord Denning and Lord Justice Megaw are a binding part of the decision in the case which follows in which they were spoken: *Thornton* v. *Shoe Lane Parking Ltd* (1971).

The plaintiff, a 'trumpeter of the highest quality', parked his car in a multi-storey car park in the City of London, where there was no attendant. Having driven his car to a barrier, a ticket was issued by a machine and bore the words: 'This ticket is issued subject to the condition of issue displayed on the premises'. The conditions of issue were, needless to say, only visible in another part of the garage, and after the ticket had been issued, one of them, buried away under a mound of verbiage, included a clause excluding liability for injury to the customer. The trumpeter was injured partly through the company's negligence.

The point of the case, as it has been in others of this nature, is whether the liability clause was a term of the contract; and the decision was that the time when the contract was made was when the ticket popped out of the machine, so that the conditions on the notice formed no part of the contract. As Lord Denning said, none of the earlier ticket cases had any application to a ticket issued by an automatic machine.

'The customer pays his money and gets his ticket. He cannot get the money back. He may protest to the machine, even swear at it; but it will remain unmoved. He is committed beyond recall.'

His Lordship seems not to know how an automatic car park works, because of course the plaintiff did not in fact pay his money before he got his ticket, but would have paid when he left the car park, but that is perhaps not material to the real basis of the decision. The contract was completed when the ticket popped out of the machine. Why? Because the Court of Appeal decided that it was. In other words, in this particular case, it was held that the motorist made the offer by driving up to the machine and his offer was accepted by the emergence of the ticket. Contrast the railway ticket cases where it is the booking clerk who makes the offer by pushing a piece of pasteboard towards the traveller.

2.17   Contracts must be evidenced in writing

From the time when the action of *assumpsit* made its appearance on the English legal scene, no special requirements were necessary to make a promise enforceable by an action. A promise made orally was as effective as one made in writing. As time has passed, however, Parliament has enacted that an increasing number of contracts have to be made in special form, usually for the protection of one of the parties.

The first enactment of this nature was the Statute of Frauds 1677 which originally required six classes of contracts to be put in writing before they were enforceable. All but one part of that enactment – that relating to contracts of guarantee – have since been repealed or re-enacted in other legislation.

What was the position if a contract was not in writing when the Statute of Frauds required it to be? For many years, judges took the view that the contracts were void and as late as 1837, for example, Lord Abinger was saying in *Carrington* v. *Roots*:

> 'The meaning of the Statute is not that the contract shall stand for all purposes except being enforced by action but it means that the contract is altogether void.'

But by 1852 in *Leroux* v. *Brown,* the judges were holding that the meaning of the Statute was the exact opposite of that attributed to it by Lord Abinger, namely that the contracts were not void but unenforceable. In other words, 'the contract shall stand for all purposes except being enforced by an action at law'.

2.18   Contracts relating to land

The effect can be seen by reference to one of the Statutes which replaced part of the Statute of Frauds, section 40 of the Law of Property Act 1925. For convenience of commentary later it is set out in separate lines:

'No action may be brought upon any contract
for the sale or other disposition
of land
or any interest in land
unless the agreement upon which such action is brought
or some note or memorandum thereof is in writing

signed
by the party to be charged
or by some other person thereunder by him lawfully authorised.

(1) 'No action may be brought upon any contract'

(a) the contract is perfectly good for every other purpose except being
sued upon. For example, if a deposit is paid on an oral contract, the
deposit can be retained. Fry gave Low a cheque for £450 as a deposit on
a contract relating to land which was not in writing. Fry repudiated the
contract and stopped the cheque. Low was able to sue successfully on the
cheque: *Low* v. *Fry* (1935).
(b) If this defence provided by section 40 of the Law of Property Act is
relied upon, it must be specifically pleaded and set up by the defendant.
If not, the court will ignore the absence of writing.
(c) It is not necessary for the written evidence to be in existence when the
contract is made; if it comes into existence before the case is heard, the
statute is complied with.
(d) Any writing with sufficient details, even in separate documents which
can be connected, will provide sufficient evidence to support an action.

(2) 'for the sale or other disposition'

Mortgages, leases – even leave to enter and take a cutting of grass (but
apparently not cultivated crops) have been held within these words.

(3) 'land'

In English law, land includes not only the soil and the buildings on it but
the air above and the minerals beneath – 'up to heaven and down to hell'
as the ancients put it.

(4) 'or any interest in land'

This includes shooting rights, partnership in a colliery, and a building
which has been purchased for the purpose of demolition. (Incidently,
apparently, some things can be 'land' for the purpose of this section and
'goods' for the purposes of the Sale of Goods Act 1979.)

(5) 'unless the agreement upon which such action is brought'

The distinction between an agreement and a memorandum is that an agreement contains all the terms of the contract.

(6) 'or some note or memorandum thereof is in writing'

This has not been defined by Statute but the courts have held that the necessary details must include:

(a) the identity of the parties
(b) the subject matter of the contract
(c) the consideration
(d) any special term, e.g. as to the date of possession. But there is a doctrine that if a material term has been omitted from the writing and it is exclusively for the benefit of the plaintiff, he can waive it and still enforce the contract.

The note or memorandum does not have to have been in the same documents and in *Stokes* v. *Whicher* (1920), the vendor's agent signed a carbon copy of a contract which contained no purchaser's name, a receipt for a cheque was given on the carbon copy, the cheque existed and there was a top copy of the contract signed by the purchaser. The courts held there was sufficient memoranda.

But a different situation existed in *Timmins* v. *Moreland St. Property Co. Ltd* (1957). At a meeting between the parties, the defendant company agreed to buy property for £39,000. They gave the plaintiff, who was the sole surviving trustee of an estate, a cheque for £3,900, drawn in favour of his employers, Messrs. Holt, Beever and Kinsley, Solicitors. Timmins gave a receipt: 'Received of Moreland Street Property Co. Ltd, the sum of £3,900 as a deposit for purchase of Nos. 6, 8 and 41 Boundary Street, Shoreditch, which I agree to sell for £39,000'.

Because the only document signed by 'the party to be charged' i.e. the defendants, was the cheque and that could not be connected with the plaintiff's receipt, it was held there was insufficient evidence to satisfy the statute. Had the cheque been drawn in favour of Timmins instead of his employers, there would have been internal evidence sufficient to link all the documents.

It should be noted that even a letter of repudiation can amount to sufficient evidence for the purpose of section 40 of the Law of Property Act 1925. So if you make an oral agreement to sell your house and you write to the proposed buyer: 'Dear Mr Buggins, I know I promised to sell you my house for £5,000 but I've changed my mind and as there is no contract in writing there is nothing you can do about it' and you sign the letter and address the envelope to him – you have provided all the memoranda necessary for an enforceable agreement.

(7) 'signed'

The signature does not need to be at the end of the memoranda; it does not have to be in full – initials alone are sufficient – and even a printed name may amount to a signature.

(8) 'by the party to be charged'

This is always the one sought to be held liable on the contract – in other words, the defendant. So, a plaintiff who has signed nothing can hold a defendant who has signed sufficient memoranda liable. Timmins would have been liable in the case mentioned above, though the contract was unenforceable against the company.

(9) 'or by some other person thereto by him lawfully authorised'

The person authorised as agent does not have to be authorised in writing, and auctioneers, for example, are authorised by law to sign memoranda for the purchaser (as well as the vendor). So if you go to an auction and bid for property which is knocked down to you, it is no good thinking you can escape by refusing to sign the agreement. The auctioneer is empowered by law to sign on your behalf, so long as he does it in the auction room or elsewhere within a reasonable time afterwards.

2.19   The equitable doctrine of part performance

The Statute of Frauds which first imposed this obligation was passed in 1677, in the reign of Charles II. Within eight weeks of the Act coming into force, however, the Court of Chancery had specifically enforced an unsigned contract for the sale of land.

'Equity,' it was said, 'would not allow a statute to become an instrument of fraud' and so came into existence the remarkable doctrine that, in spite of the Statute, even when there is no memorandum in writing as required, the contract was still enforced by the courts if there is an act of part performance. The Law of Property Act 1925, sections 40(2) and 55, has expressly preserved this equitable doctrine.

It is applicable under the following conditions:

(i)   If the contract is of such a nature that it would have been enforceable by the Court of Chancery, i.e. where the conditions for specific performance [3.01] apply.

(ii) Where the circumstances are such that it would be a fraud on the part of the defendant to take advantage of the contract not being in writing.

(iii) The act of part performance must be of such a nature that it proves the existence of some contract between the parties. Earlier law suggested that it had to prove the specific contract alleged and none other. The modern law was set forth in *Kingswood Estate Ltd* v. *Anderson* (1962), where the defendant was the rent-controlled tenant of a house owned by the plaintiffs. To get her out of the premises, the plaintiffs orally promised that if she would move into one of their flats elsewhere, she should have it for her lifetime. They thereby got her to surrender her protected tenancy. She moved into the new flat and they then gave her notice to quit. She didn't go, so the plaintiffs sued her for possession. The Court of Appeal held that 'the acts of part performance must themselves suggest the existence of a contract ... although they need not establish the exact terms of that contract'. She was therefore able to stay.

A widow gave up her council house to go and look after an elderly man in reliance on his oral promise that he would leave her his house when he died. The court held that was sufficient act of part performance to establish that there had been some contract between the parties and, that being so, they could then receive oral evidence as to the terms of the contract: *Wakeham* v. *McKenzie* (1969). Other things which have been held to be part performance have been alterations to a flat to meet the wishes of the defendant, *Rawlinson* v. *Ames* (1925), and giving notice to an existing tenant, *Daniells* v. *Trefusis* (1914).

The receipt of money can never be an act of part performance because there may be a thousand explanations other than a contract for that; but where one party is found in possession of property belonging to another with the other's consent, the implication that there is a contract between the two is very strong.

But if the alleged act of part performance is explicable on grounds other than the existence of a contract between the parties – as where a housekeeper stayed on without pay after the expiration of her contract. *Maddison* v. *Alderson* (1883), or a daughter went to live with an aged father, *N.P. Bank Ltd* v. *Moore* (unreported) – then there is no part performance.

Equity may also enforce a contract which should be evidenced by writing if the defendant has promised to put it in writing but fraudulently has not done so. 'If there was an agreement for reducing the same into writing and that is prevented by the fraud and practice of the other party' – as where instructions were given for the preparation of a marriage settlement but before it was executed the woman was induced to marry the man – then Equity could be prepared to enforce the agreement even if there were no document in writing: *Maxwell* v. *Lady Mountacute* (1720).

2.20 Contracts of guarantee and contracts of indemnity

The one extant part of the Statute of Frauds 1677 is section 4 which now reads:

> 'No action shall be brought whereby to charge the defendant upon any promise to answer for the debt, default or miscarriage of another person unless in writing and signed by the parties to be charged.'

Cases have decided that 'default or miscarriage' means promises to be responsible for the torts of others; and that this only applies to contracts of guarantees – and not contracts of indemnity. The difference between the two was aptly described by Lord Justice Harman as 'a most barren controversy which has raised many hair-splitting distinctions of exactly the kind which brings the law into hatred, ridicule and contempt with the public': *Yeoman Credit* v. *Latter* (1962), the case that decided that contracts of indemnity for infants' hire purchase contracts were enforceable.

The difference between a guarantee and an indemnity was described in the leading case of *Birkmyr* v. *Darnell* (1704):

> 'If two came to a shop and one buys and the other, to gain him credit, promises the seller "If he does not pay you, I will" ... that is a guarantee and unenforceable without being in writing. But if he says: "Let him have the goods, I will see you are paid" ... that is an indemnity and enforceable without writing.'

It is a guarantee, therefore where:

(i)   the principal debtor is primarily liable – and the guarantor only if he doesn't pay;

(ii) the principal debtor always remains liable;
(iii) the promise is given direct by the guarantor to persons giving credit.

2.21   Other contracts that need to be in writing to be enforced

(1) Solicitors' non-contentious work

It has been held in *E.T.U.* v. *Tarlo* (1964), that agreements between
solicitors and their clients relating to remuneration for non-contentious
business must be in writing to be enforceable; but that agreements
relating to contentious business – such as litigation – do not have to be.

(2) Apprentices

By the Apprentices Act 1914, section 6, all contracts of apprenticeship are
required to be in writing; normally in practice they are often made by
deed.

(3) Moneylending contracts

By the Moneylenders Act 1927, section 6, all moneylending contracts
must be in writing and contain the details specified by that Act.

(4) Marine insurance

By the Marine Insurance Act 1960, all insurances of losses resulting from
marine adventure have to be in writing and contain the details required by
that Act.

(5) Bills of sale

By the Bills of Sale Act 1878 (Amendment) Act 1882, all bills of sale
whether absolute or by way of security have to be registered at the Central
Office of the High Court within seven days of execution and have to be in
writing, containing the details required by the Act.

(6) Bills of exchange and promissory notes

Bills of exchange and promissory notes must be in writing – although not necessarily on paper as in A.P. Herbert's amusing fable about the man who wrote a cheque on a cow.

2.22 Consumer credit transactions

The Hire Purchase Acts 1938–1965 – now largely repealed and replaced by the Consumer Credit Act 1974 and subsequent enactments – introduced specific and detailed requirements as to the form in which agreements for hire purchase, conditional sales and credit sales have to be made. Consumer credit transactions are outside the scope of this book and now form a complex and involved subject, covered by another book in this series and written by an expert: *Consumer Credit* by Graham Stephenson (1987).

2.23 Jurisdiction clauses

A clause in an international contract which confers exclusive jurisdiction on a particular court or a state has to be in writing as a result of Article 17 of the Brussels Convention of 27 September 1968 on the Enforcement of Judgments. However, if the parties enter into a written agreement and then continue dealing on the same terms after it has lapsed it will be held to be complying with the Convention.

Fiat SPA entered into an agreement with Van Hool N.V. in December 1956 for one year. On 1 January 1958 another agreement was concluded, also for one year. The parties after that continued to deal with one another for twenty years on the same terms. The original written contract contained a provision that there should be exclusive jurisdiction conferred on the court of Turin.

The European Court of Justice, on a reference to it, held that where a written agreement, which included a jurisdiction clause, provided that extensions to the agreement were to be made in writing, had expired but had continued to constitute the legal basis of the contractual relationships of the parties, that jurisdiction clause satisfied the formal requirements imposed by the Article. This was based on the assumption that the sole purpose of the requirement of writing imposed by Article 17 was to ensure that that there was real consensus on the parties, as to the matter of jurisdiction: *Iveco Fiat Spa* v. *Van Hool N.V.* (1986).

Chapter 3

How the Courts Enforce Contractual Obligations

3.01 Remedies given by the courts

Contractual obligations can be enforced in a number of ways by the courts:

Debt

Sums of money due under a contract will be ordered to be paid.

Damages

The invariable remedy of the common law courts for failure to perform contractual obligations was an award of a payment of money as 'damages'. The action of *assumpsit* [1.06] which was the means whereby contractual obligations in general were enforced, was essentially an action for the compensation of a civil wrong by an award of damages; but there can be no damages unless there has first been a breach of contract.

Quantum meruit

The courts may also award a sum by way of *quantum meruit* – 'as much as they deserve'. This is described in detail later [3.03].

Specific performance

The old Court of Chancery had other and sometimes more persuasive methods. An order for the specific performance of a contract was an order that some positive obligation of a contract should be carried out; and the defendant who refused to obey such an order might remain in prison until he did. In addition, the Court of Chancery would award *injunctions*.

Injunctions

These might be either *prohibitive injunctions* (sometimes also termed 'restrictive' or 'preventative' injunctions), which are specific orders that a certain thing shall *not* be done – or *mandatory injunctions* (sometimes called 'compulsive' injunctions), which are orders that something *shall* be done.

The essential difference between specific performance and a mandatory injunction is that the first requires the performance of a positive obligation while the second requires some positive act to be done to fulfil a negative stipulation. For example, if there were a contractual obligation not to build on certain land, which is a negative stipulation, and the defendant proposed to build on it, a prohibitive injunction would be issued to stop him. If, however, he had already built on it, a mandatory injunction might be granted to make him pull down what he had erected. If on the other hand, the obligation were to convey the land to a buyer – that is, a positive act – the appropriate remedy would be an order for specific performance.

These remedies still exist today and are known as 'equitable remedies' since they were in use by the Court of Equity – that is to say, the Court of Chancery. They are always discretionary. The plaintiff may be entitled to them if the Court see fit, whereas an award of damages is something that the plaintiff is entitled to as of right for breach of a contract, even though the sum received may only be nominal.

Formerly, equitable remedies were only available from the Court of Chancery and it had no power to award damages until that power was given it by what is popularly termed 'Lord Cairn's Act', the Chancery Amendment Act 1858. That Act itself has been repealed by subsequent legislation, but the power is still vested in the High Court and an interesting use of it has been made in recent times by the grant of damages for breach of confidence. Breach of confidence is not a tort, nor is it normally a breach of contract, but it is something which would be prevented from taking place by an injunction from the courts of equity. But if it had already taken place, after Lord Cairn's Act the courts could award damages in lieu of an injunction. So, in effect, it became a legal remedy similar to those available for a tort.

It is also possible that the Act may allow a Court to award damages in lieu of an injunction even before there has been a breach of contract, but there appears to be no recorded instances of this happening.

In addition to these equitable remedies, others granted by the Court of Chancery were:

Rescission

This is an order that contractural obligations on all parties shall be discharged; or to put it another way, the revocation of a contract.

Restitution

This is closely related to rescission and is an order that the parties should be restored to their original position. It has a wider application in that it may be used outside contract to make a person with property wrongfully in his possession or to follow or trace assets which have been dispersed.

Rectification

The Courts have never rectified contracts as such, but an order for rectification is an order for the correction of a written document, to ensure that it truly expresses the intention of the parties.

Since the Supreme Court of Judicature Act 1873, there has, of course, been only one High Court and all these remedies, both damages and equitable remedies, are available in all the courts in the same action. Nevertheless, it can be important when reading reported cases before 1873 to look carefully to see which Court was hearing the case and what remedy was being sought. An example of the mistakes which can be made by neglecting to do this is to be found in Lord Wright's judgment in *Norwich Union* v. *Price* (1934), where his lordship referred to the famous case of *Cooper* v. *Phibbs* (1867), where a man entered into a thirty years'lease of fishing rights which in fact he himself owned. Lord Wright was under the impression that the decision meant that the court had held that the contract was void, 'The mere simulacrum of a contract' at common law. In reality, that case was an application to the Court of Chancery to set aside the lease on terms that the true owner recompensed the apparent owner for the money he had expended in improving the fishery. The court would only have acted in so doing if it were satisfied that the contract was *not* void at common law. In other words, the court could only grant the equitable relief of setting aside the lease, if satisfied that the contract was valid at common law.

3.02   The action for debt

Debt may, of course, arise in many other ways than out of contractual obligations – by a gratuitous promise to pay in a deed or by obligations imposed by law, such as rates and taxes.

But in so far as money is due under a contract, this must be distinguished from damages. If a man has promised contractually to pay a sum of money, however excessive it may be, the courts have no option but to condemn him in the sum to which he has agreed.

This essential difference has been made clear in some early hire purchase contracts. If the hirer broke the contract and the contract provides for a certain sum as damages as a result, the court had a discretion to decide whether the sum named was liquidated damages or a penalty. If, on the other hand, the contract allows him to terminate the contract on terms that he paid a certain sum, then the court had no discretion but to order that sum to be paid: *Associated Distributors Ltd* v. *Hall* (1938). The result might well be that he would be worse off if he performed the contract, than if he broke it.

The law has, of course, since been changed by statute regarding hire purchase, and details about this will be found in the book in this series, *Consumer Credit* by Graham Stephenson.

3.03   *Quantum meruit*

Unhappily this term, '*quantum meruit*', is used in three distinct senses:

(1) As a contractual obligation
Where there is a contract and an express or implied agreement that a reasonable price should be paid for work done or services rendered, the term is used, as Blackstone used it, to mean 'the reasonable price'.

(2) Following a breach of contract
The innocent party has the option of suing either for damages or for the value of work done. This latter applies particularly to lump sum contracts where nothing is due until the whole of the work has been completed. This is something termed the rule in *Cutter* v. *Powell* (1795). The second mate of the ship *Governor Parry* had contracted for the sum of 30 guineas to sail from Jamaica to Liverpool. He served for seven weeks, but the week before the ship arrived at Liverpool he died. His widow was held entitled to nothing, since the voyage had not been completed. So, too, in *Huttman* v. *Boulnois* (1826), where a servant engaged for a year for a fixed sum left before the year had ended. He was entitled to nothing.

But where the innocent party is prevented from earning the lump sum by virtue of a breach of contract by the other party, he is entitled to a *quantum meruit* for the work done. In *Planché* v. *Colburn* (1831), the plaintiff was engaged to write a book about armour for the sum of £100. Before he could complete it, the project was abandoned by the publishers. He was held entitled to the £50 the jury had awarded him for the work already done, as a *quantum meruit*.

But this does not apply to the guilty party. Even if he had done most of the work under a lump sum contract before he abandons it, he is entitled to nothing. Sumpter was a builder who contracted to build a house for £565. Halfway through the job, he abandoned the work. It was held he could recover nothing for what he had done: *Sumpter* v. *Hedges* (1898). The other party, however, was liable to pay a reasonable price, a *quantum valebant*, for materials Sumpter had brought to the site, and which had been used by the other party to complete the work, since he had an option as to whether he used these or not. (The law regarding building contracts has, however, since been substantially modified by the doctrines of 'divisible contracts' – see *Hoenig* v. *Isaacs* (1952) – and 'substantial performance' – see *Dakin* v. *Lee* (1916).

(3) Quasi-contractual quantum meruit

If work is done under a contract which, although believed to be valid at the time, in fact proves to be void, the party who has done the work may be awarded a *quantum meruit* for his services. In *Craven–Ellis* v. *Canons Ltd* (1936), the plaintiff became director of the defendant company and was awarded remuneration subsequently by a resolution which, for technical reasons, was void. The court held he had no claim on a contractual basis, but for the services rendered, on a quasi-contractual basis, he was entitled to remuneration on the same scale.

But, as has been mentioned earlier, in the absence of an implied or express promise, services rendered do not have to be paid for, except in exceptional cases of salvage at sea and agency of necessity. It is extremely doubtful also whether, in English law, a doctor who intended to charge for his services could recover for medical attention unsuccessfully rendered to a suicide – unlike a case which happened in Canada under French Canadian law. English law is based on promise, express or implied, not upon benefit.

3.04   The different kinds of damages

The law knows of various sorts of damages, arising out of the breach of contractual obligations.

Nominal damages are those awarded in cases where the plaintiff has proved a breach of contract by the defendant but has suffered no loss. In

Staniforth v. *Lyall* (1830), the defendant failed to provide a cargo for a ship he had chartered but the plaintiff shipowner suffered no loss because he immediately found another charterer. The defendant was held liable only for nominal damages.

In the old days, nominal damages were generally in the sum of forty shillings; no more than a 'peg on which to hang costs'. The costs, of course, might well amount to a substantial sum and up to 1954 were invariably awarded to a successful plaintiff even if he only recovered nominal damages. In recent years, however, the courts have shown a disinclination to award costs in such cases and any plaintiff who has suffered a breach of contract but has not lost thereby is well advised to restrain any enthusiasm he may feel for litigation.

General damages are those which follow the failure to perform the contractual obligation and the principles on which they are assessed are discussed in [3.05].

Special damages are specific items of loss which the plaintiff is required to set out in detail in his statement of claim.

Exemplary damages are damages in excess of the loss actually suffered, which are intended to have a punitive element – to teach the defendant not to do it again.

Damages are not recoverable in contract for a grossly insulting manner of breach nor (since the abolition of breach of promise actions) for injury to 'feelings, affections or for wounded pride'. Mr Addis was given six months'notice as manager for the Gramophone Company Ltd and a new manager immediately appointed in his place. A jury awarded him £600 damages for the humiliation suffered by the manner of his dismissal, but the House of Lords set this aside: *Addis* v. *Gramophone Company Ltd* (1909). On the other hand, according to Lord Denning in *Cook* v. *S* (1967), damages for nervous shock or anxiety state caused by breach of contract are recoverable – provided they were reasonably foreseeable. There have been numerous cases since in which this principle has been accepted, including those in which the owner-occupiers of defective houses have been reimbursed for inconvenience; and a woman recovered damages from a gas board when she suffered nervous shock as the result of seeing her house and contents burnt.

Liquidated damages are those which have been fixed in advance of the breach by agreement between the parties.

Unliquidated damages are those which fall to be assessed by the Court,i.e. the ordinary case of breach of contract where the parties have not agreed as a term of the contract what the damages should be if such a breach takes place.

3.05 The principles on which damages are assessed

The object of damages for breach of contract, in the words of Baron Parke, immortalised by constant repetition, is:

'A party sustaining a loss by reason of a breach of contract, so far as money can do it, is to be placed in the same situation ... as if the contract had been performed.' (*Robinson* v. *Harman* (1848).

In spite of their immortality, however, these words should not be taken at their face value, and must be qualified by two principles:

(i) The duty on the injured party to mitigate (reduce) his loss by such means as are within his power [3.08].

'In assessing the damages for breach ... a jury will, of course, take into account whatever ... a prudent man, ought in reason to have done whereby his loss ... would have been diminished': Chief Justice Cockburn in *Frost* v. *Knight* (1872).

(ii) The rules regarding remoteness of damages [3.10]. If Baron Parke's dictum were literally applied, the defendant would be liable for all sorts of uncontemplated, improbable and utterly unpredictable damages. The man who sold defective colour films might find himself with the entire cost of an expedition up the Nile to film wild life for television. Therefore, the courts have evolved the principle:

'In cases of breach of contract the aggrieved party is only entitled to recover such part of the loss actually resulting as was at the time of the contract reasonably foreseeable as liable to result from the breach': Lord Justice Asquith in *Victoria Laundry* v. *Newman Industries* (1949).

Since the same act may be both a breach of contract and also a tort, it is necessary to point out here that the tests of the amount of damages recoverable in tort are different. For a tort (a deliberate one, such as deceit, at any rate):

(i) the aggrieved party is to be placed, so far as money will do it, in the same position as if the tort had never been committed;
(ii) so far as remoteness of damages is concerned, the test in tort is more in favour of the injured party than in contract;

(iii) the conduct of the defendant and his motives may be taken into account, as also may the conduct of the plaintiff.

The difference between the two standards is well illustrated by the case of *Doyle* v. *Olby* (1969). Doyle bought an ironmonger's business from Olby as the result of misrepresentation which the court held to be fraudulent and a conspiracy, as well as a breach of contract. If treated as a breach of contract, by Baron Parke's definition, the plaintiff was entitled to be placed in the same position as if the contract had been performed. In other words, he was entitled to the difference between the value of the business as it was in reality and the value of the business as it was held out to be. The sum so assessed was £1,500. But since the misrepresentations were also the torts of deceit and conspiracy, he was entitled to be placed in the same position as if these torts had never taken place. He could therefore recover all losses and expenses incurred in the three years before he was able to dispose of the business and this sum was assessed at £5,500.

3.06 The breach of contract must have caused the loss and not merely have been the occasion for it, before damages can be awarded

The problem of causation is one of the most difficult that any legal system has to face; sometimes expressed (probably fallaciously) by drawing a distinction between *causa causans* – the immediate cause – and the *causa sine qua non*, some precedent event but for which the *causa causans* would not have operated.

If a burglar breaks into a house and escapes on to a rooftop, and if a police officer chasing him falls off the roof and breaks his neck, is the burglar the cause of the constable's death? This may well be a *causa sine qua non* but not a *causa causans*.

The plaintiff in an action for breach of contract must prove that his loss was *caused* by the breach. How difficult this is to define may be seen by two cases, within a year of one another, which are not easy to reconcile.

In *Weld-Blundell* v. *Stephens* (1920), the defendant was under a contractual obligation to the plaintiff to maintain confidential all correspondence received from the latter. In breach of that duty, he left lying about a letter which was defamatory of X and this letter was seen by a third party. The third party communicated the contents to X, who immediately sued the plaintiff for libel. The House of Lords held that the plaintiff was entitled only to nominal damages and he could not recover all the damages and costs he himself had to pay out in the libel action. The loss was not caused by any breach of contract, but by the action of the third party, i.e. it was a *causa sine qua non*.

But in *London Joint Stock Bank Ltd* v. *MacMillan* (1918), the defendant, in breach of his contractual duty to the bank, drew a cheque in such a way that it could be easily altered and it was altered by the criminal act of a third party. It was held that the breach of contract was the cause of the loss suffered by the bank. In both cases, the courts held that the act of the third party was reasonably foreseeable.

A similar problem arose when a building firm, in breach of their contractual obligations to the plaintiff, failed to provide him with any suitable equipment to carry out his trade. He, therefore, had to make use of improvised equipment and was injured as a result. The Court of Appeal held that these injuries were not caused by the defendant's breach: *Quinn* v. *Burch Bros (Builders) Ltd* (1966).

But what if the loss is caused by both parties to the contract? This appears to have been the situation which arose in *Government of Ceylon* v. *Chandris* (1965), where a cargo of rice was contaminated and damaged, by the defendant not providing a proper ship and by the plaintiff not shipping the goods in suitable containers. The court fell back on the normal proposition of the law that whoever alleges a thing must prove it and that damages can only be awarded where the burden of proof on the part of the plaintiff is discharged by showing that the loss was caused by the defendant. So unless the plaintiff could prove that the damage was caused by the breach, he could not recover.

Finally, can a plaintiff's damages be reduced under the Law Reform (Contributory Negligence) Act 1945, for breach of contract if the damage has been caused 'partly by his own fault and partly by the fault of some other person'?

Although the point is not free from doubt, the better view is that the plaintiff's own negligence does not preclude him from recovering the full amount of damages he would otherwise recover for a breach of contract by the defendant. This was held by Lord Justice Neill sitting as a High Court Judge in *Marintrans AB* v. *Comet Shipping* (1985) and Judge Newey sitting on Official Referee's Business (although that case was unknown to him, not then having been reported) in *Victoria University of Manchester* v. *Hugh Wilson* (1984).

3.07 Damage only for breach of contractual obligation

Damages are to be awarded in compensation solely for what the party in default was under a contractual obligation to do, and not what he would probably have done. The manager of a shop was on a five year contract at a salary of £4,000 a year. In addition, for the first three years, he received a bonus. He was then wrongfully dismissed and claimed damages, not only for the loss of salary – about which there was no dispute – but also for the loss of bonus or the increase in salary into which it had been commuted. It was held by the Court of Appeal that since there was no contractual obligation on the employers to pay the bonus or grant him an increase in salary – even though they almost certainly would have done had he remained in their employment – he could not recover these sums: *Laverack* v. *Woods* (1966).

On the other hand, expenses incurred before a contract was entered into are recoverable if they have been spent to no purpose as a direct result of the breach of contract: as, for example, where a television company incurred heavy expenses in preparing a programme for a certain artist who contracted to appear in it and then broke the contract. The artist was held liable for them, even though they had been incurred before he entered into the contract.

In assessing damages the incidence of taxation must be taken into account: *Parsons* v. *B.N.M. Laboratories* (1963), following the tort case of *B.T.C* v. *Gourley* (1955), where damages of £37,000 awarded to the plaintiff for loss of earnings were reduced by the House of Lords to £6,000 as a result of the income tax they calculated he had saved.

The fact that damages are difficult to assess will not deter the courts from determining them; and they have been willing to price the lost chance of winning a beauty contest in *Chaplin* v. *Hicks* (1911), as well as the loss of publicity to an artiste in *Clayton* v. *Oliver* (1930).

3.08 The duty to mitigate

The law 'imposes on the plaintiff the duty of taking all reasonable steps to mitigate the loss consequent upon the breach and debars him from claiming any part of the damage which is due to his neglect to take such steps'said Lord Haldane in *British Westinghouse* v. *Underground Electric* (1912). The classic illustration of this principle is the case of *Brace* v. *Calder* (1895). The plaintiff was employed by a partnership of four which came to an end, thereby wrongfully terminating his contract of employment. Two partners immediately offered him the same post and at the same salary but, out of pique, he refused it. The court held that all he was entitled to were nominal damages of 40 shillings, because he had failed to mitigate his loss by acceptance of the post offered him.

The test, however, is what 'a prudent person ought reasonably to do in order to mitigate his loss' and in this connection status and salary are both relevant factors where the cause of action arises from wrongful dismissal.

The former managing director is not expected to mitigate his loss by taking a job as a lavatory attendant. Indeed, in *Yetton* v. *Eastwood Froy Ltd* (1966) a former joint managing director was held to be entitled to refuse to accept the post of assistant managing director at the same salary of £7,500; nor was he unreasonably failing to mitigate his loss by neglecting to follow up the offer of a post at £2,500 a year.

Similarly, a client who had bought a house with a defective title as the result of the negligence of his solicitor was not to be expected, as a reasonable and prudent man, to engage in litigation against the vendor to reduce his loss: *Pilkington* v. *Wood* (1953). A prudent man could not be expected to engage in prolonged and expensive litigation for the purpose of mitigating his loss.

3.09   The duty to mitigate only arises when there has been a breach of contract

The proposition above may appear self-evident, but complications are introduced by what the judges have, most misleadingly, christened, 'anticipatory breach'; misleadingly, for an anticipatory breach is not necessarily a breach of contract.

Anticipatory breach is a repudiation of the contractual obligations before the time has come for their performance. It may be by words – as where a party expressly says he does not intend to do what he has promised to. Ot it may be by an act, as in the case of *Frost* v. *Knight* (1872), where the defendant had promised to marry the plaintiff after his father's death, but, before that event happened, he married somebody else. So if a person places it outside his power to perform the contract, as by selling a ship he has undertaken to hire out later, that is a repudiation of, or, as it used to be called earlier, a 'renunciation' of his obligations.

But a repudiation is not necessarily a breach of contract. It only becomes such if the other party accepts it as a breach; but not otherwise. 'An unaccepted repudiation is writ on water.'

Two courses are open to the promisee:

(i)   'If he pleases, he may treat the notice of intention as inoperative and await the time when the contract is to be executed and then hold the other party responsible for all the consequences of non-performance.

(ii) If he thinks proper he may treat the repudiation of the other party as a wrongful putting to an end of the contract and may at once bring his action as on a breach of it': Chief Justice Cockburn in *Frost* v. *Knight*.

Two cases will illustrate Lord Cockburn's first proposition. Mr McGregor was the Scottish proprietor of a garage and in his absence from the premises one day his sales manager was persuaded to sign a contract with White and Carter (Councils) Ltd for three years of advertisements on litter bins which that company intended to attach to lamp posts in the neighbourhood.

When Mr McGregor returned to his garage and found out what his manager has signed on his behalf, he was not pleased. The very same day he wrote repudiating the agreement. The company chose to ignore this and went ahead and prepared the necessary plates for the bins and exhibited them. They then sued Mr McGregor, not for damages, but in debt for the whole amount of rentals due under the contract; and in the House of Lords they succeeded: *White and Carter (Councils) Ltd* v. *McGregor* (1961).

The case has aroused a lot of controversey amongst lawyers; first, because it was argued that it was contrary to the duty to mitigate the loss flowing from a breach [3.08]. That is answered simply:

'It cannot be said that there is any duty on the part of the plaintiff to mitigate his damage before there is any breach which he has accepted as a breach.'

The duty to mitigate only arises when there has been a breach of contract, i.e. in the circumstances set out in Lord Cockburn's second proposition above.

The other and main objection is that the doctrine is from an ethical point of view absurd. Is an architect really entitled to spend two years preparing drawings for a town hall which he has been told will never be built? Or, to quote an example given by Lord Reid in the above case, if a company engages an expert to go abroad and prepare an elaborate report and before he sets off they tell him they no longer want it, is he really entitled to waste thousands of pounds on a trip to Australia, say, and in preparing a report, and then charge the company his full fee, when a much smaller sum by way of damages would give him full compensation for his loss? Is a printer entitled to go on and print wedding invitations even if he is told the wedding will no longer take place? It would appear so. In *Anglo-African Shipping of New York* v. *Mortimer Ltd* (1962) the plaintiffs agreed to supply the defendants with a quantity of rubber sheeting. Before the time for delivery, the defendants cancelled the order. The plaintiffs ignored the cancellation and went ahead and delivered the goods. The Court of Appeal held they were entitled to do this.

There are, however, some qualifications of this remarkable doctrine. The manager of the pop group known as 'The Kinks' was discharged by them. He claimed to have rejected their repudiation of his services and that he was entitled to his full percentage of their earnings, right up to the end of his contract, years later. He did not claim damages, because to have done so would have been inconsistent with this claim, since he would first have to accept the repudiation as a breach of contract. He, in spite of the doctrine, lost his case in the Court of Appeal. A majority of the Court, basing themselves on early nineteenth century cases such as *Smith* v. *Hayward* (1837) held that contracts of personal service are in a class of their own (*sui generis* is the legal expression) and that repudiation, even if unaccepted, ended the right to wages and converted it into a right of damages only; *Denmark* v. *Boscobel* (1968).

But this is an evasion based on an exception rather than a solution of the problem, and it may well be that the true law is that the right to refuse to accept a repudiation only exists where the injured party can go on and perform his own obligations without the co-operation of the other party. In other words, performance by the innocent party and not mere willingness to perform is necessary. Unfortunately there is a great deal of authority against this suggestion including, of course, that of Lord Cockburn, quoted above where he said the innocent party was entitled to 'await the time when the contract is to be executed'.

There is some basis for it, however, in building law. A builder who is told to stop work on a project is bound to accept these instructions. This may be because he requires the licence of the building owner to go on the land; but an interim injunction will not be granted to expel him: *Hounslow L.B.C.* v. *Twickenham Garden Developments Ltd* (1971).

And in the sale of goods, there is some authority in *British Westinghouse* v. *Underground Electric* (1912), that where a buyer has repudiated the contract for the sale of goods before the time for delivery has arrived, the seller is not entitled to reject the repudiation and hang on to the goods in a falling market until the day of delivery and so enhance the damages. But this proposition may have to be looked at again in the light of the later House of Lord's decision in *White and Carter* v. *McGregory* (*supra*).

The courts seem to have retreated somewhat from this position to judge from subsequent cases, *The Puerto Buitrago* (1976), a decision of the Court of Appeal, *The Odenfeld* (1978) and *The Alaskan Trader* (1984), so as to hold that before an innocent party rejects a repudiation, he must have reasonable grounds for so doing.

In the first case, Lord Denning vigorously dissented from principles set out by the House of Lords in *White and Carter* and said expressly

'It has no application whatever in a case where the plaintiff ought in all reason to accept the repudiation and sue for damages, provided that the damages would provide an adequate remedy for any loss suffered by him.'

He was dealing with a case where a vessel on a time charter in which the charterer was liable to do repairs had broken down. Repairs would cost US$2 million and the vessel when repaired would be worth $1 million. The charterers redelivered the vessel unrepaired. The ship owners refused to accept delivery and claimed that the charterers were obliged both to repair the vessel and pay the charter hire to the end of the charter. The Court of Appeal refused to upset an arbitrator's award that the shipowners were entitled to damages and not to the sums due under the contract. Lord Denning claimed that to hold otherwise would be to grant specific performance of the contract and he expressly refused to follow the House of Lords decision in *White and Carter* 'except in a case which is on all fours with it'.

3.10   Remoteness of damage

The question of the extent to which damages are recoverable is termed that of 'remoteness of damages'. In spite of thoroughly unsatisfactory reports of the case, the law is based on the decision in *Hadley* v. *Baxendale* (1854).

That case appears to have laid down two propositions by Baron Alderson. The first is:

'Where two parties have made a contract which one of them has broken, the damage which the other party ought to receive should be such as may fairly and reasonably be considered to arise naturally, i.e. according to the usual course of things.'

This is commonly referred to as 'the first rule in *Hadley* v. *Baxendale*'. The other proposition is:

'such as may reasonably be supposed to have been in the contemplation of both parties, at the time they made the contract as the probable result of the breach of it.'

This is referred to as the second rule in *Hadley* v. *Baxendale*.

Anson believed that a careful reading of the judgment as a whole suggested that in the so-called second rule, the court merely intended to express in other words, for the sake of greater clarity, what they had already said in the so-called first rule – i.e. that the damages which can fairly and reasonably be considered as arising 'naturally' were those which 'may reasonably be supposed to have been in the contemplation of the parties at the time when they made the contract'. Lord Denning apparently adopted this view once when he quoted this judgment but substituted for the word 'or'the words 'that is to say'.

Another difficulty about the case was that there is some confusion as to the findings of fact. The plaintiffs'mill was stopped by the breakage of a crankshaft and the broken crankshaft had to be sent to the original manufacturers as a pattern. The carriers, in breach of their contract for which they received £3, delayed delivery of the shaft and in due course the plaintiffs sued for £300 loss of profits which they would otherwise have made if the mill had been working. The reports of the case state that the defendant's clerk was told that the mill was stopped and that the shaft must be delivered immediately. In that case, one can only presume that loss of profits must have fallen under the second rule as being within the contemplation of the parties, and therefore should have been recoverable. However, the court held that they were not. Later decisions proceeded on the basis that special losses of this nature could only be recovered if there were circumstances to show that the defendant not merely knew but had also accepted liability for such losses: *Horne* v. *Midland Railway* (1873); *Bostock* v. *Nicholson* (1904).

However, the whole matter was reviewed by the Court of Appeal in *Victoria Laundry* v. *Newman Industries* (1949), in which the judgment was delivered by Lord Justice Asquith. He accepted that there were in fact two distinct rules in *Hadley* v. *Baxendale* and proceeded to reformulate them in a series of propositions, three of which are material:

(i)   'In cases of breach of contract the aggrieved party is only entitled to recover such part of the loss actually resulting as was at the time of the contract reasonably foreseeable as liable to result from the breach.'

(ii) 'What is reasonably foreseeable depends on the knowledge of the parties at the time.'

(iii) 'This knowledge may be:

(a) imputed, that is to say what everyone as a reasonable person is taken to know in the ordinary course of things. [This, Lord Justice Asquith equated to the first rule in *Hadley* v. *Baxendale*] or

(b) actual, where in a particular case there is knowledge which the defendant actually possesses of special circumstances 'outside the ordinary course of things'.

(And this, his Lordship believed to be the same as the second rule in *Hadley* v. *Baxendale*).

In *Victoria Laundry* v. *Newman Industries* the defendants agreed to supply and instal a large boiler for the plaintiff's laundry on 5th June. It was not in fact delivered until 8th November. The plaintiff claimed two items of damage:

(1) £16 a week as loss of profits from new customers they could have taken on.
(2) £262 a week as loss of profits under a special contract they had with the Ministry of Supply for dyeing battledresses.

The trial judge refused them both, finding as a fact that the special objects for which the boiler was required had not been drawn to the defendant's notice.

The Court of Appeal allowed the first item of £16 a week under the imputed knowledge rule.

'Reasonable persons in the shoes of the defendants must be taken to foresee without any express intimation that a laundry, which, at a time when there was a famine of laundry facilities, was paying £2,000 odd for plant and intended to put such plant into use immediately, would be likely to suffer in pocket from five months' delay.'

But the claim for the £262 a week under the contract with the Ministry of Supply was rejected as these were 'special circumstances outside the ordinary course of things'.

This decision of the Court of Appeal was subsequently approved by a majority in the House of Lords in the *Heron II* (1967), with some minor verbal qualifications. For ninety years, ever since *The Parana* (1877) the rule of law had been that if a ship owner diverted a ship for his own purpose and so prolonged a voyage in breach of contract, the only damages a charterer could recover was interest on the value of the cargo for the period of the delay. *The Heron II*, under charter, loaded a cargo of three thousand tons of sugar in Constanza and carried it to Basra and in breach of the contract was nine days late on arrival. Had the ship arrived on the due date the charterers would have received £32.10s a ton for their sugar; as it was, the market had slumped, and they only got £31.2s.9d, a total loss of £4,011. Interest on the cargo would have been in the region of £134. The House of Lords held that the total loss was recoverable since the shipowner knew there was a sugar market in Basra and must therefore be imputed to know that prices rise and fall on such markets.

However, this is a highly suspect decision, although undoubtedly just, in the light of facts which do not appear in any of the reported judgments. The reason *The Heron II* was nine days late was because the skipper had deviated in the Mediterranean to pick up a deck cargo of sheep and had dropped them off somewhere else in that area. There was no evidence before any court that the shipowner or master knew that the cargo of sugar they were carrying was on consignment: that is, it had not been sold in advance and still belonged to the shippers. In fact, there was an express finding in the House of Lords by Lord Reid that 'the shipowner did not know this'.

However, it was said that the shipowners 'did know that there was a market for sugar in Basra'. There was no evidence to support this proposition and in fact there was no organised commodity market for sugar in Basra. What happened was that merchants there would buy sugar as and when it arrived, and a ship from Mauritius got in before *The Heron II*.

It is difficult to know how this could reasonably be supposed to be in 'the contemplation of both parties, *at the time they made the contract*'. The case of *Hadley* v. *Baxendale* deals with actual knowledge not presumed knowledge.

3.11 Damages for late payments of monies due

The English courts had no power, until they were given it by statute to award interest on any debt or damages, however long overdue. The first right was given only to 'courts of record', so that excluded the County Court. In fact the County Court was only given power to award interest between the time when payment should have been made and judgment in 1982.

The House of Lords laid down in the *London and Chatham Railway* case, that interest as damages on late payment of monies was not recoverable. That decision still stands, but has been mitigated to some extent by the case of *The President of India* v. *La Pintada* (1984).

The present position appears to be that interest still cannot be recovered as damages on money paid late. However, if it can be established that both parties, before the contract was made, knew that the late payment would cause loss to the payee, such damages are recoverable under the second limb of the rule in *Hadley* v. *Baxendale*.

> 'A plaintiff will be able to recover damages (for late payment) if it is proved that the parties had knowledge of facts or circumstances from which it is reasonable to infer that the delay in payment would lead to that loss'

said Lord Justice Neill in *Maritime* v. *President of India* (1986). In that case, he was dealing with an exchange loss, between the US dollar and sterling caused by the late payment of demurrage due under a charter-party. The shipowner was held able to recover this.

3.12 Damages fixed by the terms of the contract

Where the contract specifies the sum to be paid in respect of any particular breach, as is quite common in building, shipping and many other contracts, these may be:

(1) *Liquidated damages* – a genuine pre-estimate, so far as one is possible at the time when the contract was made, of the loss likely to be suffered. This sum, no more and no less, is recoverable, whatever the damage suffered.

(2) *A penalty* – a sum named to intimidate the other party into performing the contract (to put him *in terrorem* is the legal jargon) and not as a genuine pre-estimate of the loss likely to be suffered. Equity would grant relief against penalties and, in that event, the aggrieved party could recover the actual damage he could prove – and no more.

(3) *Limited damages* – this happens where both parties realise that the damages may well be in excess of the sum named but one contracting party is not willing to accept any greater liability and the other agrees to this. That was the position in *Cellulose Acetate* v. *Widnes* (1932), where the contract limited damages to £600 but the plaintiff's loss was in fact £5,850. It was held they could recover no more than the sum named in the contract.

It is important to distinguish these three categories from sums payable on the happening of a certain event, i.e. under the contract. In all the cases above, a breach of contract has first to occur. In *Alder* v. *Moore* (1961), the defendant, a professional footballer, was insured against permanent total disablement. He was injured and the insurer accepted that his condition was permanent and total and paid him £500. He signed a form that he would take no part in professional football again and 'in the event of infringement of this condition he will be subject to a penalty of the amount paid him'. Two members of the Court of Appeal decided that 'there was no contractual obligation on the defendant not to play professional football again' – therefore this was simply a sum of money repayable under the terms of the contract on the happening of a certain event, and therefore recoverable. Lord Justice Devlin dissented.

3.13 How to distinguish liquidated damages from penalties

As has been seen, when a sum has been named in a contract as damages for any particular breach if it is in law liquidated damages, that sum – no more and no less – is recoverable for that breach of contract, irrespective of the loss actually incurred. Whereas, if the fixed sum is held to be in law a penalty, the sum named is not recoverable and the aggrieved party can only recover such actual damage as he can prove to the satisfaction of a court.

How does the law decide which of the two is a fixed sum named in a contract as payable in the event of a breach?

The leading authority is to be found in the judgment of Lord Dunedin in *Dunlop* v. *New Garage* (1915), which was a case where tyre manufacturers tried to maintain fixed retail prices; this time by naming a sum of £5 damages for every tyre which was sold below their listed price.

The propositions advanced by Lord Dunedin are accepted as the basis of our modern law. Paraphrased, they are:

(1) It does not matter what the parties themselves call the fixed sum – that is by no means conclusive. In the building trade, for example, the liquidated damages clause is invariably known as 'the penalty clause'. Usually it is not that at all. But on the whole, the parties may be presumed to know what they are doing, so that if they call a thing 'a penalty' there may be a disposition on the part of the court to treat it as such.

(2) The essential element of a penalty is that it is an attempt to intimidate the other contracting party into performing the contract because of the threat.

(3) By contrast, liquidated damages is an attempt to pre-estimate the loss which a particular breach may occasion. It does not matter that the parties may be way out in their calculation; provided that, when the contract was made, it was a reasonable attempt, it will be liquidated damages.

In *Dunlop* v. *New Garage (supra)* the House of Lords accepted:

(a) that some damage would result to Dunlop if people to whom they had sold tyres resold them below the manufacturer's fixed retail price list (a quaint finding in view of our modern views about retail price fixing);

(b) that the actual damage from any particular sale was impossible to forecast;

(c) therefore it was one of those cases where it was reasonable for the parties to estimate the damage at a certain figure;
(d) that £5 a tyre was not an extravagant sum and was therefore recoverable.

(4) In deciding whether or not the sum named is an honest attempt to pre-estimate the damage likely to result from a particular breach, the court will have regard to the following:

(a) If a larger sum of money is payable in default of payment of a lesser, then this is inevitably a penalty: i.e. if you don't pay me £10 by 1st June, you then have to pay me £20 – this latter sum is not recoverable.
(b) If the sum named is likely to exceed any possible loss and is extravagant, it is obviously a penalty.
(c) If the sum is payable in respect of minor breaches of contract and major ones there is a presumption – but no more – that it is a penalty.

In *Ford Motor Co. v. Armstrong* (1915), another price fixing agreement, the sum of £250 was payable for any breach of the contract including such trifling infringements as exhibiting the plaintiff's cars without their written consent. This was held to be a penalty and therefore irrecoverable.

3.14 Specific performance will only be ordered where damages are an inadequate remedy

In practice, this results in orders being made only:

(i) where the contract relates to the sale of land, which is always regarded as something unique. Both buyer and seller are entitled to such an order, but only if the seller already has the title vested in him;
(ii) where the contract is for a unique chattel. A set of Hepplewhite chairs was not held to be sufficiently unique to justify an order: *Cohen v. Roche* (1927). But an Adam-style door was so regarded in *Phillips v. Lamdin* (1949), but only because it had been taken from a particular house where it had been ever since the house had been built and was to be restored there;
(iii) where a third party might otherwise be deprived of a benefit due under a contract. No person can take a benefit under a contract to which they are not a party and for which they have given no consideration. But the House of Lords ordered specific performance at the instance of one of the parties for payments to be made to a third

party in *Beswick* v. *Beswick* (1967), because damages otherwise would be nominal.

Old Peter Beswick sold his small coal merchant's business to his nephew on terms that he himself should have £6.10s a week so long as he lived, and thereafter his widow should have £5 a week. Shortly afterwards he died, and the nephew made one payment of £5 to Mrs Beswick, the widow, and then ceased. Mrs Beswick sued in two capacities:

(a) in her personal capacity; and
(b) since her husband had left no will, she was able to take out Letters of Administration and thus become the administratrix, vested with all the rights of the deceased.

She failed in the House of Lords in her personal capacity, since she was not a party to the contract, but an order of specific performance was made in her favour as administratrix, for the nephew to pay the annuity of £5 a week to her in her personal capacity.

3.15 Specific performance will never be awarded in some cases

These include situations:

(i)   Where the obligations of the contract are not mutually enforceable. For that reason a minor will never be granted specific performance for a contract which is voidable at his option.
(ii) Where the contractual obligation would require constant supervision by the court. The earliest cases are all concerned with the cultivation of land, as where a tenant farmer has covenanted in his lease to observe a certain rotation of crops. The courts would not give specific performance in such circumstances. More recent cases include the obligations of a shipowner under a charterparty, and
(iii) contracts of personal services. The courts will not force a man to work under an employment contract or an employer to keep him on. In either case, damages are regarded as the appropriate remedy.

3.16 Specific performance may be refused in some cases

These include:

(i)   if the party which is claiming it has not behaved fairly himself;

(ii) if he is in breach of his own obligations under the contract, as in *Australian Hardwoods* v. *Railway Commissioners* (1961), where the plaintiffs sought specific performance of an option to purchase in a lease, but were greatly in arrears with their rent;

(iii) if it would cause undue hardship to the defendant, as where the defendant purchased a plot of land to which there was no lawful access over the surrounding property: *Denne* v. *Light* (1857);

(iv) if the contract has been induced by duress, misrepresentation or mistake.

3.17 Injunctions — prohibitive and mandatory

Although prohibitive injunctions are also discretionary, it was said by Lord Cairns in 1878 in *Doherty* v. *Allman* that

'if the parties for valuable consideration, with their eyes open, contract that a particular thing shall not be done, all that a Court of Equity has to do is to say by way of injunction that which the parties have already said by way of covenant – namely ... the thing shall not be done'.

But where contracts of personal service are concerned, prohibitive injunctions will not be granted unless:

(i) there is an express negative stipulation. If Tom promises to sing at the Deadbeat nightclub, that may possibly imply that he will not sing the same night at the principal rival establishment, the Beatdeads. But no injunction will be possible, unless there is an express promise not to appear anywhere else that night.

(ii) the effect of the injunction would not be the same as specific performance of the contract, i.e. to compel the person to perform the contract.

Bette Davis made a contract with Warner Bros, which included express terms that:

(i) she would not act for anybody else, and

(ii) she would not engage in any other occupation, without their consent in writing.

In breach she entered into an agreement to make a film for somebody else. The court granted an injunction to restrain her from acting for anybody else but was not prepared to grant an injunction to restrain her from engaging in any other profession. So she was free, if she chose, to earn her living as a waitress or a chambermaid. To deprive her of all opportunity of earning a living in some other capacity might have the same effect as an order of specific performance: *Warner Bros* v. *Nelson* (1936).

But when an injunction was sought against a pop group called 'The Trogs' for an express negative stipulation that they would not employ anybody but the plaintiffs as their managers, one was refused. Without a manager they would have been unable to have continued in their chosen profession and this would, the judge held, have had the same effect as an order of specific performance – in spite of the fact that they were free to find some other employment: *Page One Records* v. *Britton* (1967).

Prohibitive unjunctions may be refused when it would be contrary to public policy to enforce the covenant, e.g. where the promise is in restraint of trade.

Mandatory injunctions are granted most reluctantly, and in a case where a part of an orchard was sold, with an express negative covenant that a roadway would not be raised, and it was, the court was unwilling to order the destruction of the roadway, and adjourned the proceedings for another possible solution to be found: *Charrington* v. *Simons & Co. Ltd* (1971).

Chapter 4

The Other Contracting Party

4.01 Types of trading entities

Businessmen in general are very lax in ascertaining exactly with whom
they are dealing. There is now an Institute of Credit Controllers which is
dedicated to ensuring that credit is extended only to those worthy of it; but
they are concerned primarily with consumer credit and the sort of people
who might have County Court judgments registered against them. They
are usually ill-equipped to advise on a multi-million pound contract with
such bodies as the International Tin Council which, had become
insolvent, owing £600 million, or the agencies of a so-called but
unrecognised state called Ciskei, which had a hospital and two schools
built but was disinclined to pay the full price for them.

In Britain, unlike the situation in many other countries, a man may start
any business he chooses without the prior permission of the Government.
Except for certain types of business for which qualifications are necessary,
and others, where, usually for revenue purposes, licences are required,
there is a general freedom to engage in any enterprise. Indeed, ever since
the early eighteenth century, it has been a principle of the English Law
that restrains on trade are *prima facie* void.

Trading may take place:

(1) by individuals;
(2) by corporations. In addition to natural persons – real live human
beings – the law recognises other *personae* as they are called; that is to say,
artificial persons, recognised in law as having an identity separate from the
individual human beings who comprise them. They are usually termed
'corporations' and these corporations may consist of different types:

   (a) *The corporation sole.* The one-man corporation is something
       recognised as separate from the individual who holds the office for
       the time being. For example, the Rector of a Church of England

parish is a corporation sole – unlike a Methodist minister, or a Roman Catholic priest. So, too, is a Bishop of a Church of England diocess, unlike his Roman Catholic counterpart. The Crown is a corporation sole, as is the Public Trustee. Property vested in a corporation sole belongs to the corporation and not to the person who for the time being holds the office.

(b) *Corporations aggregate.* These are of various kinds and the most familiar is the Limited Liability Company. They, once again, are artificial persons recognised as having an identity in law separate from the individuals who comprise the corporation.

(3) by partnership firms. These are groups of persons who associate together for the purpose of carrying on a business with a view to profit. (4) by unincorporated associations. These are collections of people who come together, but whose primary purpose is not to make profit but to pursue some interest they have in common – whether it be a sport, a religion or the promotion of a special breed of cat or cattle. But many of these often engage in trading activities. The religious bodies may publish books and magazines and frequently do; the tennis club will inevitably enter into contracts and own property; and the rabbit breeding clubs may buy and sell serum or stock; and almost every other type of club with premises of its own will probably buy and sell liquor [4.03].

4.02   Trading by individuals

An individual trading is liable to the full extent of most of his assets for all debts and other liabilities incurred in trading. Some assets are exempted by sections of the Insolvency Act 1986, but they are of little value. The process of exacting these assets from an individual is termed 'bankruptcy'. There are disabilities on bankrupts, but they are outside the scope of this book. Bankrupts who can find the money to pay expensive lawyers often find it possible to continue their lifestyle as before, with a Rolls Royce and a Hampstead mansion. It is unwise to rely on being able to recover monies due from individual traders.

There is no age limit at which a person can commence trading. 'There is nothing except the commonsense of his customers to prevent a six-year-old setting up business' pointed out the Latey Committee on the age of majority. Particular care, however, is required in dealing with minors – persons under the age of 18 – as these are not liable on their trading contracts. Money paid to them for goods which are not received cannot – in the absence of deliberate fraud by the minor – be recovered, nor can they be made to pay for goods received or made to return the goods. These are not debts in law. Otherwise, of course, an individual trading as such is liable in the full extent of all his assets for the trading debts of his business. However, the Minors' Contract Act 1986 made two relevant alterations to the existing law:

(a) guarantors of a minor's obligation are liable even if the contract made with the minor is unenforceable;
(b) the court is given a discretion to order the return of property acquired by a minor under an unenforceable contract if it considers it 'just and equitable' to do so.

4.03 Unincorporated associations

A 'club' may mean a business owned by an individual, a partnership or a limited company, as are most 'night clubs', 'country clubs' and 'football clubs' etc. In all three cases they are known as 'proprietary clubs'. Most professional football clubs are owned by limited liability companies and are therefore proprietary clubs, but a local football club or cricket team will almost inevitably be a members' club and therefore an unincorporated association.

The points to note about such bodies are:

(1) They are not persons in law and cannot therefore sue or be sued.

There are exceptions by Acts of Parliament to this (such as trade unions) but this is the general principle. There is provision under Order 15 Rule 12 of the Supreme Court Rules for a Representative Action 'where numerous persons have the same interest in any proceedings', but where there is a changing membership, as with most unincorporated associations, this is not applicable.

(2) There is often a contract between each member and all the other members, in which the rules of the association constitute the terms.

This is dependant on the interpretation of all the circumstances and it may well be that there is evidence that there was no contractual intent. Where there is, however, the courts will intervene by declaration and by injunction to restrain the wrongful expulsion of members, or actions against them which are contrary to natural justice.

(3) Contracts with third parties purporting to be made on behalf of an unincorporated association do not bind the members so as to make them personally liable. This applies unless the member has expressly or impliedly pledged his personal credit.

(4) Members of the committee of an unincorporated association may be liable both in contract and tort in respect of contracts or acts which they have personally authorised. In *Bradley Egg Farm* v. *Clifford* (1943), a member of the Lancashire Utility Poultry Society – an unincorporated association – sued for damages for negligent tests carried out by the Society for white diarrhoea in hens. Judgment was given against the Executive Council.

(5) Land and buildings etc. can only be held by trustees on behalf of the members of incoporated associations. This is because the association itself is not a *persona*.

(6) In the event of dissolution of the association, property held in trust for the association is divisible amongst the existing members at the date of dissolution.

An allotment association purchased land for £210 which was conveyed to trustees but the money was raised by what were termed 'shares' of £1 each; in addition, allotment holders were members of the association and paid a small subscription. From 1961 the association became inactive, but in 1967 the land was sold for £70,000. The court held that this sum had to be distributed equally amongst all members in 1961 whether allotment holders or 'shareholders', after the shareholders' money had been refunded: *Re St. Andrew's Allotment Association Trusts* (1969).

It will be apparent from the above that there are considerable dangers for traders dealing with clubs and similar unincorporated associations, and also for members of executive committees who authorise transactions – though members of unincorporated associations may sometimes come in for unexpected windfalls.

4.04 Trading with partnerships

The members of a partnership are jointly and severally liable for its debts and liabilities if the partnership assets are incapable of meeting them.

A partnership has, in England, no separate legal personality; in Scotland, a partnership does. Partnerships, although often created by deed, can come into existence informally when there has been no formal documentation and even when the parties deny the existence of a partnership. There can also be partnerships between two or more limited liability companies and between individuals and a company. In *Eli Abt* v. *Fraiman and Ors* (1975) an architect did preliminary work on a development scheme for four men, two of them solicitors. They then told the architect to send his bill to a £100 company they had formed which had two issued shares only. The court, however, held that it was a partnership amongst themselves and with the company.

In a partnership, one partner even if unauthorised by the other, is empowered to bind the partnership; and the partnership is liable for all acts of negligence committed by all employees and all partners, irrespective of whether they were concerned in it or not.

There is no requirement for a partnership to file accounts with anybody but the Inland Revenue, and these accounts remain confidential. In general, therefore, it is not possible for outsiders, including other contracting parties, to determine the financial strength of a partnership.

Moreover, every time a partner leaves or dies or a new one joins there is a new partnership, which has no liability for the debts or liabilities of the preceding partnership, even if it may bear the same name. However, the individual members of the former partnership cannot escape liability. Being a partner, therefore, is a hazardous occupation. A vivid example of this can be seen from a 1986 case: *Lipkin Gorman* v. *Karpnale Ltd* (1986).

A partner in the firm of solicitors, whose 'punctilious orthodox Jewish observance suggested probity rather than the want of it', as the judge put it, withdrew £323,222 from the firm's clients' account. 'The vast bulk of this money was lost at the Playboy Club in Park Lane', reported the judge.

The other partners were unaware of this partner's gambling, for he even declined to take part in the office sweepstake on Derby Day. There were, it was held, no defects in the firm's accountancy system and nothing in the general conduct of its office which could have alerted the firm.

The fact that the partner in question was extradited from Israel and subsequently sentenced to a period of three years in prison; and that the partners received some sums from Lloyd's Bank as a result of the then manager of the Brook Street branch acting with 'a want of probity', could have been little comfort to the other partners called upon to replace their clients' money.

4.05 Dealing with companies

Apart from the normal perils of credit-worthiness, often difficult to ascertain since filing at Companies House is often years out of date, and even if up to date may not represent the current financial position of the company, there are three other hazards in dealing with companies.

The first is the doctrine of *ultra vires*, explained later in this section.

The second is the fact that parent companies are not liable – subject to one possible qualification – for the debts of their subsidiaries [4.07].

The third is the difficult question as to the authority of the person professing to contract on the company's behalf. At one time there was no difficulty about this: corporations, including companies, could only contract under the seal of the company; now the position is quite different. A person who professes to contract on behalf of a company may in fact have no authority to do so [4.08].

A company is required by section 2(1) of the Companies Act 1985 to include an 'objects' clause in its Memorandum of Association: previous Companies Acts since 1856 have made similar provisions.

If a company attempts to do anything outside those objects, the transaction is void as being *ultra vires*, i.e. outside the powers of the company.

The result is that

'A company incorporated under the Companies Acts can only make contracts binding on it provided that they are within the scope of the objects' clause of its Memorandum of Association. Any contracts which are outside the objects' clause are not binding on the company.'

Introductions Ltd was a company formed for the purpose of providing facilities for overseas visitors to the Festival of Britain 1951, and its objects were framed accordingly. After many vicissitudes, it ended up pig-breeding and a bank which had lent the company £29,000 on debentures for that purpose was unable to claim in the liquidation of the company: *Introductions Ltd* v. *National Provincial Bank Ltd* (1969).

Another company was by its objects clause entitled to carry on business as costumiers; it diversified into veneer panelling, and the builder of a factory, and suppliers of veneers and coke were not entitled to receive any portion of the company's assets on its liquidation: *Re Jon Beauforte Ltd* (1953).

The leading case on this *ultra vires* ('outside the powers') doctrine as it is called, is the House of Lords decision in *Ashbury Railway Carriage Co* v. *Riche* (1875) where the objects clause read

'to make and sell, or lend or hire railway carriages or waggons ... and to carry on the business of mechanical engineers and general contractors'.

The company obtained a concession to run a railway in Belgium and entered into a contract with Riche to build it for them. It was held that Riche could not recover damages for breach of contract because the apparently binding contract was outside the powers of the company to conclude.

Monies borrowed for a purpose outside a company's powers cannot be recovered as a debt, although if the money can be identified or traced, equity will assist in its recovery on a quasi-contractual basis [1.15].

To enter into contracts with limited companies therefore can be a hazardous operation since everybody is presumed to know what is contained in their Memorandum of Association. All the company documents are available for inspection for a small fee at Companies House, and a prudent man would no doubt read these carefully before he made a contract with any company; whether he would find time for any other business is, of course, debatable.

The company can rely as a defence upon its own wrong in making a contract which is *ultra vires*; but can the other contracting party also set this up as a defence? Can a defendant sued by a company on a contract that is *ultra vires* escape liability for damages for breach of contract? Can a defendant do this, even when the company has performed the whole of its own obligations? If Jon Beauforte Ltd, mentioned above, had delivered a load of veneer panels to a customer, could he have refused to pay for them?

Anglo-Overseas Agencies Ltd v. *Green* (1960) proceeded on the basis that the *ultra vires* defence was available to the other contracting party, and in 1965 Mr Justice Mocatta expressly so held in *Bell Houses Ltd* v. *City Wall Properties Ltd* (1965), but that case was reversed on other grounds by the Courts of Appeal the following year. However, Lord Justice Salmon, in passing, observed:

'It seems strange that third parties could take advantage of a doctrine, manifestly for the protection of shareholders, in order to deprive the company of money which in justice should be paid to it by the third party.'

And with that view most academic authors seem to agree.

But perhaps we shall never know the answer to the conundrum, for the Court of Appeal held in that particular case that if the objects clause included power 'to carry on any business which, in the opinion of the Board of Directors can be advantageously carried on with, in connection with, or as ancillary to, its authorised business', there was nothing that was *ultra vires* the company.

The rule was emphasised by the judgment of Lord Wensleydale in *Ernest* v. *Nicholls* (1857), shortly after the Companies Act 1856 introduced the objects clause:

'All persons must take notice of the deed and the provision of the Act.
    If they do not choose to acquaint themselves with the powers of the directors, it is their own fault ...

The stipulation of the deed ... are obligatory on those who deal with the company.

Directors can make no contract ... unless they are strictly complied with ...'

The position was altered as a result of the First EEC Directive No. 68/151 which began

'Acts done by the organs of the company shall be binding upon it even if those acts are not within the objects of the company ...'

That Directive was supposed to have been implemented by what is now section 35 of the Companies Act 1985. It is doubtful whether it does in fact do so. That section reads:

'(1) In favour of a person dealing with a company in good faith, any transaction decided on by the directors is deemed to be one which it is within the capacity of the company to enter into, and the power of the directors to bind the company is deemed to be free of any limitation under the memorandum or articles.
(2) A party to a transaction so decided on is not bound to enquire as to the capacity of the company to enter into it or as to any such limitation on the powers of the directors, and is presumed to have acted in good faith unless the contrary is proved.'

There was a discussion of the predecessor of this section, in identical words in *Barclays Bank Ltd* v. *T.O.S.G. Trust Fund Ltd* (1984) by Mr Justice Nourse. He then said:

'In the case of a transaction decided only by the directors [the section] has abolished the rule that a person who deals with a company is automatically effected with constructive notice of its objects clause. But, by retaining the requirement of good faith, it nevertheless ensures that a defence based on absence of notice shall not be available to someone who has not acted genuinely and honestly in his dealings with the company. Notice and good faith, although two separate beings, are often inseparable.'

But it will be seen that the Act appears to limit the protection solely to 'any transaction decided on by the directors'. It does not apparently cover all the multitude of contracts entered into by their authorised subordinates.

Two other points should be noted about companies. Firstly, a company cannot make a contract until it comes into existence, which is the moment when it is registered. This may appear self-evident, like saying an unborn child cannot contract, but every day, business men make arrangements for companies not yet registered. They are not binding.

Secondly, even after a company has come into existence it cannot ratify or adopt contracts made on its behalf before incorporation. There must always be a completely new contract after incorporation for it to be enforceable. This applies even to the costs of the formation and it is necessary for there to be a contract after incorporation before the promoter of the company can be reimbursed.

4.06 Dealing with subsidiaries

In most common law jurisdictions, a parent company or a group holding company has no liability for either the debts or the torts of its subsidiary companies, even if it owns all or nearly all the shares.

That is not technically entirely correct, because there may be liability on the directors in English law if the shareholders fall below the minimum number required by the Companies Act 1985 – that is, two for a private company and five for a public limited company. However, in practice, all parent companies ensure that this does not apply by appointing nominees, usually their accountants, to hold the necessary number of shares. So, if it is a private company with an issued capital of £100,000 in £1 shares, the parent will hold 99,999 shares and a nominee, holding the share in trust for the parent, will hold one share.

The effect of this could be seen in the Bhopal Gas tragedy in India. The plant which caused 2,000 deaths and untold injuries, was owned by Union Carbide, a wholly owned Indian subsidiary of a United States firm. The subsidiary's total assets were only £39 million, whereas the Indian government's own estimate of the compensation necessary was around £700 million. If the subsidiary had been put into liquidation, claimants, even if they had obtained judgment, would be relegated to the position of unsecured creditors, with the secured creditors, such as banks, no doubt taking all the assets.

Not surprisingly, some of the claimants elected to sue the parent company in one of the United States.

From their point of view this had notable advantages. To start with, in the USA lawyers are allowed to and are prepared to act on a contingency basis; that is, they conduct the whole litigation without charge to the litigant, taking part of the proceeds if successful, but charging nothing for their own expenses if they are not. British lawyers might make more of an effort on behalf of their clients if they were allowed to do the same. Indian lawyers, like British, require payment in advance for litigation and there is no legal aid system in any way comparable to even the inefficient and limited one that exists in the United Kingdom.

The United States has a sophisticated product liability and negligence law, with provision for awarding punitive damages in a case where companies have put their profits before the safety of people. These damages are still assessed by juries who are noticeably more generous with other people's money than English High Court judges. Further, in the United States, there is effective pre-trial procedures for the discovery of relevant documents which is much more effective than the English or Indian procedure.

It must therefore have been regarded as a triumph for Union Carbide when a Federal Judge in the United States stayed all the actions proceeding there and ordered that the trials should be held in India.

However, he did impose one important condition: he made this ruling expressly subject to an undertaking by the Union Carbide parent company that it would assume liability for the obligations of its subsidiary. Without this, the unfortunate plaintiffs could have been left whistling for their money even after judgment in their favour.

The value to a company of the protection afforded to subsidiaries is well illustrated by the case of Pilkingtons, the glass makers, who claim an annual turnover of £18,000 million. One of their building subsidiaries made and marketed glass cladding for buildings. This proved, after a vast amount had been sold (with the commendation of a well-known architect who later became President of the RIBA) to be thoroughly defective. However, by the time the claims came rolling in, it so happened that Pilkington had already wrapped up the subsidiary company by putting it into voluntary liquidation.

There are two good defences in law. One is 'I have no money', since no lawyer will waste powder and shot on a bird without feathers. Even better is the one: 'I don't exist any more'.

This illustrates the commercial advantages that can be achieved through trading through subsidiaries.

It also is a good illustration of the dangers of dealing with subsidiaries of companies even with famous names. If Rolls Royce can go bust leaving most of their suppliers unpaid, who cannot?

However, it now appears possible that there is a way in which holding companies may be held liable for the debts and other liabilities of a subsidiary. The Companies Act 1985 introduced into English law the concept of 'shadow director', defined in section 741 as 'a person in accordance with whose directions or instructions the directors of the company are accustomed to act'.

It is true that the same section in (3) goes on to provide that 'a body corporate is not to be treated as a shadow director of any of its subsidiary companies by reason only that directors of the subsidiary are accustomed to act in accordance with its directions or instructions'. But that recognises that there *are* circumstances in which a body corporate, such as a company, can be a 'shadow director' and, indeed, that was expressly stated in the House of Commons by the minister who was in charge of the legislation.

It has been suggested therefore that in some situations a parent company would be held to be a shadow director and, as a result of the Insolvency Act 1986, liable for the obligations of the subsidiary. But there has certainly been no case so far where this has been held.

4.07 What authority?

Another problem is knowing exactly what authority the person negotiating on behalf of the other side has.

Some of the difficulties can be seen in the House of Lords'case of *Armagus* v. *Mundogas* (1986). The chartering manager of a shipping company was authorised to sell a ship on the basis that it would be chartered back. Because he had a financial interest in the deal, he sold the ship to the new owners in a document which purported to indicate that it was to be subject to a three year charterparty back to the previous owners; to his employers, he submitted documents showing it had been sold subject to a 12-month charterparty.

When the ship was handed over at the end of the first year, the new owners claimed that they were entitled to a further two years' hire. The dishonest manager had assured the new owners that he had express authority from his employers to sell the ship.

However, the new owners were forced to concede in court that the chartering manager had neither *actual* nor *ostensible* authority to sell the ship, although they did claim that the previous owners were estopped from denying they had given him specific authority to sell the ship with a three year charterparty obligation. All courts, including the House of Lords held that he did not have that specific authority.

It was then argued that at least he had apparent authority to say that he had specific authority. Not surprisingly, this argument also failed.

It is therefore important to find out whether the person purporting to contract on behalf of a company has actual authority to do so. One way is to write to the Board of Directors and find out.

4.08   Statutory corporations

These may be created by Acts of Parliament as, for example, the British Railways Board and are subject to what is termed the *ultra vires* rule [4.06]. That is, if they make contracts outside their statutory powers the contracts are not binding on them.

In some cases, too, there is difficulty in knowing whether they contract at all where they merely carry out their statutory duty to supply consumers. The same problem applies to companies specifically created by special statute, such as water undertakings.

In a number of cases the courts have held that corporations created by Acts of Parliament and charged with specific duties are merely fulfilling their statutory obligations when they supply their customers and have no contractual obligations to them.

The earliest case of this kind appears to be *Milnes* v. *Huddersfield Corporation* (1886), where it was held that there was no *contractual* obligation by a water company created by Act of Parliament towards those it supplied.

The same thing was said in relation to a gas company later in *Clegg Parkson and Co.* v. *Earby Gas Co Ltd* (1896):

'The obligation of the Company, if any, depends on Statute and not upon contract.'

So when, in October 1937, the Croydon Corporation distributed to consumers through its mains, water that was contaminated by typhoid germs and started an epidemic in which over 300 people became infected and 43 died, the Corporation succeeded in escaping liability in contract. Had it been a contract, those injured would have been entitled to damages under the Sale of Goods Act 1983, since water (like milk) is a chattel. Damages would have been recoverable whether or not the Corporation had been negligent, since the water was clearly not fit for the purpose required. But Mr Justice Stable in *Read* v. *Croydon Corporation* (1938), held that the relationship was not a contractual one, but

'a relationship between two persons under which one is bound to supply water and the other, provided he has paid the equivalent rent, is entitled to receive.'

This principle was apparently regarded as so axiomatic that none of these cases appears even to have been discussed in *Willmore* v. *South Eastern Electricity Board* (1957). Mr and Mrs Willmore started in business as poultry farmers rearing chicks by infra red heat and the South

Eastern Electricity Board promised them an adequate and persistent supply of Electricity to maintain lamps for that purpose. This the Board failed to do, with the result that the lamps chilled, the chicks died and Mr and Mrs Willmore were ruined financially. The judge held that the representations about proper supply of electricity were not made *animo contrahiendi*, as he put it – 'with contractual intent' – and there was no contract at all between the South Eastern Electricity Board and the unfortunate consumers:

> 'I have come to the conclusion that the plaintiffs, having failed to prove a contract, can have no cause of action for damages for breach of contract.'

Presumably on the basis that it is best to ignore what you disapprove of, none of these cases finds mention in the leading practitioner's monograph on the law of contract.

Long before this principle was invented it had been held that no contractual obligations arose out of the carriage of letters by post – a principle that extends as far back as 1701. You cannot therefore sue the Post Office Corporation if they lose a valuable letter – as Triefus and Co Ltd discovered with the G.P.O. in 1957 when a registered package of diamonds dispatched to New Zealand disappeared in the course of transmission, thanks to the activities of a light-fingered member of the Post Office staff: *Triefus* v. *General Post Office* (1957).

With 'privatisation' of public utilities, such as the Gas Board, the statute and Memorandum of Association and Articles of Association will have to be carefully considered as to exactly what the obligations are. But it will be seen that many of the early cases in this topic were in relation to limited liability companies, created or licensed by statute.

4.09 Chartered corporations

Corporations may also be created under the prerogative of the Crown by Royal Charter. The Pharmaceutical Society is a body of this nature, as is the Hudson Bay Company. Such corporations are not subject to the *ultra vires* rule and they have the full capacity to do anything that an ordinary individual can. But if they exceed the powers given them in their charter of incorporation, they may be liable to forfeit the charter, and for this reason any member of such a corporation will be granted an injunction by the courts to restrain the chartered corporation from exceeding its powers: *Jenkins* v. *Pharmaceutical Society* (1921).

4.10   The perils of dealing with overseas companies

Handgate Co. Ltd S.A. was a one-ship company resistered in Panama. By a voyage charterparty, it contracted with a Hong Kong company to load rice in Rangoon for carriage to West Africa. The charterer sold the cargo to Ets Soale et Compagnie; which took delivery at Lomé under bills of lading which incorporated the terms of the charterparty.

Ets Soale alleged that there was short delivery and wet damage of the cargo and that they were entitled to damages of $32,000. But, said Lord Justice Lloyd, in the Court of Appeal:

'Service on a one-ship Panamanian company can present difficulties.

The only method of service on a Panamanian company in Panamanian law is by personal service on the company's legal representative, who is the person registered or appointed by the company as such.

Failing such registration or appointment, service may be effected on the president of the company, or in his absence, on any other director of the company.'

Needless to say, there were no directors or legal representatives actually in Panama, but the company register there provided an address in Hong Kong at which the president was allegedly located and an address in that city where the company was supposed to carry on business. Neither could be located there or at the address given in Lloyd's register of shipping. In fact, under Hong Kong law, if it were a foreign company with a place of business in that city it was required to register, just as in England by section 691 of the Companies Act 1985, a foreign company which has a place of business within the jurisdiction is required to register at Companies House. There was no registration in Hong Kong.

Eventually one director of the company was tracked down in Hong Kong and leave given to serve an English writ on him under the provisions of Order 11 Rule 1(1)(f) of the Rules of the Supreme Court which then read (it has since been altered):

'1(1) Provided that the writ does not contain any such claim as is mentioned in Order 85 Rule 2(1)(a), service of a writ out of the jurisdiction is permissible with the leave of the Court in the following cases, that is to say ...

(f) if the action begun by the writ is brought against a defendant not domiciled or ordinarily resident in Scotland to enforce rescind dissolve annul or otherwise affect a contract, or to recover damages or obtain other relief in respect of the breach of a contract, being (in either case) a contract which

(i) was made within the jurisdiction, or
(ii) was made by or through an agent trading or residing within the jurisdiction on behalf of a principal trading or residing out of the jurisdiction or
(iii) is by its terms, or by implication, governed by English law.'

Even so, a High Court judge set the writ aside on the grounds that Handgate was carrying on business in Hong Kong and should have been sued there. It required the Court of Appeal to re-establish it.

4.11   Foreign government companies

Particular care is necessary in dealing with overseas companies which are enterprises wholly owned by their governments. If those governments by decree or other legislation, enact that their companies should be exonerated from their contractual obligations, the English courts will do nothing to assist the injured party.

This became evident when a company called Settebello Ltd, a subsidiary of German steelmakers, Thyssen, sued Setenare, the Portuguese state-owned shipyard. The contract provided for a tanker to be delivered to Settebello not later than 31 January 1978. This was extended by stages until 30 April 1982 as the result of the generosity of Settebello, but eventually, out of patience, they gave notice under the terms of the contract that if it was not delivered on that date they would terminate the contract and reclaim payments made of $11 million.

Ten days before that deadline, the Portuguese government, with suspicious alacrity, passed decree No. 119/82 which gave a Portuguese company declared to be in a 'critical economic situation', the right to avoid cancellations for delay in delivery provided it made a declaration that it could deliver within two years. And, just to make sure, the decree also specified that such a declaration should be effective the day it was made and not the day it was delivered to the other contracting party – contrary to all other provisions in Portuguese law.

This, known in Portugal as the 'Setenare' decree, has never been used since it was claimed to have let the Portuguese company off the hook.

Settebello Ltd sued the Banco Totta and Acores in the English High Court on the £25 million performance bond the bank had given for due performance of the contract to build the tanker. In the Commercial Court, Mr Justice Hurst refused to allow evidence that the decree had ever been made at the instance of Setenare because, he said, it would be to interfere in the legislative process of a friendly power. The Court of Appeal upheld him and the House of Lords refused leave to appeal.

However, there were arbitration clauses in the original contract. Although Portuguese law specifically governed the contract, arbitration procedure was to be in Holland under the rules of the RNAI, the Royal Netherlands Arbitration Institute. Article 26 of those rules provides that the arbitrators shall – unlike English law – decide *ex aequo et bono,* that is, according to equity and justice, and not necessarily according to law. The three arbitrators decided that a decree made for the sole purpose of relieving one of its own enterprises of its contractual obligations (and thereby benefiting itself) was not to be given effect. It was contrary to generally accepted principles of international law and violated all concepts of public policy and morality common to all trading nations.

The moral seems to be that, if you have to contract with any enterprise of a foreign government, include a clause making the RNAI the arbitration conditions and the Netherlands the place of arbitration. An English arbitrator would have insisted that Portuguese law was given the effect intended by that government. English law, although it originally proceeded for centuries on the *ex aequo et bono* principle, now requires arbitrators to adhere strictly to the relevant law (see Parris: *Arbitration – Principles and Practice,* para. 1.04).

4.12   State entities

There are perils even in dealing with other State entities which are a separate legal persona, as Jaured Properties Ltd found in a transaction with the *Ente Nazionale per il Tourisma* (ENIT) – the Italian Tourist Board.

ENIT agreed, through its London representative, to buy from the company the long lease of a property in London. ENIT did not pay on the completion date and Jaured were granted on summary judgment an order for specific performance of the contract. ENIT appealed and were given leave to defend.

At the trial, it was not disputed that the contract for the sale of the lease was subject to English law, but it was claimed that the transaction was *ultra vires* ENIT and this question was subject to Italian law.

The English court accepted this position and received evidence as to the relevant Italian Law. The position appeared to be that a contract made by a public entity such as ENIT without the specific consent of the Minister concerned, was *millita relativa* and the Italian courts could declare it void on the application of the body concerned. But the other contracting party was bound by the contract.

This inequitable position did not meet with the approval of the English court, which found a way round it by accepting evidence that an Italian court would protect innocent third parties who made a contract with a public entity and who suffered loss from the improper conduct of public officials.

But the dangers are apparent. Contract with an Italian state company and there is no way of determining whether the contract is within its powers. Under Italian law, it can always escape from its liability by pleading that the contract was not specifically approved by the responsible Minister.

There is no way, in most cases, in which an English contractor can discover whether or not any particular contract entered into with a state corporation is *ultra vires* the powers of that body. To add to that problem is the fact that this question must be determined by the domestic law of the country concerned.

4.13   International bodies

The International Tin Council was a body set up as a cartel to rig the price of tin, by maintaining a 'buffer stock', i.e. tin that had been taken off the market. It was set up under a treaty of 22 nations, including Great Britain. When it ceased trading, it left debts of some £600 million to brokers, banks and others in Britain and led to the total collapse of the Cornish tin industry.

Mr Giles Shaw, the Minister of State for Trade and Industry, denied any liability on the part of the Government and refused to give any information to the House of Commons.

An attempt was made in 1987 by Amalgamated Metal Trading Ltd, supported by Kleinwort Benson plc. to have the International Tin Council wound up under the provisions of sections 665, 666 and 671 of the Companies Act 1985.

Section 666 (10 provides 'that any unregistered company may be wound up under this Act' and section 671 (2) provides that 'every contributory is liable to contribute' to the debts of the company.

The bankrupt International Tin Council mustered four Queen's Counsels and four junior counsels to oppose this application and so did not seem that short of money. Amalgamated Metal Trading Ltd was owed over £5.3 million pounds and had obtained an arbitration award for the sum, with interest. But the International Tin Council had failed to pay.

Mr Justice Millett in the Chancery Division of the High Court refused to make an order. He said that the Council had been established under an agreement which came into force on 1 July 1982 and that the headquarters were established in London under a Headquarters Agreement made between the UK government and the Council. Both agreements provided that the ITA should be a *persona* in law. There was a Statutory Instrument SI 1972 No. 120, which purported to confer certain immunities on the International Tin Council. Mr Justice Millett said:

'Its existence was recognised by the Order, which granted it the legal capacities of a body corporate, but was not incorporated thereby and it was not a statutory body.'

In short, his lordship was saying that ITC could sue but not be sued.

Businessmen should have great reluctance to enter into contracts with international bodies.

4.14 Unrecognised states

Even greater problems arise from dealings with unrecognised states. These cannot sue or be sued in an English court.

An unrecognised state is one that is not recognised as a sovereign state by Her Majesty's Foreign and Commonwealth Office. A certificate from that department is final and binding on all English courts and is conclusive evidence as to the facts stated in it.

In *Gur Corporation* v. *Trust Bank of Africa Ltd* (1986) the plaintiffs had entered into a contract with the Ciskei government to design and erect a hospital and two schools. Ciskei is a small territory in the eastern Cape Province of South Africa.

This government had come into existence as the result of a South African enactment, the State of Ciskei Act 1981, which purported to declare Ciskei a sovereign independent state over which the Republic had no authority.

The Foreign and Commonwealth Office certified that the United Kingdom Government did not accord recognition to the Republic of Ciskei as an independent sovereign state and had no formal position as regards the exercise of governing authority over the Ciskei territory.

For their contract, Gur Corporation had to produce an 'on demand' performance bond of US $375,000 and this was furnished by the Trust Bank of Africa Ltd. It was payable by the bank on receipt of a certificate from the Department of Public Works of the Republic of Ciskei approved and signed by a registered quantity surveyor. Shortly before the bond was due to expire, a claim was received by telex but it was not approved or signed by a registered quantity surveyor. Gur Corporation issued proceedings in the English courts against the bank claiming a declaration that the guarantee period had expired without a valid claim having been made and for repayment of US $300,000 it had deposited with the Bank for security.

The Bank initiated Third Party proceedings against the Republic of Ciskei claiming a similar declaration. The Republic served a defence and counterclaim.

On a preliminary issue, Mr Justice Steyn held that the Republic of Ciskei could not sue or be sued in the English courts. Nor could the position be cured by substituting the Department of Public Works or its Director General or a named civil servant for the Republic of Ciskei.

In some cases, the Foreign Office is prepared to issue a certificate that although the state itself is not recognised by the United Kingdom, the unrecognised state is in effect the agent of a sovereign state which the crown does recognise. It did this with the German Democratic Republic where the Foreign and Commonwealth Office contended that this was a subordinate body set up by the USSR: *Carl Zeiss Stiftung* v. *Rayner and Keeler Ltd (No. 2)* (1967).

It also accepted the Turkish Cypriot government as the agent of the Turkish State: *Hesperides Hotels Ltd* v. *Aegean Turkish Holidays Ltd* (1978).

However, the Court of Appeal held subsequently that the state of Ciskei could sue or be sued because it was a mere constituent part of the Republic of South Africa; which the UK government had recognised.

It is clear, however, that there can be difficulties in suing in the English courts either an unrecognised state or any of its authorised agencies.

Chapter 5

Obligations to the Other Party Outside the Contract

5.01 Liability in contract and tort

An important thing to notice is that the existence of a contract between the parties will not circumscribe all the obligations of the parties to each other. There can be liability both in tort and in equity to the other contracting party.

In the case of *Esso* v. *Mardon* (1976) Lord Denning laid down the principle, accepted by the other members of the Court of Appeal, that contracting parties were also liable in tort to one another. The petrol company had made representations to a potential service station that the 'throughput' of petrol in the third year of operation would reach 200,000 gallons. In fact, it never attained more than 86,502 gallons.

In the Court of Appeal, Lord Denning, having agreed that there was not a warranty in the sense that Esso had guaranteed that the throughput would be 200,000 gallons, went on to say:

> 'Nevertheless it was a forecast made by a party; Esso, who had special knowledge and skill ... They knew the facts. They knew the traffic in town. They knew the throughput of comparable stations. They had much experience and expertise at their disposal ...
>
> In the present case, it seems to me that there was a warranty that the forecast was sound, that is that Esso had made it with reasonable care and skill.'

He then went on to discuss the relationship between contracting parties and liability in tort. He continued:

> 'Assuming that there was no warranty, the question arises whether Esso are liable for negligent mis-statement, under the doctrine of *Hedley Byrne* v. *Heller and Partners Ltd*. It has been suggested that *Hedley Byrne* cannot be used so as to impose liability for negligent pre-

contractual statements; and that, in a pre-contract situation, the remedy (at any rate before the 1967 Act) was only in warranty or nothing. Thus, in *Hedley Byrne* itself Lord Reid said:

> "Where there is a contract there is no real difficulty as regards the contracting parties; the question is whether there is a warranty."

And in *Oleificio Zuccu* v. *Northern Sales* Mr Justice McNair said that:

> " ... as at present advised, I consider the submission advanced by the buyers – that the ruling in *Hedley Byrne* applies as between contracting parties – is without foundation."

As against these, I took a different view in *McInerney* v. *Lloyds Bank* when I said:

> "If one person by a negligent mis-statement, induces another to enter into a contract – with himself or a third person – he may be liable in damages."

In arguing this point, counsel for the defendant submitted that, when the negotiations between two parties resulted in a contract between them, their rights and duties were governed by the law of contract and not by the law of tort. There was, therefore, no place in their relationship for *Hedley Byrne* which was solely a liability in tort.

He relied particularly on *Clark* v. *Kirby Smith* where Mr Justice Plowman held that the liability of a solicitor for negligence was a liability in contract and not in tort, following the observations of Sir Wilfred Greene, the Master of the Rolls, in *Groom* v. *Crocker*.

Counsel for the defendant might also have cited *Bagot* v. *Stevens Scanlan & Co*, about an architect and other cases too. But I venture to suggest that those cases are in conflict with other decisions of high authority which were not cited in them. These decisions show that, in the case of a professional man, the duty to use reasonable care arises not only in contract, but is also imposed by the law apart from contract, and is therefore actionable in tort. It is comparable to the duty of reasonable care which is owed by a master to his servant, or *vice versa*. It can be put either in contract or in tort: see *Lister* v. *Romford Ice and Cold Storage Co.*, per Lord Radcliffe; and *Matthews* v. *Kuwait Bechtel Corporation*. The position was stated by Tindal C J in delivering the judgement of the Court of Exchequer Chamber in *Boorman* v. *Brown*:

> "There is a large class of cases where the foundation of the action

springs out of privity of contract between the parties, but in which the breach or non-performance is indifferently either *assumpsit* or case upon tort. Such are the actions against attorneys, surgeons and other professional men for want of competent skill of proper care in the service they undertake to render ... The principle in all these cases would seem to be that the contract creates a duty and the neglect to perform that duty, or the non-feasance, is a ground of action upon a tort."

That decision was affirmed in the House of Lords at 11 Clarke and Finelly 1, when Lord Campbell, giving the one speech, said

"Wherever there is a contract and something to be done in the course of the employment which is the subject of that contract, if there is a breach of duty in the course of that employment, the plaintiff may recover either in tort or in contract."

To this there is to be added the high authority of Lord Haldane, in *Nocton* v. *Lord Ashburton* (1914):

"The solicitor contracts with his client to be skilful and careful. For failure to perform his obligations he may be made liable at law in contract or even in tort, for negligence in the breach of a duty imposed on him."

That seems to me right. A professional man may give advice under a contract for reward; or without a contract, in pursuance of a voluntary assumption of responsibility; gratuitously without reward. In either case he is under one and the same duty to use reasonable care: [1951] 2 KB 343 see *Cassidy* v. *Ministry of Health*. In the one case it is by reason of a duty imposed by law. For a breach of that duty, he is liable in damages; and those damages should be, and are, the same, whether he is sued in contract or in tort.

It seems to me that *Hedley Byrne*, properly understood, covers this particular proposition; if a man who has, or professes to have, special knowledge and skill makes a representation by virtue thereof to another – be it advice, information or opinion – with the intention of inducing him to enter into a contract with him, he is under a duty to use reasonable care to see that the representation is correct, and that the advice, information or opinion is reliable. If he negligently gives unsound advice or misleading information or expresses an erroneous opinion, and thereby induces the other side into a contract with him, he is liable in damages. This proposition is in line with what I have said in

Candler v. *Crane Christmas & Co.* which was approved by the majority of the Privy Council in *Mutual Life and Citizens Assurance Limited* v. *Evatt.* And the judges of the Commonwealth have shown themselves quite ready to apply *Hedley Byrne* between contracting parties: see in Canada, *Sealand* v. *Ocean Cement*; and New Zealand, *Capital Motors* v. *Beecham.*

Applying this principle, it is plain that Esso professed to have – and did in fact have – special knowledge or skill in estimating the throughput of a filling station. They made the representations – they forecast a throughput of 200,000 gallons – intending to induce Mr Mardon to enter into a tenancy on the faith of it. They made it negligently. It was a 'fatal error'. And thereby they induced Mr Mardon to enter into a contract of tenancy that was disastrous to him. For this misrepresentation they are liable in damages.'

The observation about 'the judges of the Commonwealth' was disingenous. Lord Denning could not have been unaware that in the case of *Sealand* v. *Robert C. McHaffie Ltd*, that had been the decision of the judge of first instance, but it had been over-ruled by the British Columbia Court of Appeal. The New Zealand case does not support the proposition he was advancing.

However, the other judges in the Court of Appeal agreed with him, Lord Justice Shaw holding that Esso had warranted the throughput on the information available to them. He said:

'Mr Mardon complained "he had been sold a pup". I think he had. Moreover, it was a warranted pup so that Esso are in breach of warranty.'

On the duty in negligence, he said:

'There is no valid argument apart from legal technicality for the proposition that a subsequent contract vitiates a cause of action in negligence which had previously arisen in the course of negotiation.'

5.02 Misrepresentation which induces a contract

A false statement which induces a person to undertake contractual obligations is termed a misrepresentation. At one time the term was restricted to statements which had caused a party to enter a contract but which were not part of the contract itself. Some of the earliest cases deal with the sale of inns. A statement as to the amount of beer sold might induce a man to purchase an inn, but would not form any part of the contract of sale, which after 1677 would have to be in writing. This corresponds to the Roman error *in causa* – mistake as to the reason or motive for entering into the contract [7.37].

This terminology has become less exact and the expression is now used for a statement made in the course of negotiations leading up to the acceptance of contractual obligations, whether or not it is incorporated as a term of the contract. The expression 'a mere misrepresentation' is sometimes used now to distinguish those statements which form no part of the contract itself.

If the misrepresentation forms a term of the contract an action for damages will always lie, and it matters not how or why the misrepresentation came to be made.

It is often extremely hard to know whether a misrepresentation has become a term of the contract or not. The test is said to be: 'Is there evidence of an intention by one or more parties that there should be contractual liability in respect of the statement'. In *Oscar Chess Ltd* v. *Williams* (1957), a statement that a car was a '1948 model' was held to be a mere misrepresentation, and not a term of the contract: while in *Dick Bentley Productions Ltd* v. *Harold Smith (Motors) Ltd* (1965) the Court of Appeal decided that a statement that a car had done '20,000 miles'was a term of the contract as well as a misrepresentation. The modern tendency, before the passing of the Misrepresentation Act 1967 was to incorporate a misrepresentation as a contractual obligation wherever possible. The reason was that before that Act, no damages could be given for a mere representation unless it could be proved to be fraudulent, whereas damages could always be given for breach of a term of the contract.

A representation is a statement of existing fact, as distinguished from an expression of intention, a promise to do something in future, an opinion or a statement of the law. Originally, at common law, damages could only be awarded for a misrepresentation of existing facts if it were fraudent. Fraud for this purpose was defined in the leading case of *Derry* v. *Peek* (1859) as:

'a false statement made
(1) knowingly or
(2)without belief in its truth; or
(3) recklessly, careless whether it be true or false.'

Another definition is that it is one that the person who makes it does not honestly believe to be true.

5.03 'Trade puffs'

To have any effect on a contract a misrepresentation must be a statement of existing fact and not a mere expression of opinion, 'a trade puff' or a promise as to future conduct.

If you are induced to buy a certain soap by the statement that you will 'become lovelier every day' you are unlikely to have a remedy in law if you do not. Estate agents' hyperbole therefore, such as describing land as 'fertile and improvable' or 'valuable' is no more than a trade puff and is not meant to be taken seriously.

In *Bassett* v. *Wilkinson* (1926), the statement by a vendor of land in New Zealand who had never run sheep on the land himself, that it could carry 2,000 sheep was held to be no more than an expression of an opinion.

But 'it is often fallaciously assumed that a statement of opinion cannot involve the statement of a fact'. It can when:

(i) the opinion is not genuinely held, for 'the state of a man's mind is as much fact as the state of his digestion';
(ii) the person expressing the opinion has no reasonable grounds for holding it, as where it was stated that an annuitant was 'believed to have no aggregable estate'and in fact no inquiries of any kind had been made: *Brown* v. *Raphel* (1958);
(iii) the facts are not known equally by both parties. A statement of opinion by one who is in a position to know the facts very often involves a statement of material fact, for he impliedly states that he knows facts which justify his opinion. In *South* v. *Land and House Property Corporation* the plaintiffs put up for sale a hotel which was described as 'let to Mr Frederick Fleck (a most desirable tenant)'. Between contract and conveyance the most desirable tenant went bankrupt. On the facts it was held that this amounted to a misrepresentation since it was known to the seller that Fleck had paid his last quarter's rent late, by instalments and under pressure.

5.04 Silence can be a misrepresentation

Silence can also amount to a misrepresentation. Normally there is no obligation on a person entering a contract to disclose material facts but silence can amount to a misrepresentation where:

(i) what is not said, makes what is said untrue. If a man sells a block of flats asserting that all are let and produce a certain income, what he says may be falsified by knowledge that all the tenants had given notice.

(ii) the contracts are of the class termed *unerrimae fidei* ('of utmost good faith'). Most of these are contracts of insurance, where the insured is required to make full disclosure of

    (a) anything that would influence the mind of a prudent underwriter as to whether or not he would accept the risk;

    (b) anything that would influence the mind of a prudent underwriter in fixing the premium.

This applies to cases such as those where a parent insures a car in his own name, knowing perfectly well that the only, or practical user, will be his son or daughter under the age of 23.

(iii) the relationship between the contractual parties is one of the sort termed 'fiduciary'. The principle applies to family settlements, as in the case where a younger son entered into a division of property on the assumption that his elder brother was illegitimate. In fact, however, he well knew that there had been a secret marriage between his parents before his elder brother was born.

(iv) there has been a change of circumstances which has made the statement that was true before now untrue. Dr O'Flanagan in January 1934 told a prospective purchaser that his medical practice brought in £2,000 a year. In May the contract for its purchase was signed, but in the meantime Dr O'Flanagan had become seriously ill, with the result that the income of the practice had declined to not more than £5 per week. Failure to disclose this change in circumstances was a misrepresentation: *With* v. *O'Flanagan* (1936).

    The misrepresentation only affects the contract where the party deceived has relied upon the false statement and not where he has entered into the contract in reliance on his own judgment or after investigation by appropriate agents. But if a material representation is made which is calculated to induce a man to enter into a contract, it is an inference of law that he has been induced by that.

5.05 The effect of a misrepresentation on a contract

Up to 1883 a misrepresentation had no effect on a contract at common law unless it were fraudulent in the sence that the maker could be shown to have known that the statement was false at the time he made it.

The common law judges even then had no power to rescind it or set aside the contract and all they could do was to award damages in a tort action for deceit. The action was exactly the same as that in *Wilkinson* v. *Downton* (1897) where a wife was held entitled to recover damages when a joker told her falsely that her husband was lying at Leytonstone with a broken leg.

The Court of Chancery in its equitable discretion would refuse a decree of specific performance in the limited cases where that remedy might lie, if the defendant had been induced to enter the contract by an untrue representation – thereby leaving the plaintiff to his remedy for damages at common law. And it would also rescind the contract if there was 'the most clear and decisive proof of fraudulent misrepresentation'. If that did not exist, there was no remedy – as can be seen from the case of *Attwood* v. *Small* (1838) which was, up to that date the longest civil trial that had ever been held in England. It occupied various courts for no less than sixty-seven days, some twenty of them in the House of Lords. The plaintiffs failed to secure a rescission of a contract to purchase an iron mine, in part because they were unable to prove that the false statement made about the quality of the iron ore was false to the knowledge of the seller.

In 1881, however, the case of *Redgrave* v. *Hurd* (1881), fundamentally altered the law. By an ingenious piece of sophistry, Jessel MR held that

'even assuming that moral fraud must be shown in order to set aside a contract, you have it where a man, having obtained a beneficial contract by a statement which he now knows to be false, insists upon keeping that contract. To do so is moral delinquency; no man ought to seek to take advantage of his own false statements.'

In that case a solicitor had inserted an advertisement in The Law Times for a partner 'an efficient lawyer and advocate, about forty, who would not object to purchase advertiser's suburban residence'. The defendant replied to the advertisement and the plaintiff assured him that the business was worth £300–£400 p.a. In reliance on that statement the defendant agreed to purchase the house and a share in the practice for £1,600, paying £100 deposit. After contract but before conveyance, the defendant found out that the gross takings of the practice were less than £200 per annum. This was held to be an innocent and not a fraudulent misrepresentation – presumably only because of the court's tenderness to those of its own ilk – and at first instance the defendant was ordered specifically to perform the contract and was refused rescission, the judge holding that he had not relied on the oral representation. However, the Court of Appeal refused the plaintiff's application for specific performance and granted an order for rescission in favour of the defendant. Henceforth the courts would set aside (grant rescission) of contracts for innocent misrepresentations.

However, rescission could only be granted in limited circumstances. The right to rescind for innocent misrepresentation was lost if:

(i)   the parties could not be restored to their original position – if what the law termed *restitutio in integrum* could not be granted;
(ii) the contract had been fully performed. (If, for example, the application for rescission in *Redgrave* v. *Hurd* had been made after the conveyance had been completed; or in the case of goods, if they had been accepted and the property passed to the buyer.)
(iii) possibly, where there was a great interval of time between the contract and the discovery of the falsity of the misrepresentation;
(iv) the misrepresentation was also a term of the contract, but only a subsidiary one. (In that case, the injured party had no right to rescind but could only sue for damages.)
(v)   an innocent third party had acquired rights as the result of the contract;
(vi) the contract had in any way been affirmed after knowledge of the falsity of the misrepresentations.

5.06   The Misrepresentation Act 1967

The first thing the 1967 Act did was to remove two of the bars to rescission mentioned above.

Section 1 enacts removal of certain bars to rescission for innocent misrepresentation

> 'where a person has entered into a contract after a misrepresentation has been made to him and
>> (a) the misrepresentation has become a term of the contract or
>> (b) the contract has been performed or both,
>
> then, if otherwise, he would be allowed to rescind the contract without alleging fraud, he shall be so entitled, subject to the provisions of this Act, notwithstanding the matter mentioned in paragraphs (a) and (b) of this section'.

The Law Reform Committee recommended that sales of land should be excluded from the proposed Act but, as will be seen, there is no such exemption. Even where the land has been conveyed to the purchaser the conveyance is now liable to be set aside for innocent misrepresentation. But no such case has yet occurred, and it is much more likely that in these circumstances the court would take advantage of section 2(2) not to allow rescission but to award damages in lieu of it.

Section 2(1) gives a right to damages for innocent misrepresentation

'where a person has entered into a contract after a misrepresentation has been made to him by another party thereto and as a result thereof he has suffered loss, then if the person making the misrepresentation would be liable to damages in respect thereof had the misrepresentation been made fraudulently, that person shall be so liable notwithstanding that the misrepresentation was not made fraudulently, unless he proves that he had reasonable ground to believe and did believe up to the time the contract was made that the facts represented were true.'

That means, in plain language, that damages will be awarded for innocent misrepresentation except where the defendant satisfies the court that he believed on reasonable grounds that what he said was true.

Section 2(2) confers on the courts a discretion to grant damages in lieu of granting a degree of rescission

'where a person has entered into a contract after a misrepresentation has been made to him otherwise than fraudulently, and he would be entitled by reason of the misrepresentation, to rescind the contract, then, if it is claimed in any proceedings arising out of the contract that the contract ought to be or has been rescinded, the court or arbitrator may declare the contract subsisting and award damages in lieu of rescission if of the opinion that it would be equitable to do so, having regard to the nature of the misrepresentation and the loss that would be caused by it if the contract were upheld, as well as to the loss that rescission would cause to the other party.'

The Act is silent as to what measure damages are to be given – whether the standard should be that for a deliberate tort or as if for breach of contract. The general view is that it is the tort standard that is appropriate.

Section 3 limits the right to exclude misrepresentation by an exemption clause.

'Avoidance of certain provisions excluding liability for misrepresentation – if any agreement (whether made before or after the commencement of this Act) contains a provision which would exclude or restrict
  (1) any liability to which a party to a contract may be subject by reason of any misrepresentation made by him before the contract was made, or

(2) any remedy available to another party to the contract by reason of such a misrepresentation,

then that provision shall be of no effect except to the extent (if any) that in any proceedings arising out of the contract, the court or arbitrator may allow reliance on it as being fair and reasonable in the circumstances of the case.'

The present position, therefore, is that for all mere misrepresentations, i.e. those which are not terms of the contract, whether fraudulent or innocent, the aggrieved party can do the following:

(1) Sue for damages
If fraudulent, damages are for deceit.
If innocent, the damages are:

(i) under section 2(1) of the Misrepresentation Act 1967;
(ii) and/or for the tort of the negligent mis-statement.

In the case of innocent misrepresentation the defendant has a defence if under section 2(1) he can satisfy the court that he has reasonable grounds for believing and that he did in fact believe what he said, to be true.

(2) Refuse to perform his side of the contract

(3) Claim rescission of the contract
save that there is now no absolute right to rescind in the case of innocent misrepresentation and the court has the discretion to order damages in lieu of rescission. The Misrepresentation Act 1967 was intended to simplify the law by applying the remedies available at common law for fraudulent misrepresentation to innocent misrepresentations which had induced a party to enter into a contract. It has, in fact, made it much more complicated. But it can be confidently said that if the misrepresentation is not incorporated as a term of the contract, a plaintiff can recover damages under this section of the Misrepresentation Act 1967 and rescind the contract unless the defendant can prove that he had reasonable grounds for believing and did in fact believe that the facts he represented were true.

Even if the defendant can prove that, an action may lie in equity for rescission of the contract and an indemnity. If rescission of the contract is not possible, section 2(2) of the Misrepresentation Act 1967 allows a court, if it is equitable to do so, to award damages in lieu of rescission.

5.07 Fiduciary responsibility to the other party

A company may also have fiduciary obligations imposed on it by the way it engages in negotiations. It may incur a fiduciary obligation not to profit by matters disclosed confidentially in the course of those negotiations

In a Canadian case, Corona Resources Ltd had discovered some promising gold deposits on land adjacent to some that they owned. The company entered into negotiations with Lac Minerals Ltd to form a joint venture to exploit those resources, in the course of which they disclosed confidential information to the other company. However, Lac Minerals, instead of entering into a joint venture, went off and bought the land itself and began to mine it.

The Supreme Court of Ontario held that Lac Minerals had made use of confidential information and that they had been in breach of their fiduciary obligations to Corona Resources. It therefore awarded the not inconsiderable sum of the equivalent of £350 million profit to Corona; alternatively, it decreed that if Corona paid £8 million to Lac, that company was to convey the property in question to Corona.

The basis of this judgment was that between parties who are in negotiation for a contract, there are fiduciary duties whereby they are obliged to act fairly and not prejudice the other.

A minor gloss on this doctrine was the case of a Toronto lawyer who took on the case of a businessman who had lost his job, and who claimed that as a result he had become impotent. The lawyer took advantage of the knowledge to seduce the client's wife. The court awarded the injured client £10,000 damages for breach of the fiduciary relationship which existed between a lawyer and a client.

5.08 What is a fiduciary relationship?

Certain specific relations give rise to fiduciary relationships: directors and companies; solicitors and clients; partners; bailee and bailor.

In the Court of Appeal in the USSC case [5.09] one judge suggested that:

'a fiduciary relationship exists where the facts of the case in hand establish that in a particular matter a person has undertaken to act in the interests of another and not in his own.'

The Court of Appeal added:

'that it is not inconsistent with this principle that a fiduciary may retain that character although he is entitled to have regard to his own interest in particular matters. The conclusion was that in matters concerning the development of USSC's market in Australia for its surgical stapling products, and its protection from competition, HPI undertook to act in USSC's interest and not in its own.'

In *Reading* v. *A.G.* (1949), a British soldier had made use of his British uniform and Army vehicle to aid Middle East smugglers and had made a vast sum of money. In that case, Lord Justice Asquith said:

'A consideration of the authorities suggests that for the present purpose "a fiduciary relation" exists

(a) whenever the plaintiff entrusts to the defendant property, including intangible property as, for instance, confidential information, and relies on the defendant to deal with such property for the benefit of the plaintiff or for the purposes authorised by him, and not otherwise ... and
(b) whenever the plaintiff entrusts to the defendant a job to be performed, for instance, the negotiation of a contract on his behalf or for his benefit, and relies on the defendant to procure for the plaintiff the best terms available ...'

That decision was approved in the House of Lords (1951) although Lord Porter said that the words 'fiduciary relationship' in that setting were used in 'a wide and loose sense'.

The soldier was held liable to disgorge all his ill-gotten gains.

5.09　An example of fiduciary responsibility

A Mr Blackman became an employee of the United States company, United States Surgical Corporation, which manufactured and sold patented devices for surgeons under the USA trademark of 'Auto Suture' in 1973. Later the same year, he left to run his own business selling these products as a dealer with an exclusive area in New York City.

In August 1978 he visited Australia, where USSC already had a distributor, for twelve days. During this visit he found out that the name 'Auto Suture' was not registered in Australia and the device was not patented there. On this visit, he instructed local solicitors to register the trademark in Australia of 'Autosuture'. Less than a year later he applied for an Australian patent based largely on particulars filed by USSC in the

United States for a 'surgical skin and fascia stapler and disposable staple carriage for use therewith'.

On the same visit in August 1978, he instructed a metallurgist to investigate and report on the composition and physical properties of the wire staples and other metal parts in USSC devices.

On another visit in November, he took further steps, as the trial judge found, to be able:

(a) to manufacture components similar to USSC-made components of the types required to be used with USSC-made demonstration cartridges;
(b) to repackage and sterilise USSC-made demonstration cartridges accompanied where necessary by components made by himself; and
(c) to market the resulting products in competition with USSC-made clinical products.

On his return from Australia on this occasion, he immediately entertained the President and Vice-president of USSC to a meal in a restaurant. He proposed that they sack the existing distributors of their products in Australia, and that he gave up his New York dealership and be appointed their exclusive Australian distributor. To this they agreed under contractual terms about which there was subsequently much dispute.

He took over the stock of the sacked distributors and on 1 April 1979 started to market USSC products in Australia. By that time he had already engaged an engineering consultant who was busy with reverse engineering – i.e. from the finished USSC product producing tools, mould and dies identical to those used to make the original product.

By October of the same year, 1979, he was ready surplanting USSC goods he had bought with his own products. He wrote on Christmas Day 1979 to end his distributorship of USSC goods 'on spurious grounds'and widely advertised that his company were phasing out all goods manufactured in the United States and substituting a product manufactured in Australia.

He was over-optimistic. He had production problems and was forced by subterfuge to obtain further USSC supplies.

The Court of Appeal concluded that all Mr Blackman's operations had largely been financed by USSC since the necessary finance would have not been available but for monies provided by USSC and the fact that the Bank of New Zealand extended credit to him and his companies only because it was USSC's distributor.

It was important for USSC to establish that there had been a breach of fiduciary duties because if so, they could recover not just damages but all the profits from selling non-USSC brand stapling products secured by an equitable lien over Mr Blackman's companies' assets.

That was the order the trial judge made which was over-ruled by the Court of Appeal. Incredibly, the High Court of Australia, by a majority of three to two held there were no fiduciary duties. Of all the judges who heard this case, a majority of six to three thought there were fiduciary obligations.

The real issue in this case was a simple issue of fact, which could have been resolved in two terse questions to a jury:

(1) In all the circumstances of this case, was Mr Blackman, in addition to the contractual obligations he had undertaken, under a duty to behave so that he did not imperil the patents, the trademarks, the confidential information, and the product goodwill of USSC?
(2) Was he in breach of that duty?

There can be little doubt what verdict any sensible jury would have returned.

5.10   Collateral contracts

For several years there was an inclination on the part of judges to hold that observations made by one party which induced the other to enter into the contract constituted a collateral contract. In part this was due to two factors: no action would lie for damages for anything except fraudulent misrepresentation; and the numerous frauds perpetrated by car dealers in selling cars where the only contract was between the purchaser and the finance company.

In *Karsales (Harrow) Ltd* v. *Wallis* (1956), for example, the plaintiff agreed to acquire on hire-purchase from the defendants a Buick car which was described to him as being 'in perfect condition' and 'good for thousands of trouble-free miles'. Later the car was delivered outside his house in the dead of night for the excellent reason that it was incapable of moving under its own steam and had to be towed there. The defendants disowned all responsibility. The only contract, they claimed, was between the plaintiff and the finance company and that excluded all liability for the condition of the vehicle. As for any contract of warranty, there was no consideration moving from the promisee (the plaintiff) to the promisor (the defendants).

The Court of Appeal adopted the view expressed by Justice McNair and held that there was in fact a unilateral collateral contract [2.01] between the plaintiff and the defendant in these terms:

'If you enter into a contract with the finance company, I promise you that the goods are as I say they are.'

The defendants were therefore held liable not only for the cost of putting the vehicle into the condition they had warranted it to be, but also for loss of use during the period necessary.

Car dealers are the spiritual descendants of the old horse dealers, one of whom said to a purchaser who sought a stallion for stud purposes:

'You need not look for anything: the horse is perfectly sound. If there was anything the matter with the horse I would tell you.'

The House of Lords, in 1913, held this to constitute a collateral contract of warranty.

'It would be impossible, in my mind, to have a clearer example of an express warranty where the word "warranty" was not used.

The essence of such warranty is that it becomes plain by the words and action of the parties that it is intended that in the purchase the responsibility of the soundness shall rest upon the vendor; and how in the world could a vendor more clearly indicate that he is prepared and intends to take upon himself the responsibility of the soundness than by saying: "You need not look at that horse, because it is perfectly sound" and sees that the purchaser thereupon desists from his immediate independent examination.'

Collateral in this sense means 'lying alongside' so that when a man is in bed with his wife or girlfriend he is collateral to her. So there may be contracts which lie alongside other ones. These may be between the contracting parties themselves so that in addition to their major contract there is a collateral one; or it may be that there is a collateral contract where one party is by the promises of another induced to enter into a contract with a third party. Both are commonly unilateral contracts in the sense that there is an undertaking 'if you enter into a synallagmatic contract with me (or with X) I promise you ...'

There are numerous cases where it has been held that there was a contract of warranty between parties who did not enter into any other contract.

In *Shanklin Pier Ltd* v. *Detel Products Ltd* (1951) the owners of a pier entered into a contract with painters to paint the pier with two coats of bitumen paint. A director of the defendant company assured the plaintiffs that the paint they manufactured, called D.M.U. would protect the pier for seven to ten years. In reliance on these warranties, the company specified that the painting company should use D.M.U. It lasted less than three months.

The pier company sued the paint manufacturers and succeeded.

Mr Justice McNair said:

'This case raises an interesting and comparatively novel question whether or not an enforceable warranty can arise between parties other than parties to the main contract for the sale of the article in respect of which the warranty is alleged to have been given ...

In the result, I am satisfied that, if a direct contract of purchase and sale of the D.M.U. had then been made between the plaintiffs and the defendants, the correct conclusion on the facts would have been that the defendants gave to the plaintiffs the warranties substantially in the form alleged in the Statement of Claim.

In reaching this conclusion, I adopt the principles stated by Holt CJ in *Crosse* v. *Gardner* (1689) Comb. 142, and *Medina* v. *Stoughton* (1700) 1 Salk. 210, that an affirmation at the time of sale is a warranty, provided it appears on evidence to have been so intended.

Counsel for the defendants submitted that in law a warranty could give rise to no enforceable cause of action except between the same parties as the parties to the main contract in relation to which the warranty was given. In principle, this submission seems to me to be unsound. If, as is elementary, the consideration for the warranty in the usual case is the entering into of the main contract in relation to which the warranty is given, I see no reason why there may not be an enforceable warranty between A and B supported by the consideration that B should cause C to enter into a contract with A or that B should do some other act for the benefit of A.'

This was followed by *Wells (Merstham) Ltd* v. *Buckland Sand and Gravel Ltd* (1964), where the defendants induced the plaintiffs, who were chrysanthemum growers, to purchase their sand from a third party by asserting that it had a low oxide content and was suitable for growing these plants. The sand, however, turned out to have a high iron oxide content which caused damage, agreed at £2,500, to the plaintiffs.

Mr Justice Edmund-Davies, finding for the plaintiffs, said:

'As between A (a potential seller of goods) and B (a potential buyer), two ingredients, and two only, are in my judgment required to bring about a collateral contract containing a warranty:

(1) a promise or assertion by A as to the nature, quality or quantity

of the goods which B may reasonably regard as being made *animo contrahendi* and

(2) acquisition by B of the goods in reliance on that promise or assertion.

As K.W. Wedderburn expressed it in *Collateral Contracts* in Cambridge Law Journal, 1959, at p.79:

> "... the consideration given for the promise is no more than the act of entering into the main contract. Going ahead with that bargain is sufficient price for the promise, without which it would not have gone ahead at all".

And a warranty may be enforceable notwithstanding that no specific main contract is discussed at the time it is given, though obviously an *animus contrahendi* (and, therefore, a warranty) would be unlikely to be inferred unless the circumstances show that it was within the present contemplation of the parties that a contract based upon the promise would shortly be entered into. Furthermore, the operation of the warranty must have a limitation in point of time which is reasonable in all the circumstances. But none of these considerations gives rise to difficulty in the present case.'

Some doubts now exist about these principles following the refusal of the House of Lords in *I.B.A.* v. *E.M.I. and Anor.* (1980), to hold that there was a collateral contract of warranty between the parties. There is a tendency now to reject collateral contracts between parties who enter into a subsequent contract, especially where that contract is in writing.

Chapter 6

Negotiations for a Contract

6.01 Invitations to treat

Not every indication that a person is prepared to enter into a contract will constitute an offer which can be accepted.

If there is a particular item displayed in a shopkeeper's window, is a member of the public entitled to walk in and demand it as the price marked?

According to English law (but not Continental law) he is not. For the exhibition of the goods in the window is not an offer to sell the goods which can be accepted, but is an indication that the shopkeeper is prepared to receive offers for them – at the price stated.

'In the case of an ordinary shop, although goods are displayed and it is intended that customers should go and choose what they want, the contract is not completed until, the customer having indicated the articles which he needs, the shopkeeper or someone on his behalf, accepts that offer. Then the contract is completed.'

It follows that if a fur coat is offered by mistake in the window for £100 instead of £1,000, the shopkeeper is entitled to refuse to sell it for the marked price.

In a self-service shop the goods are not offered for sale by being exhibited on the shelves. The offer to buy them is made by the customer who presents them at the cash desk. Boots had in one of their shops a self-service section with goods subject to Part 1 of the Poisons List, and which therefore could only be sold under the supervision of a qualified pharmacist. It was not disputed that a pharmacist was stationed at the cash desk, but the Pharmaceutical Society contended that the contract was made, and the property passed, when a customer took an article from a shelf and put it into a receptacle, the taking of such an article being an acceptance of the trader's offer. This contention was rejected by the judge of first instance and by the Court of Appeal. As Lord Justice Somerville said:

> 'I can see no reason at all … for drawing any different implication as a result of the layout from that prevailing in an ordinary shop.'

As a result, the goods had been dispensed under the supervision of a qualified pharmacist: *Pharmaceutical Society* v. *Boots* (1953).

Advertisements in newspapers and periodicals which offer goods for sale are also not offers but invitations to treat. They are an indication that the would-be seller will receive offers. A Mr Partridge advertised in the classified advertisements column of the magazine *Cage and Aviary Birds*: 'Quality British bramblefinch hens for sale'. It was a criminal offence under the Protection of Birds Act 1954 to, *inter alia*, offer for sale certain species of birds, of which this was one. A customer replying to the advertisement was supplied with a bird, and as a result Partridge was prosecuted under the Act. The court held that he had not made an offer for sale by his advertisement. It was only an invitation to treat: *Partridge* v. *Crittenden* (1968). It was the customer who had made the offer.

6.02 'Undertakings'

It is common practice in some commercial situations for one party to give an 'undertaking'. In a takeover bid for an independent brewery company in Great Yarmouth, the bidders gave an 'undertaking' that the local brewery would not be closed down. It was, within a year.

Similarly, when the Guinness company made an offer for the shares of the Distillers Company, it gave undertaking to appoint a specified gentleman as chairman of the joint company and to transfer the main offices of the company to Scotland. Both undertakings were broken as soon as Distillers was taken over.

In 1960, when the Ford Motor Company acquired the minority shareholdings in its British subsidiary, Ford gave undertakings about the management of the subsidiary. Chrysler did the same when it took an interest in Rootes motors, the Hillman-Humber concern, in 1964, and again in 1967, when it took the majority shareholding. Peugeot gave similar undertakings in 1978 about the operation of Chrysler UK/Talbot.

All these 'undertakings' were broken, as were those made in 1986 when Sikorski Helicopters took a minority shareholding in the insolvent Westland concern.

There are two reasons why such 'undertakings' are not contractually binding. They may be promises, but they are not promises to any other specific party. Secondly, they are not intended to have any contractual effect. They are promises made only for what is now termed 'presentational purposes', that is, to secure acceptance of what would otherwise have been unacceptable. In other words for 'public relations purposes', i.e.lying propaganda.

6.03 'Gentlemen's agreements'

Similar considerations apply to what are known as a 'gentleman's agreement', which one judge aptly described as an 'agreement made between two persons, neither of whom is a "gentleman" and neither of whom intends to be bound by it unless it suits his convenience'.

The law allows parties to make agreements which otherwise would have all the characteristics of a contract, but to specify that it shall be 'binding in honour' only. However, business deals will be presumed to be intended to have legal effects.

Skyways Ltd made an agreement with the British Airline Pilots Association that they would pay '*ex gratia* payments' to any of their pilots who was made redundant. A Mr Edwards, one of their pilots, was dismissed but was not paid the agreed sum. Skyways sought to escape from their promise by contending that the agreement was not intended to create legal relations.

Mr Justice Megaw held that:

(a) since the agreement related to business matters, the burden of proof that it was not intended to create legal obligations fell on Skyways;

(b) the use of the words '*ex gratia*' simply meant that Skyways did not accept that they were under any obligation under their contract of employment with a pilot to pay him any sum if he were dismissed with due notice.

As a result there was a binding contract: *Edwards* v. *Skyways Ltd* (1964).

But if the parties clearly indicate that it is their intention not to enter into contractual obligations, the courts will respect their intentions.

Crompton Bros were an English firm which manufactured carbon paper. In 1913 they entered into a written agreement with Rose and Frank Co., whereby the latter were made their sole agents for sale in the United States for a period of three years, with an option to extend. The agreement, which had all the appearance and formality of a written contract, contained the clause:

'This agreement is not entered into ... as a formal or legal agreement and shall not be subject to legal jurisdiction in the law courts either of the United States or England, but it is only a definite expression and record of the purpose and intention of the three parties concerned to which they each honourably pledge themselves with the fullest confidence, based on past business with each other, that it will be carried through by each of the three parties with mutual loyalty and friendly co-operation.'

This clause was headed 'The Honourable Pledge Clause'.

The Court of Appeal and the House of Lords held that there was no contractual obligation.

In the Court of Appeal Lord Justice Scrutton said:

'It is quite possible for parties to come to an agreement by accepting a proposal with the result that the agreement concluded does not give rise to legal relations. The reason of this is that the parties do not intend that their agreement shall give rise to legal relations ... In Sir Frederick Pollock's language, an agreement to become enforceable at law must

"be concerned with duties and rights which can be dealt with by a court of justice. And it must be the intention of the parties that the matter in hand shall, if necessary, be so dealt with, or at least they must not have the contrary intention."

... the particular clause in question shows a clear intention by the parties that the rest of their arrangement or agreement shall not affect their legal relations, or be enforceable in a court of law, but in the words of the clause, shall be "only a definite expression and record of the purpose and intention of the three parties subject to which they each honourably pledge themselves, and shall not be subject to legal jursidiction".'

6.04 'Letter of intent'

A declaration of intent, or what is now commonplace in commercial practice, the letter of intent, *prima facie* does not constitute an offer and has no contractual significance. So where a father wrote to the man who was considering marrying his daughter, 'My daughter will have a share of what I leave after the death of her mother', this was held to be a mere expression of intention and not a promise intended to create contractual obligations: *Farina* v. *Fickins* (1900). But where a 'letter of intent' is of such a nature that serious obligations are incurred as a result of it, or the parties subsequently acted as if it were a binding contractual obligation, it would be open to a court to find that contractual obligations were intended.

Cleveland Bridge and Engineering Co. Ltd (then an independent company) was involved in the construction of a bank in Saudi Arabia. It sent a letter to the British Steel Corporation, which read:

> 'Samma Bank: Damman
> We are pleased to advise you that it is our intention to enter into a sub-contract with your company for the supply and delivery of the steel castings which form the roof nodes on this project ...
> We request you to proceed immediately with the works pending the preparation and issuing to you of the official form of sub-contract.'

British Steel, on receipt of this request, started work. But no 'official form of sub-contract'was ever received. Despite this, British Steel manufactured and delivered the nodes to Cleveland Bridge.

It was held by Mr Justice Robert Goff that no contractual obligation had been created by the letter of intent: *British Steel Corporation* v. *Cleveland Bridge and Engineering Co. Ltd* (1981). He said in his judgment:

> 'There can be no hard and fast answer to the question whether a letter of intent will give rise to a binding agreement; everything must depend upon the circumstances of a particular case ...
> As a matter of analysis the contract (if any) which may come into existence following a letter of intent may take one of two forms: either there may be an ordinary executory contract, under which each party assumes reciprocal obligations to the other; or there may be what is sometimes called an 'if' contract, i.e. a contract under which A requires B to carry out a certain performance and promises B that, if he does so, he will receive a certain performance in return, usually remuneration.'

He then commented that Judge Fay had been able to find a contract with reciprocal obligations in the letter of intent in *Turriff Construction Ltd* v. *Regalia Knitting Mills Ltd* (1971). But he added:

> 'Everything must depend on the facts of the particular case.'

In the instant case, he drew attention to the fact that when the letter of intent was issued, the parties were in a state of negotiation 'not least on the issues of price, delivery dates and the applicable terms and conditions'. He then said:

'Since the parties were still in a state of negotiation, it is impossible to say with any degree of certainty what the material terms of the contract would be ...

In the course of argument, I put to [counsel] the question whether BSC were free at any time after starting work to cease work.

His submission was that they were not free to do so, even if negotiation on the terms of the formal contract broke down.

I find this submission to be so repugnant to common sense and the commercial realities that I am unable to accept it.'

He then turned to consider whether there was a unilateral contract, an 'if' contract [2.01]. He concluded that there was not because the parties had proceeded on the basis that work was being done *pending* a formal sub-contract. He drew attention to the fact that one element of the dispute was whether the work was being done on C.B.E.'s standard terms or B.S.C.'s. Those of C.B.E. provided that the seller had unlimited and indefinite damages for delay, including consequential losses. Those of B.S.C. excluded all such liability.

'It would be an extraordinary result if, by acting on such a request in such circumstances, the [seller] (the law reports say "buyer" but this is clearly incorrect) were to assume an unlimited liability for his contractual performance, when he would never assume such liability under any contract which he entered into.

For these reasons, I reject the solution of the "if contract".'

He concluded therefore that the only effect of the letter of intent was that the party making the request was liable to pay for any work done on a *quantum meruit* basis [3.03].

He referred with approval to the 'crisp *dictum*' of Mr Justice Parker in *O.T.M. Ltd* v. *Hydranautics* (1981) where the judge said of a letter of intent:

'its only effect would be to enable the defendants to recover on a *quantum meruit* for work done pursuant to the directions contained in the Letter of Intent.'

The result is that in general, as Judge Fay said in the *Turriff Construction* case (*supra*):

'Such a letter is no more than the expression in writing of a party's ... present intention to enter into a contract at a future date. Save in exceptional circumstances it can have no binding effect.'

However, in that case he was able to hold that there had been an oral agreement made at a meeting that if Turriff did preliminary design work, Regalia would pay for it, even if the project was abandoned.

However there may be circumstances where a letter of intent is held to have been incorporated as part of the terms of a subsequent contract.

A letter of intent issued on 10 September 1981 by Peter W. Turner Ltd to John Worman Ltd, contractors, indicating the company's intention to appoint the latter as main contractors under a design and build contract for the refurbishment of Turner's abattoir, to comply with EEC standards, was made subject to these conditions:

(i)   All building works, materials and installation planning permission and Nijhuis' equipment [a sub-contractor] to be supplied by Worman at a maximum cost of £500,000.
(ii) All work, existing and new, to be eligible for red meat grant aid, to have the approval of the Ministry veterinary officers and on completion the abattoir to be to E.E.C. standard.'

Judge John Davies held that these conditions were incorporated into the terms of a contract between Turner and Worman subsequently entered into on 27 January 1982. He said in his judgment:

'The guiding principles for construing a contract were laid down by Lord Wilberforce in *Penn* v. *Simmonds* (1971). I need do no more than summarise them here: the idea that English law is left behind in some island of literal interpretation has long been discarded; one has to have regard to the genesis and aim of the transaction as elicited from the surrounding circumstances, especially when the consequences of too literal an interpretation would be to make the transaction futile.

These observations are all the more pertinent when it comes to dealing with rudimentary agreements such as the ones in this case.'

He referred to the contract, which he described as 'all too obviously a scissors and paste effort', and said:

'The terms of reference defined the main purposes of the transaction. So did the letter of intent and the reply to it. It would be quite unrealistic to seek to construe the former without regard to the latter.

This was a contract where the obligation to design and build was upon the contractor and his consultants. There is nothing in the conditions, specifications or plans which would negate the interpretation which I put upon the contract or, were it necessary to do so, the implications of a term to a similar effect. In fact, the contract particulars, in my judgment, allow more than ample room for the inclusion of what I think should be read into the contract, not only to make it workable, but also to give effect to what I regard as the indisputable object of the whole bargain, which was not merely to produce an abattoir that would work to scheduled capacity, but which would also achieve the necessary standards for UK and EEC financial aid: *Consultants Group International (a firm)* v. *John Worman Ltd* (1985).

However, this must be subject to the principles set out in [9.01] and the cases quoted therein, none of which was quoted to the learned Official Referee.

6.05   Uncomfortable 'letters of comfort'

These are documents which have the superficial appearance of being guarantees but are in reality nothing of the sort. Typical examples were the letters addressed by the Vatican Bank to various other banks which enabled vasts sums of money to be siphoned via those banks to dubious South American companies.

A specific example may be found in the one Rediffusion Ltd sent to Chemco Leasing SpA of Italy in respect of its subsidiary Computer Machinery Company Italia. As has been pointed out [4.06] a holding company has no liability in English law for the obligations of a subsidiary, even if it owns, directly or through nominees, all the shares of the subsidiary.

Leasing facilities were to be provided by Chemco to Computer Machinery of Italy. The 'letter of comfort' sent to Chemco by Rediffusion Ltd on 21 December 1979 pointed out that the Computer Machinery Company of Italy was 99.9 per cent owned by the Computer Machinery Company of France, which was 100 per cent owned by Rediffusion Ltd.

The so-called 'letter of comfort' went on to say

'We assure you we are not contemplating disposal of our interest and undertake to give Chemco prior notification should we dispose of our interest during the life of the leases. If we dispose of our interest we undertake to take over the remaining liabilities to Chemco of Computer Machinery Italy should the new shareholders be unacceptable to Chemco.'

The letter was less than accurate. In fact, the Computer Machinery Company of France was not 100 per cent owned, or owned at all, by

Rediffusion Ltd but by a Dutch company, the Computer Machinery Company Europe, in which Rediffusion Ltd had a controlling shareholding.

On 16 December 1981 Rediffusion Ltd sold the entire shareholding in the Computer Machinery Company Europe but did not advise Chemco. They learned of this fact but, believing that they held letters of guarantee from Rediffusion Ltd, continued to finance the Computer Machinery Company Europe.

On 23 July 1982 the Computer Machinery Company Italia went into liquidation, having defaulted on its obligations to Chemco.

In an action brought by Chemco against Rediffusion Ltd in the English jurisdiction, it was held by the High Court and the Court of Appeal that the letter of comfort was neither a guarantee of the debts of the Italian subsidiary nor an indemnity and that Rediffusion's obligation to take over the liabilities of the Computer Machinery Company Italy did not arise until Chemco Ltd had given notice that the new owners were unacceptable.

It was an offer to take over the liabilities only if Chemco found the new owners unacceptable. As that offer had not been accepted within a reasonable time, there was no obligation.

In the Court of Appeal, Lord Parker said:

'It is well settled that if an offer is not limited in time by its express terms, it lapses after a reasonable time.

Alternatively ... such a term must be implied.'

The result was the 'letter of comfort' gave no rights whatsoever to the unfortunate holder: *Chemco Leasing SpA* v. *Rediffusion Ltd* (1986).

Any businessman offered such a document by a holding company for a subsidiary should not only scrutinise the terms carefully but should, if possible, obtain a guarantee, preferably under seal. In truth, most 'letters of comfort' are worthless pieces of paper because there is usually no consideration [7.25] to support the promises made in them.

6.06   Tenders

Few English words can have more meanings. As a noun, it might mean a waiter at an inn or the guard of a train. Also as a noun, it means a boat which attends on a larger ship or that part of a steam engine which carries the fuel. As an adjective, it means delicate, gentle, or soft.

More relevantly, it has two distinct legal meanings. In the expression 'legal tender' it means currency that cannot be refused in payment of a debt; in the law regarding performance of a contract, it may mean the offer of coins of the realm in satisfaction of a debt.

But it also has a meaning in the formation of contracts, as where a local authority invites 'tenders' for work. In this connection, the word is less than precise and examiners who invite students to distinguish a tender from 'an offer' betray their own ignorance. For a tender may simply be an offer in writing. If a body invites tenders for the supply of a new ambulance they are doing no more than inviting offers, and each tender is an offer.

In other senses, however, a tender may be a continuing offer to supply goods at a price 'as and when' required by the buyer. If so, like any other offer it can be withdrawn at any time before acceptance; that is, before any particular order is placed, but not after.

Much will depend on the wording of the contract, but in this sort of case there is no obligation on the party inviting the tender to place an order at all. But if the party inviting the tender promises to take all his requirements from the party submitting the accepted tender, he will not be entitled to obtain any of them from anybody else. Nor will he be entitled to make use of this contractual arrangement to obtain goods not for his own requirements but for resale.

In all these situations, the meaning to be attached to 'tender' depends on the terms of the documents in question and there is no legal or standardised definition that can be ascribed to the word.

Not every invitation to tender constitutes an offer to accept the highest tender. In *Spencer* v. *Harding* (1870) the defendants sent out a circular which read:

'We are instructed to offer the wholesale trade for sale by tender the stock-in-trade of Messrs G. Eilbeck & Co. amounting as per stock book to £2,503 13s. 1d. and which will be sold at a discount in one lot. Payment to be made in cash. The stock may be viewed on the premises ... up to Thursday the 20th instant, on which day, at 12 o'clock, noon precisely, the tenders will be received and opened at our offices ...'

The judge held:

'The question is whether there is here any offer to enter into a contract at all, or whether the circular amounts to anything more than a mere proclamation that the defendants are ready to chaffer for the sale of goods, and to receive offers for the purchase of them. In advertisements for tenders for buildings, it is not usual to say that the contract will be given to the lowest bidder, and it is not always that the contract is made with the lowest bidder. Here there is a total absence of any words to intimate that the highest bidder is to be the purchaser. It is a mere attempt to ascertain whether an offer can be obtained within such a margin as the sellers are willing to adopt.'

The placing of orders on a tender may constitute a binding contract. Great Northern Railways advertised for supply of stores such as they might order during one year. Witham & Co. made a tender offering to supply them for that period at fixed prices, and the company accepted it. However, Witham & Co. refused to supply the goods and pleaded that the contract had no right to recover damages because the contract was unilateral. Mr Justice Brett said:

'The objection to the plaintiffs' right to recover is that the contract is unilateral. I do not, however, understand what objection that is to a contract. Many contracts are obnoxious to the same complaint.
    If I say to another "If you will go to York, I will give you £100" that is in a certain sense a unilateral contract. He has not promised to go to York. But if he goes, it cannot be doubted that he will be entitled to receive the £100. His going to York at my request is a sufficient consideration for my promise.
    So, if one says to another "If you will give me an order for iron, or other goods, I will supply it at a given price"; if the order is given, there is a complete contract which the seller is bound to perform.'

The terms on which tenders are invited are paramount in determining the commercial effect of a tender. Commonly, those who invite tenders make it clear that there is no obligation on them to accept the highest or any tender. When bids are invited and the indication given that the highest bid will be accepted, that will be enforced normally. However, referential bids are excluded. In *Harvela Investments Ltd* v. *Royal Trust of Canada* (1985), sealed bids were invited for the shareholding held by the bank in another company. Sir Leonard Outerbridge made an offer – 'Can. $101,000 in excess of any other you may receive which is expressed as a fixed monetary amount'. The bank accepted that as a valid offer of Can. $2,175,000.
    The case went to the English High Court, the Court of Appeal and ultimately the House of Lords, where their Lordships adopted the observations in the New York Court of Appeals (1932) 449 NYW 2d 173 where it was said:

'A submission by one bidder of a bid dependent for its definition on the bids of others is invalid and unacceptable as inconsistent and potentially destructive of the very bidding on which it is submitted.'

6.07   Auctions

The position regarding auction sales in England is now codified in section 57 of the Sale of Goods Act 1979. This provides:

'57(1) Where goods are put up for sale by auction in lots, each lot is *prima facie* deemed to be the subject of a separate contract of sale.
(2) A sale by auction is complete when the auctioneer announces its completion by the fall of the hammer, or in other customary manner; and until the announcement is made any bidder may retract his bid.
(3) A sale by auction may be notified to be subject to a reserve or upset price, and a right to bid may also be reserved expressly by or on behalf of the seller.
(4) Where a sale by auction is not notified to be subject to a right to bid by or on behalf of the seller, it is not lawful for the seller to bid himself or to employ any person to bid at the sale, or for the auctioneer knowingly to take any bid from the seller or any such person.
(5) A sale contravening subsection (4) may be treated as fraudulent by the buyer.
(6) Where, in respect of a sale by auction, a right to bid is expressly reserved (but not otherwise) the seller or any one person on his behalf may bid at the auction.'

Section 57(2) merely codifies the old common law right that a bidder could withdraw his offer at any time before the hammer fell.
As Lord Kenyon said in *Payne* v. *Cave* (1789):

'The auctioneer is the agent of the vendor, and the assent of both parties is necessary to make the contract binding; that is signified on the part of the seller by knocking down the hammer, which was not done here till the defendant had retracted. An auction is not inaptly called *locus poenitentiae*. Every bidding is nothing more than an offer on one side, which is not binding on either side until it is assented to. But according to what is now contended for, one party would be bound by the offer, and the other not, which can never be allowed.'

However, sales can be conducted under conditions different from the common law and statutory terms, and the National Conditions of Sale provide that the auctioneer, in the event of a dispute about a bid:

'may determine the dispute or the property may, at the vendor's option, either be put up again at the last undisputed bid or be withdrawn.'

However, it would appear that a provision that 'No person shall retract his bidding' is void for want of consideration: *Routledge* v. *Grant* (1828).

6.08   The lapse of offers

If one party makes an offer to another, it remains open until it is brought to an end by lapsing or by revocation.

An offer may lapse:

(1) *By non-acceptance within a prescribed time.*
A man offered another six weeks in which to decide whether he wanted to make a lease. After the expiration of that period, the offeree purported to accept it. He could not do so. The offer had come to an end with the expiration of the period.

It should be noted that a promise to keep an offer open for a fixed time is not, however, binding on the offeror. If he cares to, he can withdraw it by notice of revocation a minute later. The reason for this is that there is no consideration for his promise. But if consideration, however trifling, is accepted, whether it be a cigarette or a peppercorn, in return for the promise to keep the offer open, it is termed an 'option' and is binding. The promisor will be liable in damages if he withdraws his offer or contracts with some other party.

(2) *After the lapse of a reasonable time.*
What is a reasonable time is an issue of fact for the court to decide in the circumstances of any particular case. A Mr Montefiore applied for shares in the Ramsgate Victoria Hotel Company Ltd in June. Such applications have been held to constitute an offer. In November, a letter of allotment, which is the acceptance, was sent to him. It was held that the offer had lapsed, and there was therefore no contract: *Ramsgate Victoria Hotel Co. Ltd* v. *Montefiore* (1866).

(3) *Where a state of affairs, in reliance on which an offer made, ceases to exist.*
There is as yet little authority for this proposition except observations, which were *obiter*, made by Lord Denning in *Financings Ltd* v. *Stimson* (1962):

'Suppose an offer is made to buy a Rolls Royce at a high price on one day, and before it is accepted, it suffers the next day severe damage. Can it be accepted, and the offeror bound? My answer is no, because the offer is conditional on the goods at the moment of acceptance remaining in substantially the same condition as at the time of the offer.'

This seems an eminently sensible proposition, especially since by virtue of section 6 of the Sale of Goods Act 1979, where specific goods have perished without the knowledge of the seller, the contract is void. In France, in the case of partial loss or deterioration, the buyer has the choice of either rescinding the contract or, if he accepts the goods, securing abatement of price on a valuation; but this is not yet English law and unfortunately there seems to be express authority against it, to the effect that rotten potatoes are still potatoes for the purpose of section 7 of the Sale of Goods Act 1979 goods perishing after an agreement to sell but before sale: *Horn* v. *Minister of Food* (1948). But there are so many objections to this decision that it seems hardly likely that the case will be followed by a superior court; or any other, for that matter.

6.09 The revocation of offers

In addition to these situations, an offer may be revoked at any time before acceptance by the offeror; and that, notwithstanding he has promised to keep it open for a fixed period.

Revocation – the withdrawal of the offer – is not effective unless it has been communicated to the offeree. In the case of *Byrne* v. *Van Tienhoven* (1880), on 1 October Van Tienhoven and Co. posted from Cardiff a letter to Byrne in New York, offering him 1,000 boxes of tinplate. On 8 October the company posted a letter revoking their offer. On 11 October Byrne received the letter of 1 October and immediately telegraphed acceptance. On 20 October the letter of revocation was received – and it was held that there was a binding contract made on 11 October.

To this principle there is said to be an exception, based on the case of *Dickinson* v. *Dodds* (1876). On Wednesday Dodds made Dickinson an offer to sell certain houses 'this offer to be left open until Friday 9 o'clock'. On Thursday Dodds made a contract for the sale of the same property to Allan. Dickinson was informed that negotiations with Allan were going on and therefore hurried and accepted the offer. On Friday before 9 o'clock his acceptance had been communicated to Dodds.

On those facts, Bacon VC made a decree of specific performance against Dodds. In that he was clearly wrong, because the contract with Allan was first in time. But Dickinson should have been entitled to damages against Dodds in that there was a contract between the two for the sale of the property which Dodds had broken by placing it outside his power to perform. On appeal, however, the Court of Appeal held there was no contract between Dickinson and Dodds. The headnote to the Law Report read:

'*semble* the sale of the property to a third party would of itself amount to withdrawal of the offer, even though the person to whom the offer was first made had no knowledge of the sale.'

That is in fact what the judges in the Court of Appeal decided. Lord Justice James said:

'To constitute a contract, it must appear that the two minds are one, at the same moment of time that is, that there was an offer continuing up to the time of acceptance.

Lord Justice Mellish said:

'If it be the law that, in order to make a contract, the two minds must be in agreement at some time ... If a man makes an offer to sell a particular horse in his stable, and says "I will give you until the day after tomorrow to accept the offer" and the next day goes and sells the horse to somebody else ... can the person to whom the offer was originally made, then come and say I accept, so as to make a binding contract and so as to be entitled to recover damages for the non-delivery of the horse?'

Lord Justice Mellish did not answer his own question and implied that the answer was 'No'. But clearly on principle the correct answer is 'Yes'. There can be two contracts relating to the same subject matter, and even if the vendor cannot perform both contracts, he is liable to damages to one party. But, apparently, the learned judge thought the obvious answer was 'No' – which is in defiance of the well-established principle that an offer remains open until it lapses, is revoked or is rejected.

Ridiculous as the reasoning is in *Dickinson* v. *Dodds*, the case has passed into the body of law in support of the proposition that a man cannot accept the offer that he knows – from any source – to have withdrawn. The American Restatement of the Law of Contract adopts this position in a slightly modified form, limiting it to contracts of sale and where reliable information has been received. But in *Cartwright* v. *Hoogstoel* (1911) a judge followed the earlier case. It may therefore appear to be reasonably well-established law, but there is no ground for believing that a modern court would follow a decision so patently rooted in fallacy, and so contrary to the principle that revocation of an offer must be communicated to the offeree by the offeror.

6.10 The rejection of offers

An offer may also come to an end by rejection of the offeree. A counter-offer is rejection of the offer.

In *Hyde* v. *Wrench* (1840) Wrench offered on 6 June to sell his farm to Hyde for £1,000. Shortly afterwards Hyde's agent called on him and offered £950, which offer Wrench asked for time to consider. On 27 June Wrench wrote and refused the £950. On 29 June Hyde wrote purporting to accept the offer of £1,000; but Wrench refused to accept it. Hyde brought an action for specific performance of the contract of sale.

The court held that there was no contract; 'there exists no obligation of any sort between the parties'. Therefore, unless acceptance corresponds exactly with the offer, it is a counter-offer.

A company in North Wales sent a telegram to one in Canada: 'Confirming sale to you Grummond Mallard aircraft. Please remit £5,000'. The Canadian company cabled back: 'Confirm purchase of Grummond Mallard aircraft terms set out your cable … £5,000 sterling forwarded your bank to be held in trust for your account pending delivery. Please confirm delivery to be made thirty days within this date'. The trial judge construed the first telegram as an offer and the second as a counter-offer because it introduced two new terms:

(i) the £5,000 asked for was only to be released on delivery;
(ii) there was no reference to delivery within 30 days in the original telegram

Therefore there was no contract: *Northland Aircraft Ltd* v. *Dennis Ferranti Ltd* (1970).

This is an example of the erroneous application of a correct principle to the facts. Clearly, the first telegram was not an offer but the confirmation of a concluded oral contract.

The principle is correctly seen in *Neale* v. *Merett* (1930). Merett offered land to Neale at £280. Neale replied accepting, and enclosed £80 and a promise to pay the balance by four monthly instalments of £50. This variation of the offer was held to be a counter-offer and therefore a rejection.

With more reality, the Uniform Law on the Formation of Contracts for the International Sale of Goods, which has become part of English law by virtue of the Uniform Laws on International Sales Act 1967, but which has still not yet been put into force, says that an acceptance which contains additional or different terms not materially different from the offer constitutes a valid acceptance unless promptly rejected by the offeror.

6.11 Acceptance of offers

Acceptance must correspond exactly with the offer and be unconditional. Acceptance must also be communicated to the offeror for there to be a binding contractual obligation. There is, so far as synallagmatic contracts are concerned, only one exception to that rule – contracts made by post. These were discussed earlier [2.06].

These rules only apply where the offeror expressly or by implication makes known to the offeree that he will accept acceptance by post: *Quenerduaine* v. *Cole* (1883). They may be said to apply by implication where the offer is made by post and no other mode of acceptance is specified, but they would equally apply if the offer were by telephone and an acceptance by post requested.

In those cases, the posting of the letter constitutes the acceptance: *Adams* v. *Lindsell* (1818). It is still a binding contract even if the letter does not reach the offeror: *Household Fire Insurance* v. *Grant* (1879). Compare also *Adams* v. *Lindsell*. On 2 September Lindsell at St. Ives wrote offering wool to Adams. The letter was wrongly addressed to Bromsgrove, Leicestershire instead of Bromsgrove, Worcestershire so that it did not reach Adams until 5 September at 7 P.M. The same evening a letter of acceptance was posted.

On 8 September Lindsell, not having received a reply in the time anticipated, sold the wool. On 9 September he received the letter of acceptance. The court held there was a binding contract made when the letter of acceptance was posted.

Interesting questions arise out of these decisions. If the offeror's letter, by the date or postmark, indicates to the offeree that it had been long delayed in the post, could the offeree still accept it in law by letter? If the acceptance is wrongly addressed, is the contract still binding as soon as it is posted? If a postal strike intervenes, between the posting of the acceptance and the receipt of it, does the rule still apply? And what if the offeree rejects the offer by post and then changes his mind and posts an acceptance; is the contract still complete when the letter of acceptance is posted, so long as the letter of rejection has not been received by the offeror? If a letter of acceptance has been posted, can it be withdrawn by a telegram or a telephone call? In the United States it has been held that there was no contract when a subsequent telegram was received before the letter of acceptance, but that might turn on the postal regulations of that country. In England, it would appear that if the contract is being concluded when the letter is posted, a subsequent telegram which arrives before the letter cannot have any effect on it.

To these, and other intellectual exercises of a similar nature, there is no satisfactory answer, for it is impossible to predict what attitude a modern court would adopt to a rule formulated in 1818 which rejects a fundamental principle of the law of contractual obligations. They might even come to their senses and decide that in these days when the Post Office is very much less reliable and swift than it used to be, it is wrong to saddle an offeror with contractual obligations without express knowledge of them. The same rule apparently applies to telegrams. The contract is made when the telegram is handed in: *Cowan* v. *O'Connor* (1888). But it does not apply to telephone or telex communications [2.09]; there the contract is not concluded until the acceptance has been received by the offeror and the place where it is concluded is at the recipient's end: *Entores* v. *Miles Far East Corporation* (1955).

6.12   The mode of acceptance

It is open to the offeror to lay down the manner in which his offer may be accepted. If the offer is accepted in some other fashion, is there a contract?

An early American case presents an interesting example. Eliason and Co. sent an offer to purchase 300 barrels of flour at $9.50 a barrel in a letter sent by wagon to Henshaw. In the letter they asked for an answer by the return of the wagon which was to Harper's Ferry. Instead, Henshaw sent his acceptance by post to Georgetown, where Eliason also had an office. As it happened, it arrived later than a reply by the wagon would have done, but that was immaterial. The Supreme Court of the United States held that there was no contract since not only had the letter not been sent by the method required, it had not been sent to the place required: *Eliason* v. *Henshaw* (1819).

English cases have never gone as far as that, and in *Tinn* v. *Hoffman* (1873), the court held that an acceptance 'by return of post' did not mean exclusively by letter by return of post. 'A telegram or verbal message or ... any means not later than a letter written and sent by return of post' was sufficient.

The present position therefore appears to be that it is only where the offeror expressly makes it clear that he wants an acceptance in a prescribed form, and none other, that there will not be a contract if some other method of acceptance is adopted; provided, of course, that the acceptance arrives not later than it could have by the method asked for.

6.13   Is offer and acceptance essential to a contract?

Older textbooks, and the most elementary and inaccurate ones of today, describe offer and acceptance as being essential to a contract. This is just not true. There are many cases where it is impossible to find any offer and acceptance, and still more where the so-called offer is an artificial invention of the courts.

A fair example of the case where there is no discoverable offer or acceptance is *Clarke* v. *Dunraven* (1897). Two yachts were entered in a race run on the Clyde by the Mudhook Yacht Club when one collided with the other as the result of the breach of the rules by one of the yachts, the *Satanita*, but without negligence on the part of the owner or the skipper. If there was no contract between the two owners, the damages the owner of the *Satanita* would be liable to pay would be, by the Merchant Shipping Act Amendment Act 1862, limited to the trifling sum of £8 per ton for the small tonnage of the *Satanita*. If, however, there was a contract between the various owners entered in the race, the owner of *Satanita* was liable for 'all damages arising therefrom'.

That there were contracts between the Club and each individual entrant is obvious. But the House of Lords held that there was also 'a contractual relation between the parties to this litigation', i.e. between one entrant and another. Some ingenuity has been expended in discovering an offer and acceptance in this case, but the truth of the situation is that there is none. The House of Lords addressed itself to the correct crucial issue; on the facts of the case, did the parties accept contractual obligations one to the other?

The same result followed in *Brogden* v. *Metropolitan Railway* (1877), where the plaintiff sent a signed copy of a proposed contract to the defendants' agent who altered it in a minor particular and put it in his desk unsigned. The parties behaved as if there was a concluded contract between them, by the plaintiff supplying coals on the terms of the contract to the defendants. The court held that they had assumed contractual obligations to one another in the terms of the unsigned contract.

More recently, a contract for a telephone answering service was found to exist even though the written document had not been signed on the part of the owner as required: *Robophone Facilities Ltd* v. *Blank* (1966).

In the case of contracts in writing for the sale of land, the contractual obligations are assumed not when the contracts are signed but when the last signed counterpart is received: *Eccles* v. *Bryant and Pollock* (1947).

In many cases too, the so-called offer is an entirely artificial concept and no more than a matter of business convenience. Who, except English judges, would have thought of finding that the pushing of a piece of pasteboard towards an intending passenger by a booking clerk is the offer of a contract and that the taking up of the piece of pasteboard is the acceptance of the contract, with a multitude of conditions quite unknown to the acceptor? And who but English judges would have held that, when a shopkeeper puts goods in his window for sale, he is not offering to sell them?

As has been suggested earlier, the real test is whether an independent observer would conclude that the parties had accepted contractual obligations one to the other.

6.14 Mistake as to the subject matter of the contract

The Romans described this as one form of error *in consensu*, a mistake in undertaking, one aspect of which was *error in corpore*, mistake as to the subject matter of a contract – as where Gaius sells Tiberius the slave Strichius. Gaius thinks he is selling one Strichius, where Tiberius thinks he is buying a quite different slave of the same name.

In English law, if there is a latent ambiguity of this nature there is no contract.

Two merchants entered into an agreement, the one to sell and the other to buy a cargo of cotton 'ex Peerless from Bombay'. One merchant had in mind a ship called *Peerless* sailing from Bombay in October. The other was referring to another ship, also called the *Peerless*, which was sailing from Bombay in August. The court held that there was no contract between the two; clearly there were no obligations that any court could enforce, in the absence of further indications as to which '*Peerless*' was intended. Therefore the buyer could not recover damages for non-delivery. The reality of the situation is that no court could possibly decide what to enforce; *Raffles* v. *Wichelhaus* (1864).

This is not because there is no agreement between them, because the law demands not real agreement – a true meeting of minds – but only the outward appearance of it.

Lord Atkin in the leading case on mistake, *Bell* v. *Lever Bros* (1932) said 'if mistake operates at all, it operates so as to negative or in some cases nullify consent'. By negative, he meant the situation where the parties have misunderstood one another in the process of negotiation, so that although there is an appearance of agreement, there is in reality none. But this proposition does not apply to all cases where there is apparent agreement. It only applies where there is latent ambiguity in what the parties have agreed and therefore no contract that the court can find to enforce it. If there is apparent agreement which the courts could enforce, one party cannot be heard to say that it does not represent his true intentions.

A man, by telegram, ordered three rifles. In the course of transmission this became altered to 'the' rifles and, from previous negotiations, was assumed by the recipient of the telegram to be fifty.

Fifty rifles were therefore despatched. The court held that there was no contract between the parties, for the excellent reason that although there appeared to be outward agreement on 'the rifles', no court could possibly say whether it was three or fifty: *Falck* v. *Williams* (1900).

And where the parties enter into an agreement when it is known that there is no consensus between them, they are bound by the apparent terms as interpreted by the courts. In *I.C.C.* v. *Henry Boot and Sons Ltd* (1959) the parties disagreed, before they signed a written contract, about the meaning of an 'up and down' clause in it but did nothing to clarify the situation. Later, one party set up that there was no contract, because there was no true agreement between them – an indisputable fact – in spite of the apparent agreement. The House of Lords held that the apparent agreement, as interpreted by the courts, was the only material thing. Subjective intent and the consensus theory play no part in the modern law.

To summarise: *error in corpore* only affects the contractual obligation in English law if there is ambiguity in the apparent agreement, and the courts are unable to decide which contract to enforce; and that only because the promises are too uncertain to enforce.

6.15 The battle of the forms

It not infrequently happens that an intending purchaser of goods or services writes to a supplier requesting a quotation. He receives a document which contains a quotation, that is an offer, to supply goods on the 'terms set out overleaf', all too often numerous and set in miniscule type.

The intending buyer then places an order on his standard form which excludes all other terms and states that these are the only ones which shall govern the contract. The goods are then supplied with a delivery note which contains a replication of the supplier's terms and conditions. The buyer's gateman signs for the goods and takes them into stock.

The question is, is there a contract for the sale of goods, and if so, on what terms? On basic principles, the answer may be that there is no contract of any kind. Traditionally, unless the parties are agreed as to all essential terms, there is no contract. That, at least, is what students are taught, in accordance with the cases of *Hyde* v. *Wrench* (1840); *Neale* v. *Merett* (1930); *Northland Aircraft Ltd* v. *Dennis Ferranti Ltd* (1970) etc.

The learned editor of the 9th edition of *Cheshire and Fifoot on the Law of Contract* (page 151) appears to support this view, while conceding that in practice the courts will not adopt it, but try to give some commercial effect to what the parties have done. (The 11th edition, however, on page

155 seems to evade the issue.) The learned editor of *Anson on Contract* (24th edition, page 37), however, supports the view that there should be held to be a binding contract in spite of the old rules.

It is, however, clear that there is no *consensus ad idem* such as Pollock and Anson laid down as essential to a valid contract.

Of course, if goods are actually supplied, but on the facts there is no express contract, the courts may imply a quasi-contractual obligation on the buyer to pay for goods received on the basis of a *quantum valebant* (i.e. the market value of the goods which may not be the agreed price), and in that case the transaction will not incorporate any terms (see also section 8(2) of the Sale of Goods Act 1979).

Excluding 'no express contract' and 'no implied contract' as answers to the problem, if there is a contract is it on

(a) the seller's terms; or
(b) the buyer's terms?

In general the courts in England have inclined to the view that the winner of the battle of the forms is 'the last past the post'. In other words, if goods are accepted by the buyer on certain conditions put forward by the seller, those conditions apply.

Those were the findings of the court in *British Road Services Ltd* v. *Arthur V. Crutchley & Co. Ltd* (1968) where, however, there had been previous dealings between the parties. A load of whisky was delivered by British Road Services to a warehouse belonging to the defendants who stamped the plaintiff's delivery note: 'Received on AVC's conditions'. The whisky was stolen while in the defendant's possession. On whose conditions were the goods stored: on those contained in the plaintiff's printed delivery note or on the defendant's condition annexed by the rubber stamped words? Needless to say, the conditions were entirely incompatible. The Court of Appeal held that the defendants' conditions were incorporated in their contract with the plaintiffs by reason of the rubber stamp. But had the lorry driver power or authority to bind his employers?

In the later case of *Butler Machine Tool Co. Ltd* v. *Ex-Cell-O Corporation (England) Ltd* (1979) the court again opted for the 'last past the post' solution.

Round one: the plaintiffs offered a machine tool to the defendants on terms containing a price fluctuation clause.

Round two: the defendants accepted the offer on their own standard order form which had no price fluctuation clause but which had a tear-off section which read 'We accept your order on the Terms and Conditions stated thereon'.

Round three: the plaintiffs completed and returned this slip to the defendant.

Round four: the plaintiffs supplied the machine tool without imposing other terms on their delivery note.

Later, the plaintiffs sought to claim an escalation in price under their price fluctuation clause. The Court of Appeal held that the goods had been brought on the buyer's (the defendants') terms and those terms contained no provisions for escalation.

6.16   The battle of the forms in the USA

In the United States a not entirely satisfactory attempt has been made to resolve the problem by article 2–207 of the Uniform Commercial Code.

(1) A definite and reasonable expression of acceptance or a written confirmation which is sent within a reasonable time operates as an acceptance even though it states terms additional to or different from those offered or agreed upon.

(2) The additional terms are to be construed as proposals for addition to the contract. Between merchants such terms become part of the contract unless:
   (a) the offer expressly limits acceptance to the terms of the offer;
   (b) they materially alter it; or
   (c) notification or objection to them has already been given or is given with in a reasonable time after notice of them is received.

(3) Conduct by both parties which recognises the existence of a contract is sufficient to establish a contract for the sale, although the writings of the parties do not otherwise establish a contract. In such a case the terms of the particular contract consist of those terms on which the writings of the parties agree, together with any supplementary term incorporated under other provisions of the Code.

Chapter 7

Agreements Which Cannot Be Enforced

7.01 Reasons why agreements may not be actionable

Although there may be agreements which have all the appearance of being binding contracts, there are various reasons why these will not be enforced by the English courts.

English lawyers divide agreements of this nature into four categories:

(a) non-contractual agreements;
(b) void contracts – that is, contracts which have no effect and are a nullity;
(c) voidable contracts – those which are legally effective until one of the parties exercises a right to rescind it;
(d) unenforceable contracts – that is, those which, although perfectly valid, cannot for some reason (such as the Limitation Act 1980 or the want of writing) be enforced through the courts.

The consequences in each case are quite different but it is not proposed here to go into detail. This chapter deals in general with the various reasons why some agreements cannot be enforced by an action.

One good reason for this is that the terminology of the courts is totally confused, the words 'illegal', 'void', 'unenforceable', 'immoral', '*contra bonos mores*' being used inconsistently and with no logical uniformity.

A classic example of total incoherence is to be found in Lord Denning's judgement in *Bennett* v. *Bennett* (1952), when his lordship said:

'They are not "illegal" in the sense that a contract to do a prohibited or immoral act is illegal. They are not "unenforceable" in the sense that a contract within the Statute of Frauds is unenforceable for want of writing. These covenants lie somewhere in between. They are invalid and unenforceable. The law does not punish them. They are void, not illegal.'

7.02   Non-contractual agreements

One reason may be that the parties have decided themselves that the agreement between them should not be subject to enforcement by the courts.

As Lord Justice Atkin said in *Balfour* v. *Balfour* (1919):

'There are agreements which do not result in contracts within the meaning of that term.'

He was dealing with an agreement between a civil servant who left his wife behind in the United Kingdom when he was posted to Ceylon and promised to pay her £30 a month housekeeping allowance until he returned. He never did return or pay her, and when she obtained a decree of divorce, she sued him for the unpaid allowance. She failed because the court held that such agreements could not be sued upon 'because the parties never intended that they should be sued upon'. It is therefore open to the parties not only by implication but expressly to agree that their agreement should not be enforceable by the courts.

Business deals are normally presumed to have contractual intention; but it is possible for the parties to agree to the contrary on terms that indicate clearly that it is not their intention to assume contractual obligations. If the agreement is ambiguous, the courts will assume that a contract is intended.

In *Edwards* v. *Skyways Ltd* (1964), a redundant pilot was promised an appropriate sum of money as an *'ex gratia* payment' and the court held that, in spite of these words, the promise created a contractual obligation. (See also 'gentlemen's agreements' [6.03].)

If, in business transactions, the parties wish to ensure that the agreement is not to be taken as a contractual obligation it is always open to them to say so in language which is unmistakeable.

In *Rose and Frank* v. *Crompton Bros* (1925), the parties entered into an agreement, no doubt to avoid United States law regarding monopolies, which contained what was termed the 'Honourable Pledge Clause' (see [6.03] for details). The Court of Appeal held that this clause was not legally binding (see [6.03] for Lord Justice Scrutton's judgment).

Similarly, every time a man fills in a football coupon he expressly agrees with the promoters that the agreement is 'binding in honour only' or some such words that are carefully chosen to exclude contractual obligations. It follows that even if he claims to have won the first prize and the promoters refuse to pay him, he cannot sue them successfully. Mr Appleson discovered this when he brought an action against Littlewoods for £4,335 which he alleged was due to him: *Appleson* v. *Littlewoods Ltd* (1939).

7.03 Sufficient precision for the courts to enforce

Before there can be contractual obligations enforceable by the courts it is essential that the obligations are specified with sufficient precision for the courts to be able to enforce them. This of course is obvious; it is no use the parties making promises to one another which are of such a nature that no court can tell definitely what they mean or when they have been broken. The parties must make their own agreement and specify the terms with sufficient certainty to enable them to be enforced if necessary by the courts. If the terms are too vague, there is no contract. As Lord Maugham put it:

> 'In order to constitute a valid contract, the parties must so express themselves that their meaning can be determined with a reasonable degree of certainty.'

The Law Reports abound in cases where parties have not specified their agreement with sufficient particularity. In *Guthing* v. *Lynn* (1831) the defendant promised to pay the plaintiff a further sum of money, in addition to the purchase price, 'if the horse proves lucky'. The court declined to enter into speculation as to what was or was not 'a lucky horse'. In *Davies* v. *Davies* (1887), one partner promised to retire from a business 'in so far as the law allows'. In *Montreal Gas* v. *Vasey* (1900) one term of the contract was that 'favourable consideration' would be given to its renewal. All these words were held to be too vague to be enforceable.

The difficulty of deciding what exactly the parties meant arises particularly where they refer to terms or conditions not specifically set out and of which there are several forms in current use. An agreement was made to buy a van 'on hire purchase terms' (*Scammell* v. *Ouston* (1941)). This was held to be too vague to impose contractual obligations since there were numerous hire purchase terms in common usage. Words, therefore, which are capable of having a number of different meanings cannot bind the parties at all. 'Subject to strike and lock-out clauses' (*Love and Stewart* v. *Instone* (1970), 'Subject to ... war clause' (*Bishop and Baxter* v. *Anglo Eastern* (1943)), 'Subject to ... *force majeure* conditions' (*British Electric* v. *Patley* (1953)) are similar examples. No court could possibly say what strike clauses, what war clauses or what *force majeure* conditions were incorporated in these agreements.

7.04 'Meaningless clauses'

On the other hand it is said that the court may ignore a clause which is not one that has a number of possible meanings, but is one that is completely meaningless – provided the meaningless words can be deleted from the agreement and still leave a perfectly valid and enforceable contract. In *Nicolene* v. *Simmons* (1953), there was an agreement to buy and sell a quantity of iron reinforcing bars. The seller failed to deliver and, when sued for damages, set up the defence that there was no binding agreement because the agreement contained the words 'we are in agreement that the usual conditions of acceptance apply'. There were no usual conditions of acceptance: and hence this was not an obligation which the court could enforce. But the Court of Appeal refused to accept that argument. Lord Denning said on that occasion:

> 'A distinction must be drawn between a clause which is meaningless and a clause which has yet to be agreed ... a clause that is meaningless can be ignored, whilst still leaving the contract good, whereas a clause which has yet to be agreed may mean there is no contract at all, because the parties had not agreed on all the essential terms.'

7.05 No agreement to make an agreement

It is for the parties themselves to make their own agreement on all essential points; and if they fail to do so there are no contractual obligations. 'A concluded contract is one that settles everything that is necessary to be settled and leaves nothing to be settled by subsequent agreement between the parties', said Lord Dunedin in *May and Butcher* v. *R* (1934). The parties had entered into what they no doubt thought at the time of making was a binding agreement for the purchase of First World War surplus tents; but the agreement read 'the price to be paid ... shall be agreed upon from time to time between the Commission and the purchasers'. The Court of Appeal held that this meant that a reasonable price was to be paid, and therefore there was an enforceable contract since, in the absence of an agreement between the parties as to what was reasonable, the court could decide. But the House of Lords reversed this decision and held there was no binding obligations at all. As the parties had yet to agree the essential element of price, there was no contract. In that, the House of Lords followed an earlier decision. An actress made an agreement with a producer for her engagement 'at a West End salary to be mutually arranged ... between us' but it was held there was no contract: *Loftus* v. *Roberts* (1902).

7.06 'That is certain which can be made certain'

But these principles are subject to the important qualification that is expressed in the maxim: *certum est quod certum reddi potest* – 'that is certain which can be made certain'.

If in *May and Butcher* v. *R*, for example, instead of leaving the price to be settled by future agreement themselves, the parties had elected to allow the price to be fixed by a third party, there would have been a valid contract. Although Lord Buckmaster, dissenting, in the House of Lords, in that case said 'I find myself unable to understand the distinction between an agreement to permit the price to be fixed by a third party and an agreement to permit the price to be fixed in future by the two parties themselves', the difference in fact is quite clear. The two parties may never agree on the price.

If an arbitration clause is included in the agreement it may have the same effect as reference to a third party, for it provides machinery whereby such details can be decided in the absence of agreement. A Mr Foley sold land to Classique Coaches Ltd for the erection of a motor coach garage, and, in a separate document, the company agreed to buy all their requirements of petrol from him at a price 'to be agreed by the parties from time to time'. One clause provided for an arbitrator to be appointed to settle disputes arising out of the contract. It was held that this was a binding contract for the supply of petrol of reasonable quality at a reasonable price and the provision regarding an arbitrator provided a method of arriving at this, even when the parties, as it in fact had happened, failed to agree the price: *Foley* v. *Classique Coaches Ltd* (1934).

Similar reasoning was applied when Fine Fare Ltd entered into an agreement for the supply of broiler chickens from F. & G. Sykes (Wessex) Ltd for a period of five years. The agreement provided for the supply of between 30,000 to 80,000 chickens each week during the first year but failed to specify how many chickens were to be supplied in subsequent years. There was an arbitration clause and the court held there was a binding contract because the number could be decided by the arbitrator: *F. & G. Sykes (Wessex) Ltd* v. *Fine Fare* (1967).

Also, of course, if in *May and Butcher* the agreement allowed *one* of the parties to fix the price in future, there would have been a valid contract, since a certain method of arriving at the price would have been specified.

The absence of expressed agreement between the parties on all essential terms of a contract is not always fatal. 'The general presumption is that the parties have expressed every material term which they intended should govern their agreement, whether oral or in writing. But if there are gaps, the court may be able to close these by reference to either:

(i) previous dealings between the same parties or
(ii) an implied term, which may be imported by the custom and usage of a trade, or by statute, or to give commercial effect to the intention of the parties.

Somewhat surprisingly, the House of Lords found itself able to complete a contract for the parties in *Hillas* v. *Arcos* (1932). There was an agreement between the plaintiffs to buy from the defendants, the Trading Agency of the Soviet Government, 22,000 standards of timber in one year with an option to take 100,000 in the following year. The Court of Appeal held the option too vague to be enforceable at law 'considering the number of things left undetermined: kinds, sizes and quantities of goods, times and port and manner of shipment ...' but the House of Lords reversed this decision. The absence of agreement about the details of the second year's trading could be completed by reference to the terms of the first year's.

Even where an agreement is entirely silent about price, it is not fatal unless the contract relates to land or an interest in land. For the court must imply in the agreement a promise that a reasonable price shall be paid. So far as the sale of chattels is concerned the Sale of Goods Act 1979 enacts:

'Section 8(i) The price in a contract of sale may be fixed by the contract, or may be left to be fixed in manner thereby agreed, or may be determined by the course of dealing between the parties.

(ii) Where the price is not determined in accordance with the foregoing provisions, the buyer must pay a reasonable price.'

So, if in *May and Butcher*, the parties had not said a word about the price of the goods, there would have been a good contract because by reason of this section, the price would have to be a reasonable one. And if the parties could not themselves agree on what was a reasonable price, the Courts would do it for them.

The present position, therefore, in regard to the sale of goods appears to be:

Price to be fixed in future by third party – GOOD CONTRACT.
Price to be fixed in future by one of the parties – GOOD CONTRACT.
No method of fixing price specified – GOOD CONTRACT.
Price to be fixed in future by agreement between both of the parties with arbitration clause – GOOD CONTRACT.

It is not surprising therefore that the decision of the House of Lords in

May and Butcher v. *R* has not received universal approbation. As Lord Scrutton observed dryly about that case and *Hillas* v. *Arcos*:

'The two decisions of the House of Lords are not easy to fit into one another'.

He, of course, was one of the judges of the Court of Appeal which had been overruled in both cases.

The tendency nowadays, when the parties have made a business agreement intending it to impose contractual obligations, is to uphold it wherever possible. *Verba ita sunt intelligenda ut res magis valeat quam pereat*: 'words are to be so understood that the object may be carried out and not fail'.

The principles that are applied by the Sale of Goods Act 1979, and by the common law for centuries before that, to chattels, have been applied to contracts of service. In *British Bank* v. *Novinex* (1949), there was a term that an agreed commission should be paid on certain transactions. This, the court held, meant that there was an implied term that the defendants would pay a reasonable commission and what was a reasonable commission the court itself was able to decide in the light of previous dealings between the parties. Similarly, a promise to a secretary to pay her a bonus if she undertook extra duties was held to carry the implication that it would be a reasonable sum and what that sum was the court itself decided: *Powell* v. *Braun* (1954).

7.07 Illegal contracts

Contracts which are tainted with illegality will not be enforced by the courts.

The word 'illegality' is used with a considerable lack of precision. It used to cover at least six different situations.

(1) Where the agreement itself and/or the acts it contemplates are perfectly lawful in themselves but it is against the policy of the law to enforce such obligations on the ground that it is contrary to public policy. There is nothing wrong in a garage proprietor entering into an agreement with a petrol company to sell only their brand of petrol for 30 years but, in certain circumstances, it may be against the policy of the law to enforce such obligations.

(2) Where the contract is perfectly lawful but the intention of the parties is to use it to break the law; as in the old case of *Ewing* v. *Osbaldiston*

(1836), where the two parties were partners for the management of a London theatre licensed for music and dancing but not licensed for the production of plays – for which purpose they proposed to use it.

(3) Where the agreement itself is specifically caught by common law or statute. The Gaming Act 1845, for example, declares 'all contracts or agreements ... by way of gaming or wagering, shall be null and void'.

(4) Where the agreement between the parties has as its object the furtherance of a criminal offence. Nobody would expect the courts to enforce as a contractual obligation an agreement between bank robbers but difficulties arise where the 'crime' is of a technical nature such as infringing the provisions of a statute.

An agreement by a limited liability company to purchase its own shares, apart from the express provisions of the Companies Act 1985, or to indemnify against loss those who they have induced to purchase its shares (as appears to be the position regarding the takeover by Guinness of the Distillers Company) violates several sections of the Companies Act 1985 and would not be enforced by the courts.

(5) Where the agreement has as its object the furtherance of an act which is not criminal but is unlawful.

Fornication, whether for money or pleasure, has always been unlawful in England, though no longer punishable by the Ecclesiastical Courts as a crime. As a result, when a prostitute was sued on a contract to supply her with a brougham on hire purchase terms which a jury found the plaintiffs knew would be used for the purpose of her profession, a Victorian court held that no action would lie on it: *Pearce* v. *Brooks* (1866). A landlord in 1911 was held unable to recover two quarters' rent for a flat let to a man's mistress, after one of the judges in the King's Bench Divisional Court had received guidance from the Book of Common Prayer:

'The law will not allow a contract which is tainted with immorality to be enforced. It was urged that prostitution is one thing and living as one man's mistress is quite a different thing. They may differ in degree but they both stand upon the same plane.'

(Perhaps he meant lie upon the same plane.)

If that indeed be the law, then every lease must be void where the landlord knows the premises are going to be occupied by a couple who will cohabit together although unmarried or a couple of homosexuals living together. If so, there must be many thousands of void leases in London alone: *Upfill* v. *Wright* (1911), but there have been no recent cases. (In fact, it has been suggested in legal journals that agreements between unmarried cohabitors regarding properties acquired during cohabitation would be enforced by the courts.)

From these past cases it might well be concluded that joint agreements by unmarried partners to purchase property are unenforceable at law, as also the mortgages granted to unmarried partners. Currently, the income tax rules allows unmarried couples who jointly purchase property taxation relief on £30,000 a head, namely £60,000, as opposed to a married couple's £30,000. It is curious that English income tax statutes should so favour fornication and for that matter, the cohabitation of homosexual couples, who get tax relief that those who dwell in lawful matrimony do not enjoy. Between 1979 and 1985 tax relief on mortgages escalated by 400 per cent to reach £4,500 million while expenditure on housing went down by 60 per cent.

In fact, of course, if this issue were to be raised today, a judge would find some expedient reason for evading the law as set out in the cases above. In fact, it has even been suggested that English courts would uphold and enforce a cohabitation agreement between a couple.

7.08 The effect of illegal contracts

With so many different concepts tucked away in the portmanteau word 'illegality' it is not surprising that the law to be applied is confused.

Mr Justice Devlin (as he then was) made some attempt to sort the practice out in *Elder* v. *Averback* (1949) 'by laying down some propositions as to how the courts should approach the whole problem':

'(i)   Where the contract on the face of it is illegal the courts will not enforce it, whether illegality is pleaded by the defendant or not.
(ii) Where the contract is not on the face of it illegal, evidence of extraneous circumstances tending to show illegality ought not to be admitted unless specifically pleaded by the defendant.
(iii) Where unpleaded facts emerge in the course of hearing a case which suggest that the contract was illegal, the court should not act on this information unless it is satisfied that all relevant facts are before it.
(iv) Where unpleaded facts emerge in the course of the hearing and the court is satisfied that all the relevant facts are before it and can clearly see that the contract had an illegal objection the court is bound to take notice of the fact and refuse to enforce the contract.'

But, since that date, it has been held that if counsel has reason to suspect that a contract may be illegal, he is under a duty to draw the attention of the court to all the relevant facts in order that the court may not enforce illegal transactions; and the Court of Appeal in *Small* v. *Unity Finance Co.* (1963) felt itself bound to take the point of illegality of a contract even though the matter had not been pleaded or raised in the County Court.

7.09   Contracts which are void

In most cases the effect of illegality on contracts is to make them void.

The unfortunate first printer of a book called *The Memoirs of Harriet Wilson* was held not able to recover his remuneration from the publishers because the court held that the book, being the autobiography of a harlot, amounted to a criminal libel: *Poplett* v. *Stocklade* (1825). Possibly this was because of the entertaining account she gives of how the Duke of Wellington, straight from the battlefield of Waterloo, was kept waiting outside her door while she was engaged with another client. Printers of pornography are therefore well advised to get their remuneration in advance. In *Napier* v. *National Business Agency Ltd* (1951), the plaintiff was engaged to act as secretary of the defendant company for £13 per week plus £6 a week expenses. Both parties knew that his expenses would not amount to £6 a week and that it was a device to avoid income tax on that part of his salary. The Court held that no part of his remuneration was recoverable.

But in other cases, where the unlawful part can be severed from the rest of the contract, and the judges regard it as proper to do so, that alone will be void. This normally is the case in contracts where a particular covenant only is in restraint of trade and the rest of the contract is unobjectionable [7.11].

Normally, if the whole of a contract is void, money or goods which have passed as the result of the void contract are recoverable. But where the contract is void for illegality, money or goods which have passed under it are (subject to the exemptions noted below) not recoverable.

Ex turpi causa non oritur actio is said to be the maximum that applies: 'no action will lie in an evil cause'. The principle is well settled that if the plaintiff requires any aid from an illegal transaction to establish his cause of action, then he shall not have any aid from the court. In one case, the plaintiff sued for the recovery of a half bank note which he had deposited with the defendant as security for money due; it was undoubtedly his property but he was unable to recover it when evidence was accepted that the 'money due' was for wine and food supplied in a brothel: *Taylor* v. *Chester* (1869). A plaintiff who was on the 'stop list' of a trade association got somebody else to order cigarettes for him, for which he paid money over. He did not get the goods, nor could he recover the money, since to do so he would have to set up his own fraudulent scheme: *Berg* v. *Sadler and Moore* (1937).

7.10   Exceptions to the rules as to void contracts

There are three exceptions to the rules as to void contracts:

(1) If a right of property quite apart from the contract can be established

Bowmakers Ltd were able to recover from Barnett Instruments Ltd certain machine tools which were leased to the latter company, notwithstanding that the contract of leasing was illegal by S.R. & O. (1940) No. 1784 etc.

'Why should not the plaintiffs have back what is their own?'

asked Lord Justice Du Parcq:

> '*Prima facie* a man is entitled to his own property and it is not a general principle of our law ... that where one man's goods have got into another's possession in consequence of some unlawful dealing between them, the true owner can never be allowed to recover those goods by action': *Bowmakers Ltd* v. *Barnett Instruments Ltd.*'

It is even said that a right of property can pass under a void illegal contract. In other words, the contract is void while performance is executory, but once it has been performed the property has passed. In *Feret* v. *Hill* (1854) a lease of a house was taken and the premises converted into a brothel, which had been the intention of the lessee all the time, unknown to the lessor. It was held that the lease was good. And where goods were delivered as the result of an illegal and therefore void contract, the property in them was held to pass to the purchaser (*Kingsley* v. *Sterling Industrial Securities Ltd* (1966); so that the buyer could maintain an action for damages against anybody – even the seller – who took the goods from him.

Ali knew that he could not obtain a haulier's licence required by government regulations; so he got Singh to buy a lorry on hire purchase and register it in his name. Ali then bought the lorry from Singh, who had obtained the necessary licence, but Singh took it from him. It was held that Ali could recover it since his case rested not upon an illegal contract, even though the whole purpose of the transaction was to evade the regulations, but on a property right which had passed: *Sajan Singh* v. *Sardara Ali* (1960).

So, when the word 'void' is used in connection with illegal contracts, it does not in two respects have the same meaning as usual. By this time, the reader will be no doubt wishing that semantics were required study for lawyers who became judges.

(2) If the parties are not in pari delicto

This means that goods or money which have passed under the void contract may be recovered if the plaintiff is not a willing party to infringing the law. Therefore if a man parts with money or property under an illegal contract as the result of fraud or pressure by the other party, he is able to recover it. 'It can never be predicated as *par delictum* where one holds the rod and the other bows to it' was said in *Smith* v. *Cuff* (1817).

The same principle applies where the statute which makes the contract illegal has been passed for the purpose of protecting one party to the contract. A tenant is able to recover illegal premiums exacted by a landlord, even though he knew that they were illegal when he paid them: *Craig* v. *Southouse* (1949).

(3) If one of the parties has withdrawn before the illegal transaction is carried out

There is, it is said, a place of repentance for all parties to an illegal contract, If, therefore, a man has paid money out under an illegal contract before 'substantial performance' has taken place, he may be allowed to recover it. In order to defraud his creditors, Taylor assigned all his goods to another; this man then assigned and delivered the goods under a bill of sale to Bowers who was aware of the fraud. It was held that Taylor could recover them from him because the fraudulent purpose of the transaction had not been carried out, and no creditor had been defrauded: *Taylor* v. *Bowers* (1876).

But if the only reason why the illegal transaction is not carried out is that one party refuses to perform it, the other party cannot claim that he has repented: *Bigos* v. *Bousted* (1951).

7.11   Contracts in restraint of trade

Until the early seventeenth century, the common law allowed and vigorously supported all sorts of restrictions on trade. Men could not practise a trade unless they had been apprenticed and served their time and unless they were members of the local guild. Monopolies could be created and sold, and under the Tudors they frequently were. Sir Walter Raleigh, for example, held the monopoly of sweet wines. The modern law, as we know it, is largely the invention of Coke and his friends and was a political measure directed at the Royal Prerogative and the right to create monopolies (though there is one earlier case in the last year of Elizabeth's reign).

The tailors of Ipswich tried to stop a man who was not a member of their guild from plying his craft in the town. Coke, then Chief Justice of the King's Bench, held that:

'At common law, no man could be prohibited from working at any lawful trade, for the law abhors idleness, the mother of all evil ... And therefore, the common law abhors monopolies which prohibit any from working in any lawful trade.' *The Tailors of Ipswich* (1615).

It was not a doctrine that commended itself to his royal master; for this and many other matters, the following year Coke was sacked by the King. But what he had invented in this respect, as in much else, passed into the common law.

Prima facie all contracts in restraint of trade are unenforceable. A contract in restraint of trade is one that limits competition or prevents one of the parties from exercising his trade or profession however and wherever he may wish:

'Any contract which interferes with the free exercise of a trade or business by restricting [a man] in the work he may do, or the arrangement which he may make with others is a contract in restraint of trade': Denning MR in *Petrofina (G.B.) Ltd* v. *Martin* (1966).

But a contract in restraint of trade will be enforced, provided that:

(1) it is reasonable as between the parties;
(2) it is not contrary to the public interest.

How the law applies these principles is best studied in three contexts:

(1) Contracts of employment where the employee ('the servant' – as the

law still slightingly calls him) promises that, after leaving his master's employment, he will not engage in that particular occupation within a certain geographical area.

(2) Contracts of sale, of, *inter alia*, goodwill of a business where the vendor promises that for a certain period he will not compete with the business in a specified area.

(3) Other agreements between traders, particularly what are termed 'solus' agreements whereby a trader undertakes to sell only the product of one particular manufacturer.

7.12 Restrictive covenants in contracts of employment

The law scrutinises these with care, conscious that there is no equality of bargaining power between a man seeking employment and an employer selecting, perhaps from numerous applicants, an employee. The employee, in his eagerness to get a job, will readily agree to almost any restriction being made on his activities after he has left the employment. The employee has very little choice in the matter. Therefore, such conditions are only enforceable provided three conditions are fulfilled. These are:

(a) The master must have a proprietary interest to protect.
That is, the object of the clause of restraint must be to protect his trade connections or his trade secrets. It must not be merely to prevent competition from his former employee. A Mr Saxelby was employed as an engineer by Morris Ltd and a term of his contract was that for seven years after leaving the employment he would not work in the sale or manufacture of various kinds of machinery. The House of Lords held this term to be invalid because it merely sought to restrain competition with the employer's business and not to protect his trade connection or his secrets: *Morris* v. *Saxelby* (1916).

A prohibition of practice as a 'medical practitioner' was too wide – because it would exclude consultancy – to protect the proprietary interest of a firm of general practitioners: *Lyne-Perkis* v. *Jones* (1969).

But in the *Home Counties Dairies* v. *Skilton* (1970) a milk roundsman promised that he would 'not at any time during the period of one year after the determination of his employment under this agreement ... either on his own account or as representative or agent of any person or company, serve or sell milk or dairy produce to any person or company who at any time during the last six months of his employment shall have been a customer of the employer and served by the employee in the course of his employment'. This Court of Appeal held to be enforceable as 'precisely the area the employer was allowed to protect', i.e. his trade connection.

(b) The restraint must be limited in area to that reasonably necessary for the protection of that proprietary interest.

There are a host of decisions that show that an excessively wide area makes the whole clause void. 'Twenty-five miles from London' was too wide for a canvasser who had been employed in one particular area of London: *Mason* v. *Provident Clothing* (1913); 'twenty miles from Sheffield' was too wide for a reporter: *Leng* v. *Andrews* (1909); five miles from a butcher's shop was too wide for a manager: *Empire Meat* v. *Patrick* (1939); and ten miles from a tailor's shop was too wide for a tailor's assistant: *Attwood* v. *Lamont* (1920). But seven miles from Tamworth Town Hall was reasonable for a solicitor's managing clerk: *Fitch* v. *Dewes* (1921); and ten miles from a doctor's surgery was held good: *Lyne-Perkis* v. *Jones* (1969).

The test is entirely one of what is reasonable for the protection of the legitimate proprietary interests of the employer. A world-wide prohibition could in certain circumstances be valid though none appears to have been recorded in the courts, in the case of employees as distinct from vendors of a business.

(c) The restraint must be limited in time to that reasonably necessary for the protection of that proprietary interest.

A credit drapery salesman covenanted that he would not for five years following the termination of his employment, canvas or solicit orders from any of his employer's customers. It was held that this period was longer than was necessary for the protection of employers' legitimate interests and was therefore void: *M. & S. Drapers* v. *Reynolds* (1956).

7.13 Vendors of businesses

Different considerations apply in cases where a man sells his business and the goodwill of it and promises that he will not compete with it. Here the principle is that a vendor should 'not derogate from his grant'. Obviously, if he sells a business and then opens up again in close proximity the purchaser of the business is likely to lose his customers to the former owner.

Notwithstanding the above:

(a) There must be a proprietary interest to protect.

So, when a company which had a licence to brew beer, but did not in fact brew any, sold the goodwill of its business and promised that for a period of fifteen years it would not compete in beer brewing, this clause was invalid. It amounted to no more than a restriction of competition; no part of the goodwill that the purchasers had bought was due to beer brewing: *Vancouver Malt* v. *Vancouver Breweries* (1934).

(b) The protection afforded by such clauses will be strictly limited to protection of the actual business sold. In *British Reinforced Concrete* v. *Schelff* (1921), the vendor had sold a business based in Leicester and engaged in the manufacture of 'hoop' road reinforcements. He covenanted not to engage in the manufacture of road reinforcements of any kind anywhere in Britain. It was held that this was too wide and was aimed at restriction of competition rather than the legitimate protection of the business goodwill acquired.

(c) General restraints, although unlimited in area or time, may well be reasonable.
Nordenfelt, the patentee and manufacturer of weapons of war sold throughout the world, sold his business interests to a limited company and covenanted that he would not for 25 years anywhere in the world engage in the business of a manufacturer of arms or ammunition. It was held that the business he had sold being worldwide (unhappily!) the restriction was binding as reasonable: *Nordenfelt* v. *Maxim Nordenfelt Co.* (1894). And a restriction for the whole of the Dominion of Canada and unlimited in time was held reasonable in *Connors Bros Ltd* v. *Connors* (1940).

Once again, it is a question of fact: what is reasonably necessary for the protection of the business sold?

7.14 Solus agreements

Formerly the law was little interested in what arrangements businessmen made amongst themselves; liberty to make what contract they wished and to restrict themselves in any way was not regarded as contrary to the public interest. Solus agreements have been a feature of the licensed liquor trade for many years and often tie publicans to taking only one brand of beer and to taking all their wines and spirits from one brewer – even though they can often obtain them cheaper elsewhere. Such agreements have been enforced certainly since 1792 and probably earlier.

But changes in political and economic ideas have influenced the courts, particularly in relation to the distribution and sale of petrol. For what was satisfactory for the sale of beer was not considered satisfactory for the sale of petrol.

Garages distributing petrol in this country have often entered into solus agreements which formerly contained four basic provisions:

(a) 'the tying covenant' – to purchase all their requirements of petrol from one supplier;
(b) 'the continuity covenant' – a clause that if they sold their business to a third party they would insert a similar clause in the contract with him;
(c) 'the compulsory trading'covenant – an undertaking to keep the petrol stations open, sometimes during minimum hours;
(d) 'the fixed retail price covenant' – an undertaking not to sell the petrol below the manufacturer's fixed retail price. Such covenants are now illegal and unenforceable as a result of the Resale Prices Act 1964.

The Monopolies Commission report, *The Supply of Petrol to Retailers* (1965), led to a voluntary undertaking by the petrol companies to the then Board of Trade which radically changed the position and, in effect, was changed by something that was not law but belonged to the shadowy hinterland where Government pressure is exerted and the industries submit rather than endure legislation.

One result of the Commission's Report was that the courts the following year, in *Petrofino (G.B.) Ltd* v. *Martin* (1966), held that the doctrine of restraint of trade was applicable to solus agreements. There, the tying covenant was for twelve years. The continuity covenant was also criticised as an unnecessary restraint and both were held to be void. This case was followed by *Esso Petroleum* v. *Harper's Garage* (1967) where a tying covenant of twenty-one years was held void as too long a period, but one which was effective for four years and five months was regarded as valid. The House of Lords in so holding paid regard to the recommendations of the Monopolies Commission that there should be a five year limit to solus agreements. But this was limited by the decision in *Cleveland Petroleum* v. *Dartstone* (1969), where it was held that if the solus agreement was accepted by the buyer of a garage as a term on which he obtained possession, it was enforceable against him. In 1968 the defendant bought an underlease of a garage from X and accepted solus covenants originally framed in 1960 for twenty-five years.

'Where a man takes possession of premises under a lease, not having been in possession previously and on taking possession he enters into a restrictive covenant tying himself to take all his supplies from the lessor, *prima facie*, the tie is valid,' said Lord Denning.

It would appear therefore that the doctrine does not apply to clauses in leases.

The present legal position therefore seems to be that if the owner or existing tenant of a petrol station, in return for a mortgage at a low rate of interest, improvements to his garage, or an increased discount rate, or any of the other inducements commonly given by the petrol companies for such covenants, freely covenants to buy nothing but Mogul's petrol for twenty-one years, together with a continuity covenant, he is not bound by either promise. The next day, if he so wishes, he can sell somebody else's petrol. But if the only terms upon which he can obtain possession at all are by having to accept a lease containing the self-same unreasonable covenants, he is bound by them.

Neither the logic nor the justice of this situation will be immediately apparent to everybody.

If the clause in restraint of trade is unreasonable it is wholly void. So if a man sells his butcher's business and covenants that he will not for the rest of his life engage in the same trade anywhere in the world and this clause is held unreasonable he may safely set up business next door to his former shop. The courts are not there to rewrite the parties' contracts for them. But even so he may be precluded by equity from canvassing his old customers or holding out that he is carrying on the same business: *Trego* v. *Hunt* (1896).

This is subject to what has been termed 'the blue pencil rule', if it still exists. A London dealer in artificial jewellery sold his business and covenanted not to compete with the buyer 'as a dealer in real or imitation jewellery in ... any part of the United Kingdom ... the United States of America, Rome or Spain'. This was obviously too wide for the protection of the proprietary interests in the business sold and therefore *prima facie* void. But the court held that the covenant was severable and they would uphold a covenant which excluded the words 'real' and all places outside the United Kingdom: *Goldsoll* v. *Goldman* (1914).

As Lord Justice Pearson commented in *Commercial Plastics Ltd* v. *Vincent* (1964):

'A good deal of legal "know how" is required for the successful drafting of a restrictive covenant.'

7.15 Horizontal agreements

The sort of agreements which have been discussed in the previous paragraphs are sometimes termed 'vertical agreements' because the agreements are between a supplier of goods and those he supplies. Equally important are those termed 'horizontal agreements', namely those between members engaged in a similar trade, whereby they all participated in what has come to be termed 'restrictive agreements'. This refers to the sort of agreement or 'undertakings' whereby all or most of the members of a particular business agreed to restrict:

(i)   prices to be charged for goods;
(ii) terms on which goods are to be supplied;
(iii) amounts of goods to be produced;
(iv) process of manufacture;
(v)   persons to whom the goods are to be supplied.

British industry had become burdened with an overlaid criss-cross network of restrictive practices between traders. In 1956 the Restrictive Practices Act was passed, and this established the Restrictive Practices Court to deal with what the economist would no doubt describe as 'cartel agreements'.

The common law gave no relief against this sort of conspiracy against consumers. Indeed, if a group of traders combined to force a competitor out of business, no action in tort would lie unless he could prove that what they had done was not in furtherance of their business interests, but out of malice – an impossible task. The leading case is the *Mogul S.S. Co. Ltd v. McGregor, Gow and Co.* (1892), where a newcomer attempted to break into the closely organised China-England carrying trade. The fact that all those already engaged in the business ganged up against him and refused to accept any goods for shipment from those who dealt with the newcomer did not confer a right of action on him, although calculated, and indeed intended, to damage him.

The law remains unaltered so far as transactions outside the United Kingdom are concerned. All the ferry services that take passengers and vehicles from the United Kingdom to Europe are at liberty to, and in fact did until recently, agree to fix and maintain minimum prices. But, so far as these practices within the United Kingdom are concerned, they were for long unlawful.

They were struck at by legislation in the United States and Canada as early as 1890; but it was not until 1948 that Britain was willing to recognise that the problem existed. In the slovenly way in which legislation is enacted in Britain, the Monopolies and Restrictive Practices (Inquiry and Control) Act was passed in 1948; to be amended by the Restrictive Practices Act 1956. After that, resale price maintenance was made illegal by the Resale Prices Act 1964, except as expressly approved by the Restrictive Practices Court.

The 1956 Act requires all parties operating a 'restrictive trading' agreement, as there defined, to register it with a new officer termed the Registrar of Restrictive Trading Agreements. It is his duty to bring all such agreements before the Restrictive Practices Court, which is concerned only whether such practices are in the public interest or not. An agreement includes any agreement or arrangement whether or not it is intended to be enforceable by legal action. So all sorts of bargains between parties are caught by the Act besides formal contracts. As Lord Justice Dankwert commented in 1964: 'Heaven help the lawyer who has to advise a client'. Heaven has helped the lawyers, not least of all in the multiplicity and duration of fees for such cases. A test of 'an arrangement' is whether the party would consider himself under a moral obligation to do what he has undertaken to do. It will be seen therefore that agreements which are far removed from the normal concept of contractual obligations may be caught by this Act. 'A wink is as good as a nod.' Even an arrangement whereby manufacturers notified one another of the prices they were charging may be held to be caught by the Act. Section 6(1) specifically applies to situations where the parties have by some such 'arrangement' limited their freedom to contract with others.

If the agreements between the parties are contractual, failure to register them does not apparently make them unenforceable in the courts.

The Resale Prices Act 1964 made minimum price agreements void except in so far as they are approved by the Restrictive Practices Court. Where they are so approved – as in the case of books, for example, by the *Net Book Agreement* 1957 (1962) – these minimum prices are binding on retailers irrespective of whether there is any privity of contract between them and the manufacturers or publishers and regardless of any absence of consideration.

7.16   Agreements to oust the jurisdiction of the courts

While it is always open to the parties to make an agreement expressly excluding contractual intent it is not open to them to exclude the jurisdiction of the courts. The historical background to this is the long (and losing) battle that the courts fought to prevent the parties substituting arbitration for litigation. An arbitration results from an agreement between the parties to submit any dispute to a tribunal of their own choice, and to abide by its decision. So fond are business men of arbitration, that clauses to this effect are to be found in every building contract, every commodity contract and every shipping contract. The advantages are apparent to businessmen. The tribunal sits in private at a time and place convenient to the parties; the arbitrators are the servants of the parties and therefore much more courteous and considerate than the

High Court judges who still regard themselves as 'lions under the throne'and not as servants of the public. There is a minimum of formality and no recourse to the thousand pages of 'The White Book' – the Practice of the Supreme Court. Anybody can appear as advocate for the parties – and the dispute is usually settled more speedily and at less cost than in any court. The partiality of businessmen for arbitration is well-founded and, in spite of all the efforts of the courts to prevent it, it has become the most favoured method of settling commercial disputes; so much so that the lawyers have decided that 'if you can't beat 'em – join 'em!'. High Court judges are now empowered to sit as arbitrators.

The long battle of the lawyers against arbitration eventually ended in 1855 when the House of Lords – by a majority of one – held that a clause which made arbitration a condition precedent did not supplant or oust the jurisdiction of the English Courts; *Scott* v. *Avery* (1855). Later it was held in the case of *Atlantique Shipping* v. *Dreyfus* (1922) that there was no objection to a clause which deprived a party of an action if he did not go to arbitration within a certain period, e.g. within six weeks after goods have been landed from a ship. The Arbitration Act 1950 recognised the reality of the situation and retains some measure of control by the courts over arbitration. The Arbitration Act 1979 increased the courts'power to interfere in arbitration while professing to limit it.

But the same principle has been applied in recent times to cases where clubs or associations have purported to deprive their members of access to the courts; see *Lee* v. *Showmen's Guild* (1952) and *Baker* v. *Jones* (1954).

7.17 Agreements contrary to the interests of justice

Formerly, agreements not to prosecute for a criminal offence – such as embezzlement – if the money was restored, were not binding because they were in themselves the criminal offence of 'compounding a felony'. But the Criminal Justice Act 1967 abolished this crime, and although it made the acceptance of any consideration for nondisclosure of an arrestable offence a crime, there is an express exception in favour of a consideration which is 'the making good of loss or injury occasioned by the offence'. It would appear, therefore, that such promises may now be binding.

But any other contract which tends to interfere with the course of justice is not binding; and a contract, for example, whereby one person who has stood bail for another should be indemnified against loss is not merely void but an indictable offence in itself.

7.18   Agreements for trading with an enemy

Quite apart from any statute passed relating to this subject, on the outbreak of war, all contracts with enemy nationals are dissolved and any contract made with them is void. Any enemy for this purpose is anybody who resides in enemy country, or any territory under the control of the enemy. But if there is 'an accrued right' this may, in some circumstances, be merely suspended and not discharged – as where a husband was held liable for instalments under a separation agreement to a wife who was in enemy-occupied territory: *Bevan* v. *Bevan* (1955).

7.19   Agreements for the procurement of honours

A Colonel Parkinson was promised by the secretary of the College of Ambulance that, if he made a large donation to that body, he would receive a knighthood. The Colonel paid up but did not receive his knighthood and sued for the return of his money: *Parkinson* v. *The College of Ambulance Ltd* (1924). He could not recover.

7.20   Gaming and wagering contracts

The common law had no objection to enforcing promises to pay money lost at gaming or on a bet by the action of *assumpsit*, except that the judges occasionally protested when they were called upon to decide which of two flies had reached the top of a window first, and matters of that nature.

But the aristocracy were very much concerned with relieving their offspring from the consequences of their own folly, with the result that Parliament began to intervene to protect those who had wagered and lost. An Act of 1710 made all securities (such as cheques) given for money lost on gaming absolutely void, but this was in due course replaced by the Act of 1835 to which reference is made later. Gaming is now defined by section 52(1) of the Gaming Act 1968 as:

'the playing of any game of chance for winnings in money or money's worth, whether any person playing the game is at risk of losing money or money's worth or not.'

It is therefore presumably not gaming if you stake your wife or fiancée at roulette, since the money element is essential. The same section also provides that 'a game of chance' includes a game of chance and skill combined, or a pretend game of chance; but it excludes 'an athletic sport or game'.

For the purpose of the other Acts, a more extensive definition has been adopted, wide enough to include playing any game for winning money or money's worth and it includes horse racing.

A wager is simply a bet and wagering was defined by Mr Justice Hawkins in *Carlill* v. *The Carbolic Smoke Ball Co.* (1892) as:

'one by which two persons, professing to hold opposite views touching the issue of a future uncertain event, mutually agree that, dependent upon the determination of that event, one shall win from the other, and that other shall pay or hand over to him, a sum of money or other stake, neither of the contracting parties having any other interest in that contract by either of the parties. It is essential to a wagering contract that each party may under it either win or lose, whether he will win or lose being dependent on the issue of the event and therefore remaining uncertain until that issue is known. If either of the parties may win but cannot lose, or may lose but cannot win, it is not a wagering contract.'

It is generally held that the use of the words 'future uncertain events' is too narrow, and that there can be a wager on past events, e.g. which footballer scored most goals last year, or any present fact, e.g. whether Jupiter is inhabited or even certain future events, e.g. what time the sun rises tomorrow, provided that the parties hold different views. But one thing has been decided beyond peradventure – there can only be two parties to a wager. 'You cannot have a multipartite agreement for a bet.'

Stock Exchange and Commodity Market transactions are excluded from wagering, even though there may never be an intention to take up the shares or the commodity, and all the transactions are done on margins. The court will scrutinise them to see whether they are really commercial transactions or bets.

A bet between two people on the result of a game is a gaming wager.

The statutes and gaming and wagering

The Gaming Act 1835
By this Act all securities for money lost on gaming or in repayment of money lent for gaming are deemed to be given for an illegal consideration.

They are not void, but if the drawer of a cheque, for example, stops payment the drawee cannot successfully sue on the cheque.

Cases on the Act have held that a third party who takes the cheque and gives value for it can sue the drawer on the cheque if it be dishonoured, provided he does not know that it was received in payment of money won on gaming. But even if he does know it is the proceeds of money won on a wager (that is, not a gaming wager) he can recover, for this Act deals only with gaming and not wagering. So if you give your grocer a bookmaker's cheque for a case of champagne and tell him you have won it by a bet on the results of the Cup Final, he can sue on it; but not if you tell him you have won it on the Grand National.

Since the Gaming Act 1968 cheques given in licensed gaming houses for play are valid, provided they are not post-dated, that they are exchanged for cash or tokens, and that they are presented to a bank within two days.

The Gaming Act 1845
This Act provides:

> 'All contracts or agreements whether by parol or in writing, by way of gaming or wagering shall be null and void and no suit shall be brought or maintained in any court of law and equity for recovering any sum of money or valuable thing alleged to be won upon any wager – or which shall have been deposited in the hands of any person to abide the event on which any wager shall have been made ...'

There are three limbs of the section. The first makes contracts for gaming or wagering null and void – but that does not mean that the contract is illegal, therefore collateral transactions are valid.

The effect, of course, is that you cannot sue your bookmaker if he fails to pay you your winnings, nor can he sue you if he allows you to bet on credit and you lose.

For a long time it was thought that subsequent promises to pay some or all of the money lost on bets were enforceable provided that there was fresh consideration, such as a forbearance to report the defaulter to Tattersalls, but this was held, in *Hill* v. *William Hill (Park Lane) Ltd* (1949), not to be the case. Subsequent contracts are as much caught by the second limb of the 1845 Act as the original bargain. The money is still money 'alleged to have been won on a wager'.

The effect of the Act on stakeholders has been held to be that if both parties hand their stakes to the stakeholder, and if he pays over both stakes to the winner, he cannot be sued by the loser. But if, before he does this, the loser (or the winner for that matter) sues to recover his stake he can do so, as money 'had and received' to his benefit. But the winner cannot sue both for his stake and the loser's stake, i.e. his winnings.

The Gaming Act 1892
This Act does two things:

(i)   It prevents an action being brought for money paid in settlement of bets or gaming bets by somebody other than the principal. If out of charity, you pay off your friend's debts to the bookmaker, you cannot recover it from your friend.
(ii) It prevents a betting agent suing his principal for remuneration.

Loans for gaming bets
Money lent for this purpose may fall into three classes:

(i)   Where the loan consists of paying betting losses direct to the winner, e.g. settling a bookmaker's account. This is clearly caught by the 1892 Act and is irrecoverable.
(ii) Where A lends B money to pay B's losses. Here the law appears to be that even if A knows the purpose for which the loan is required, it is recoverable provided that A has not imposed a stipulation that it shall be used only for that purpose and none other: *McDonald* v. *Green* (1950).
(iii) Money lent for the purpose of laying a bet or playing a game. It is sometimes said on the basis of the decision in *Carlton Hall Club* v. *Lawrence* (1929) that this money is irrecoverable. But that is a highly doubtful decision, because there was in fact no loan of money. A cheque was accepted for chips in an illegal gaming house and the action was framed as 'a loan' since obviously the cheque which was stopped could not be sued upon by reason of the 1835 Act. The better view is that a loan is recoverable even though the lender may know that the borrower intends to use it for backing a horse or playing roulette. But this does not apply if the loan is made within a licensed gaming house: that is an illegal act by virtue of section 16(b) of the 1968 Act.

7.21   Agreements induced by duress

A contract induced by duress or undue influence is voidable.

In *Williams* v. *Bayley* (1866), a father was induced to grant an equitable mortgage in his property in consideration of the return to him of promissory notes which had been forged by his son and under the threat that the son would get 'transportation for life' when sentenced. He applied to the courts for a cancellation of the agreement. In the House of Lords, Lord Westbury said

'The security given for the debt of the son by the father under such circumstances, was not the security of a man who acted with that freedom and power of deliberation that must, undoubtedly, be considered as necessary to validate a transaction of such a description ...'

He referred to: 'the great folly, nay impropriety, of the bankers proceeding to take this security from the defenceless old man after his solicitor had left him, protesting in such an emphatic manner against the proceedings which he knew they were about to enter upon.'

7.22 Agreements induced by undue influence

In the case of *Lancashire Loans Ltd* v. *Black* (1934), a daughter without independent legal advice had been induced by her mother and her solicitor to give promissory notes to cover her mother's debts to moneylenders.

When sued upon the notes, she contended that she had acted under the undue influence of her mother. Mr Justice du Parcq rejected that contention and held that since she was married she was 'emancipated'.

The Court of Appeal unanimously revised that finding. In his judgment, Lord Justice Greer said:

'The following principles of law seem to me to be well established:
(1) In the case of certain relationships involving trust and confidence by one person in another the law requires that the court shall presume that a gift or voluntary settlement or obligation entered into without consideration in favour of the party in whom trust or confidence is placed by the other party to the transaction has been induced by undue influence.
(2) The relationship of parent and child is one of the relationships to which the presumption applies.
(3) The presumption continues to apply after the child has come of age for a period which has not been defined by the decisions, but has been referred to in some of the decisions as either just after or in a short time after the child has come of age.
(4) The presumption ceases to apply if it be proved that the child has been emancipated from the relationship which gives rise to the opportunity for the exercise of undue influence, i.e. a relationship in which trust and confidence is placed on the good faith and integrity of the parent when the latter is exercising his or her influence as a parent.

(5) The presumption may be rebutted by proving that the gift or instrument whereby benefits are conferred on the parent by the child is the result of the "pure, voluntary, well understood acts" of the child's mind. I have quoted these words from the judgment of Lord Eldon in the leading case of *Huguenin* v. *Baseley* (14 Ves. 273,296)

> "... the evidence in this case establishes that the mother continued to exercise over her daughter the power which her relationship gave her to persuade her daughter to say 'yes' to any course of action, however much it was against the interests of the daughter and for the benefit of the mother."'

7.23 Inequality of bargaining power

An elderly farmer, not experienced in commercial matters, gave guarantees to Lloyds Bank to cover an overdraft of a limited company engaged in the plant hire business which his son was running. In 1970 the bank called in the guarantee and contracted to sell the father's house and brought an action for possession against the father.

In a judgment which was highly innovative, to put it mildly, Lord Denning (with whom other members of the Court of Appeal agreed) said:

> '... in the vast majority of cases a customer who signs a bank guarantee or a charge cannot get out of it. No bargain will be upset which is the result of this ordinary interplay of forces. There are many hard cases which are caught by this rule.
>
> 'Yet there are exceptions to this general rule. There are cases in our books in which the courts will set aside a contract, or a transfer of property, when the parties have not met on equal terms, when one is so strong in bargaining power and the other so weak that, as a matter of common fairness, it is not right that the strong should be allowed to push the weak to the wall.
>
> 'The first category is that of "duress of goods". A typical case is when a man is in a strong bargaining position by being in possession of the goods of another by virtue of a legal right, such as by way of pawn or pledge or taken in distress. The stronger demands of the weaker more than is justly due and he pays it in order to get the goods. Such a transaction is voidable. He can recover the excess.
>
> 'The second category is that of the "unconscionable transaction". A man is so placed as to be in need of special care and protection and yet his weakness is exploited by another far stronger than himself as to get

his property at a gross undervalue. The typical case is that of the "expectant heir". But it applies to all cases where a man comes into property or is expected to come into it, and then being in urgent need another gives him ready cash for it, greatly below its true worth, and so gets the property transferred to him.

'Even though there be no evidence of fraud or misrepresentation, nevertheless the transaction will be set aside: see *Fry* v. *Lane* (1888) 40 Ch.D. 312 at 322 where Kay J said:

> "The result of the decisions is that where a purchase is made from a poor and ignorant man at a considerable undervalue, the vendor having no independent advice, a Court of Equity will set aside the transaction."

'The third category is that of "undue influence" usually so called. These are divided into two classes as stated by Cotton LJ in *Allcard* v. *Skinner* (1887) 36 Ch.D 145 at 171.

'The first are those where the stronger has been guilty of some fraud or wrongful act – expressly so as to gain some gift or advantage from the weaker.

'The second are those where the stronger has not been guilty of any wrongful act, but has, through the relationship which existed between him and the weaker, gained some gift or advantage for himself. Sometimes the relationship is solicitor over client, doctor over patient, spiritual adviser over follower. At other times, a relationship of confidence must be proved to exist. But to all of them the general principle obtains which was stated by Lord Chelmsford LC in *Tate* v. *Williamson* (1866) 2 Ch. App. 55 at 61:

> "Wherever the persons stand in such a relation that, while it continues, confidence is necessarily reposed by one, and the influence which naturally grows out of that confidence is possessed by the other, and this confidence is abused, or the influence is exerted to obtain an advantage at the expense of the confiding party, the person so availing himself of his position will not be permitted to retain the advantage, although the transaction could not have been impeached if no such confidential relation had existed".

'The fourth category is that of "undue pressure". The most apposite of that is *Williams* v. *Bayley* where a son forged his father's name to a promissory note and by means of it, raised money from the bank of which they were both customers.

'Other instances of undue pressure are where one party stipulates for an unfair advantage to which the other has no option but to submit. As where an employer – the stronger party – had employed a builder – the weaker party – to do work for him. When the builder asked for payment of sums properly due (so as to pay his workmen) the employer refused to pay unless he was given some added advantage. Stuart VC said: "Where an agreement, hard and inequitable in itself, had been exacted under circumstances of pressure on the part of the person who exacts it this Court will set it aside": see *Ormes* v. *Beadel* (1860) 2 Giff. 166 at 174; *D & C Builders Ltd* v. *Rees* (1966) Q.B. 617 at 625.

'The fifth category is that of salvage agreements. When a vessel is in danger of sinking and seeks help, the rescuer is in a strong bargaining position. The vessel in distress is in urgent need. The parties cannot truly be said to be on equal terms. The Court of Admiralty have always recognised the fact. The fundamental rule is "If the parties have made an agreement, the Court will enforce it, unless it be manifestly unfair and unjust – but if it be manifestly unfair and unjust the Court will disregard it and decree what is fair and just". See *Akerblom* v. *Price* (1881) 7 Q.B.D. 129 at 133 per Brett LJ applied in a striking case, *The Port Caledonia and The Anna* (1903) p. 184, when the rescuer refused to help with a rope unless he was paid £1,000.

'Gathering all together, I would suggest that through all these instances there runs a single thread. They rest on "inequality of bargaining power". By virtue of it, the English law gives relief to one who, without independent advice enters into a contract on terms which are very unfair or transfers property for a consideration which is grossly inadequate, when his bargaining power is grievously impaired by reason of his own needs or desires, or by his own ignorance or infirmity, coupled with undue influences or pressure brought to bear on him by or for the benefit of the other.

'I have no doubt that the assistant bank manager acted in the utmost good faith and was straightforward and genuine. Indeed, the father said so. But beyond doubt he was acting in the interests of the Bank – to get further security for a bad debt. There was such a relationship of trust and confidence between them that the Bank ought not to have swept up his sole remaining asset into their hands – for nothing – without his having independent advice.'

Sir Erich Sachs, a former Lord Justice of Appeal, agreed that the appeal should be allowed, but did not go all the way with Lord Denning's analysis. He limited his judgment (with which Lord Justice Cairns agreed) to the simple point:

'The assistant manager had acknowledged that "the defendant relied on

me implicitly to advise him about the transactions as Bank Manager".
Since the Bank would derive benefit from the defendant's signature
there was a conflict of interest between them. There was a duty on the
bank to advise the defendant to get independent advice and a manifest
breach of duty. It was therefore contrary to public policy that the bank
should retain the benefit of the transaction.'

But the principles of the case were applied in *Clifford Davis Management Ltd* v. *W.E.A. Records Ltd* (1975), where two members of a pop
group who wrote songs entered into a contract with their manager
whereby they assigned the copyright in their works to him. The manager
obtained an interim injunction restraining the group from infringing the
copyright. The Court of Appeal set it aside. Lord Denning said:

'But there are ingredients which may be said to go to make up a case of
inequality of bargaining power. The composers can urge these points.
1. That the terms of the contract were manifestly unfair. Each
composer was tied for ten years without any retaining fee and no
promise to do anything in return save for a promise by the publisher to
use his best endeavours. Such a promise was so general as probably to
be of little use to the composers. See what Lord Reid said in *Instone's*
case (1974) 3 All E.R. at 621, 622. And the tie of ten years for a
composer seems to be just as unfair as a tie of twenty-one years in a solus
agreement for a garage: see *Esso Petroleum Co. Ltd* v. *Harper's Garage
(Stourport) Ltd*.
2. That the property (the copyright in every one of the works over ten
years) was transferred for a consideration that was grossly inadequate.
It was 1 *s*. for each work. It is true that if the publisher chose to exploit
a work, he was to pay royalties – but if he did not do so he got the
copyright for 1 *s*.
3. That the bargaining power of each of the composers was gravely
impaired by the position in which he or she was placed *vis à vis* the
manager. Each composer was in a group which was managed by him.
They wanted to get their songs published. It was their ladder to success.
In order to get the songs performed – and to get them published – they
were dependent on the manager. Their needs and desires were
dependent on his will. He could say Aye or No. He was skilled in
business and finance. They were composers talented in music and song
but not in business. In negotiation they could not hold their own. That
is why they needed a manager.
4. That undue influence or pressures were brought to bear on the
composers by or for the benefit of the manager.
'It may be inferred that the manager took a stock form, got the blanks

filled in and asked the composer to sign it without reading it through or explaining it. One thing is clear from the evidence. The composer had no lawyer and no legal advisers. It seems to me that if the publisher wished to exact such onerous terms or to drive so unconscionable a bargain, he ought to have seen that the composer had independent advice.'

7.24 'Economic duress'

The case of *Pau On* v. *Lan Yur Long* (1980), before the Privy Council on Appeal from the Hong Kong Court of Appeal, dealt with an indemnity given in a complex situation regarding shares. However, Lord Scarman took upon himself to summarise the position where one party enters into a contract as the result of 'economic duress' which he defined as being like all duress, as 'a creation of the will so to vitiate consent'.

He further said:

'At common law, money paid under economic compulsion could be recovered in an action for money had and received: *Astley* v. *Reynolds* (1731) 2 Str. 915. The compulsion had to be such that the party was deprived of his "freedom of exercising his will".'

It is doubtful however whether at common law any duress other than duress to the person sufficed to render a contract voidable: see *Blackstone's Commentaries*, Book 1, 12th edition, pp. 130–131 and *Skeate* v. *Beale* (1841) 11 Ad. & E. 983.

American law (*Williston on Contracts*, 3rd edition) now recognises that a contract may be avoided on the ground of economic duress. The commercial pressure alleged to constitute such duress must, however, be such that the victim must have entered the contract against his will, must have had no alternative course open to him, and must have been confronted with coercive acts by the party exerting the pressure: *Williston on Contracts*, 3rd edition, vol. 13 (1970) s. 1603.

American judges pay great attention to such evidential matters as the effectiveness of the alternative remedy available, the absence or fact of protest, the availability of the independent advice, the benefit received and the speed with which the victim has sought to avoid the contract.

Recently, two English judges have recognised that commercial pressure may constitute duress the pressure of which can render a contract voidable: Kerr J in *Occidental Worldwide Investment Corporation* v. *Skibs A/S Avanti* (1976) and Mocatta J in *North Ocean Shipping Co. Ltd* v.

Hyundai Construction Co. Ltd (1979). Both stressed that the pressure must be such that the victim's consent to the contract was not a voluntary act on his part. In their lordships' view, there is nothing contrary to principle in recognising economic duress as a factor which may render a contract voidable, provided always that the basis of such recognition is that it must amount to a coercion of will, which vitiates consent. It must be shown that the payment made or the contract entered into was not a voluntary act.

In the latter case, which is also known as *The Atlantic Baron*, there was a contract by shipbuilders to build a tanker for a fixed price. In the middle of construction the yard demanded an increase of 10 per cent.

The shipowners, who were desperate to obtain the tanker at the due date, because they had contracted to charter it to Shell Oil for three years, sent a telex to the shipyard which read:

'We are in receipt of your telex dated 26th June 1973. Although we are convinced we are under no obligation to make additional payments which you ask, we are prepared as you demand in your telex of the 26th June 1973 and in order to maintain an amicable relationship and without prejudice to our rights to make an increase of 10 per cent in instalments payable subsequent to the 12th February 1973. No doubt you will arrange for corresponding increases in the letter of credit, provided for in article XI(2)(iii).'

Mr Justice Mocatta said:

'A threat to break a contract may amount to such "economic duress".

The facts found in this case do establish that the agreement to increase the price by ten per cent reached at the end of June 1973 was caused by what may be called 'economic duress'. The yard were adamant in insisting on the increased price without having any legal justification for doing so and the owners realised that the yard would not accept anything except an unqualified agreement to the increase. The owners might have claimed damages in arbitration against the yard with all the inherent unavoidable uncertainties of litigation, but in view of the position of the owners *vis à vis* their relations with Shell it would be unreasonable to hold that this is the course they should have taken: see *Astley* v. *Reynolds* (1731) 2 Str. 915. The owners made a very reasonable offer of arbitration coupled with security for any award in the yard's favour that might be made, but this was refused. They then made their agreement which can truly I think be said to have been made under compulsion, by the telex of 28th June without prejudice to their rights. I do not consider the yard's ignorance of the Shell charter material. It may well be that had they known of it they would have been even more exigent.'

However, incredibly, he found in favour of the shipyard on the ground that the owners had affirmed the variation of the contract by making the final payment without qualification.

7.25   The English doctrine of consideration

Even if a promise be intended to amount to a contractual obligation it will not be enforced unless there is consideration for it. But this only applies to what are termed 'parol' or simple promises – those not contained in a deed under seal; that is to say, those made orally, in writing, or by conduct. English law has a superstitious reverence for deeds, even though nowadays the act of executing a deed consists of nothing more than signing it and putting a finger on a circle while proclaiming 'I deliver this as my act and deed'; or, more probably, just signing a bit of paper which purports to be a deed.

But if a man promises another £10 at Christmas in writing, that cannot be sued upon successfully; if he does so by deed, it can be. And it can be too, if, in return for the promise of £10, he requires a peppercorn, or, apparently, a couple of used chocolate wrappers.

In the nineteenth century lawyers were given to defining consideration in terms of profit or loss. The classic oft-repeated definition of consideration is that given by the Court in *Currie* v. *Misa* (1875):

'some right, interest, profit or benefit accruing to one party, or some forbearance, detriment, loss or responsibility given, suffered or undertaken by the other'.

In other words, consideration is a benefit to the promisor or a detriment to the promisee.

But this definition is defective in that:

(i)   it does not make it clear that a promise given in exchange for a promise is adequate consideration. This has been the law ever since, in *Strangborough* v. *Warner* (1589) the reporter noted 'a promise against a promise will maintain an action on an *assumpsit*'. (Probably what he really meant, however, was that the plaintiff need show no loss other than the fact that he had bound himself by promise in return for the defendant's.)

(ii)   a detriment to the promisee incurred at the request of the promisor is sufficient consideration even though no benefit is conferred on the promisor; and

(iii) there is consideration if the promisor does benefit (or some third party at the request) even though it costs the promisee nothing.

Another well known definition is that of *Dunlop* v. *Selfridges* (1915), a case which, as Lord Dunedin said in the course of it, 'is apt to nip any budding affection one might have for the doctrine of consideration':

> 'An act or forbearance of one party, or the promise thereof, is the price for which the promise of another is bought and the promise thus given for value is unenforceable.'

How this extraordinary doctrine originated is a matter of some controversey amongst legal historians, but about its purpose there can be no dispute. It was thought originally to provide a test of which promises the law could enforce. If a man got something for his promise it could be assumed that he had intended his promise to be enforceable at law and therefore had undertaken contractual obligations, i.e. it was purely of evidential value in determining contractual intent. But, as is abundantly apparent from *Jones* v. *Padavatton*, this function has entirely disappeared.

It should also be remembered that right up to the middle of the last century there were two sorts of consideration sufficient to support a promise. As J. T. Powell put it in his *Essay on Law of Contract and Agreement*, the first legal monograph on the subject, which went through successive editions both here and in the United States after the first in 1788:

> 'A contract may be supported either by a valuable consideration as marriage, work done etc., or by a good consideration: as that of blood or natural affection between near relations.'

Today, what Powell called 'good consideration' is bad consideration. An antecedent moral obligation, family reasons or affection is not sufficient to make a promise binding. The facts of the case which was largely responsible for this change in law as it had been understood and established for two hundred and fifty years are, in themselves, sufficient condemnation of the present doctrine. Sarah Sutcliffe had been left an orphan and Eastwood, her guardian, spent his own (borrowed) money on her education and the preservation of her small estate. When she came of age she promised to reimburse him. Later she married a Mr Kenyon, bringing to him of course by the laws of those days, all her estate, and he also promised in writing the same. When they were sued, however, it was held that there was not sufficient consideration to support these promises: *Eastwood* v. *Kenyon* (1840).

How long shall we have to live with this legal coelacanth is difficult to say. The Law Revision Committee in 1937 recommended the abolition of the rule in its present form, but no action has been taken on that report.

One result is that today there is neither logic nor juridicial justification for many of the decisions on consideration. If the judges want to uphold a promise they find consideration, or discreetly ignore the absence of it; if they don't want to, they find there is no consideration. The Court of Appeal have even found a contractual licence where a woman was allowed to live in a house rent-free for the rest of her life: *Binions* v. *Evans* (1972). The reader will find more of the real reason for the decision in *Combe* v. *Combe* (1951) in Lord Denning's comment: 'I do not think it right for this wife, who is better off than her husband, to take no action for six or seven years, and then demand from him the whole £600, than in the legal reasons ones advanced in the judgment.'

The reader must not therefore expect to find in the decisions that follow any connection at all with logic and little with justice.

7.26 Past consideration is no consideration

By executed consideration is meant performance by one party contemporaneous with the promise of the other. If a man gives another a pot of paint in return for the promise, express or implied, of the other to pay for it, the consideration on the seller's side is executed.

Executory consideration is consideration which lies in the future – something still to be performed. The consideration on the part of the man who has yet to pay for this pot of paint is executory. So it is, of course, on both sides in all contracts where a promise is exchanged for a promise.

Past consideration is something that has happened before the promise is made. A man rescues a boy from drowning in a canal and the grateful father promises him £10 when he gets his pay packet on Friday. The promise is unenforceable. The act was completed before the promise was given. Mr Eastwood in the case cited earlier spends his own money to educate Sarah and prevent her cottages falling down. Too bad, says the law. Her promise and that of her husband who is now enjoying the fruits of Mr Eastwood's expenditure, do not create a contractual obligation to reimburse him. For by the time when the promises were given, it had all been done.

A doctor called to an unconscious man gives expensive injections and when the patient recovers he promises to pay the doctor a reasonable fee. The doctor cannot sue – the consideration was past.

This is 'The Law of the Ingrates' as a European writer, reared in the Roman law tradition, has called it, as will be seen from *Re McArdle* (1951). When Mr McArdle died he left a will under which his widow was entitled to live in the house for her lifetime and after her death their five children were to be entitled to it in equal shares. One daughter-in-law expended money on repairs and improvements to the house in question and later the five children all signed a document promising to repay her when the house was eventually sold. It was held that since this agreement came into existence after the money had been expended, it was not binding. The five children were entitled to take the house with the benefit of the improvements and not pay the daughter-in-law a penny.

There is one situation, however, where the common law still retains some of its original virtue. If the plaintiff does something at the request of the defendant and if the thing is of such a nature that a promise to pay can reasonably be implied at the time, a subsequent promise will be binding.

Braithwait had killed a man and asked Lampleigh to obtain a pardon from the King for it. This Lampleigh succeeded in doing and the other then promised him £100 for his services. The court held that 'The previous request and subsequent promise were to be treated as part of the same transaction': *Lampleigh* v. *Brathwait* (1615).

Two inventors assigned a third of their joint patents to a Mr Casey 'on consideration of your services as the practical manager in working on both our patents'. It was argued that the assignment was not valid because all that Casey had done took place before the assignment and therefore the consideration was past. Lord Justice Bowen, in rejecting this argument, said:

> 'The fact of a past service raises an implication that at the time it was rendered it was to be paid for, and if so ... when you get a subsequent promise to pay, the promise may be treated either as an admission which evidences, or as a positive bargain which fixes the amount of that reasonable remuneration, on the faith of which the service was originally intended': *Re Casey's Patents* (1892).

7.27 Consideration need not be adequate

Provided a promisor got something for his promise, the common law always refused to inquire into whether it was an adequate recompense. That was up to the parties. If one chose to sell a Rolls Royce in return for a packet of cigarettes, well – that was his contract and he had to stick to it.

The Court of Chancery, however, would formerly grant relief for what it termed 'unconscionable bargains' as in the case of commodity loans of

Elizabethan times, where young men with expectations were induced to give their bond under a seal for a consignment of goods which were then sold for a fraction of the price they had undertaken to pay for them – a moneylending device at extortionate rates of interest. Equity would also grant relief where a man sold his reversion in an estate for a trifle, or, like the Earl of Aylesford in 1873 who, at the age of 22, borrowed money at 60 per cent interest per annum against his large expectations. Much of this equity jurisdiction has now been replaced by either the Moneylenders Acts or by the Infants' Relief Act, although it would perhaps be premature to describe the equity doctrine as completely obsolete (see [7.19] and [7.20]). But even as early as 1676, it was being said that 'The Chancery mends no man's bargains'.

The present legal position seems therefore to be that the courts will not interfere with 'unfair' contracts, except in those situations set out above. Miss Frances Day, the then well-known comedienne, made a contract with Gaumont-British which, her counsel complained showed 'a want of mutuality'– in other words, the contract she had made was unfair. But she was held to it: *Gaumont-British* v. *Alexander* (1936).

Nestlé, the chocolate manufacturers, offered gramophone records for 1s. 6d., plus three used chocolate wrappers. A question having arisen under the Copyright Acts whether the 1s. 6d. was the sole consideration, the court decided that the used chocolate wrappers comprised further consideration: *Chappell and Co. Ltd* v. *Nestlés* (1959). Logically, therefore, even three used chocolate wrappers can constitute the sole consideration for a contract – even if they are thrown away immediately they are received.

Provided a man gets that for which he stipulated, and it is of some value, the courts will not enter into whether a consideration was adequate or not. As Lord Somerville said in the Nestlé's case:

> 'A peppercorn does not cease to be good consideration even if it is established that the promisee does not like pepper and will throw away the corn.'

The second half of the proposition above, that the 'consideration' must be of some value in the eyes of the law' is much more difficult to justify or explain.

In the first place, it means in these days that 'good considerations' – that is to say moral obligation, affection or family duty – is not valuable consideration sufficient to support a promise. It means, too, that the consideration must not be entirely illusory – so that, at present, the promise of a fortnight's holiday on the moon is hardly likely to rank as valuable consideration. What is more, unlawful or illegal consideration –

whether it be a promise to pay a girl £20 per week while she cohabits with the promisor, or to divide in equal shares the proceeds of a bank robbery – is not valuable consideration in the eyes of the law.

In the last century, one could have said with some confidence that valuable consideration meant something of some value – however trifling – in a commercial or economic sense. But our mercenary ancestors of the nineteenth century have given way to more humane theories and, as we shall see, the Court of Appeal apparently is prepared to hold that a promise to keep a child 'well and happy'afforded valuable consideration.

It is also somewhat difficult to see what valuable consideration exists in other cases. *Godfrey Davis* v. *Culling* (1962) arose out of the collapse of an insurance company called Fire, Auto and Marine. A motorist took his car in for repairs under the policy of insurance with this company, and the company specifically authorised the garage to effect the repairs at its expense. When the company became insolvent after the work was done, and the garage knew they were unable to recover their expenses from the insurance company, the garage sued the motorist. The court held there was no obligation on the motorist, on the impeccable grounds that (a) he had never promised, expressly or implied, to pay for the repairs and (b) there was no consideration to support a contract between the garage and the motorist.

A somewhat different situation arose in *Charnock* v. *Liverpool Corporation* (1968). Here the motorist had taken his car into a garage for repairs at the charge of his insurance company but the garage negligently delayed executing the work, and the motorist sued for the hire of a substitute vehicle. The Court of Appeal this time held there was a contract between the motorist and the garage. What constituted valuable consideration moving from the promisee was glossed over, and it is difficult to see how the mere act of leaving a car with a garage for them to effect repairs to it could possibly constitute valuable consideration. It was nothing more than a condition precedent to his receiving a benefit.

7.28　Forbearance to sue is consideration

After a good deal of hesitation, and numerous conflicting decisions, it was eventually decided that a promise to refrain from instituting legal proceedings amounts to valuable consideration, as does the compromise of the action which has already begun. So that if Tom offers Harry that if Harry will promise not to sue Bert for an outstanding debt then he, Tom, will pay the debt, the promises are binding.

Even the surrender of a possible but somewhat nebulous right to bring an action for the rectification of a document has been held to provide valuable consideration. When Mr and Mrs Horton separated, the husband executed a separation agreement whereby he promised to pay his wife 'the monthly sum of £30'. A later, supplemental agreement was signed by the husband whereby the monetary consideration was made '£30 a month free of tax'. The only consideration the Court of Appeal could discover to make this second promise binding was a forbearance by the wife from suing to correct the first agreement: *Horton* v. *Horton No. 2* (1960).

But this principle does not apply where the forbearance is entirely illusory – as where a bookmaker agrees to refrain from suing an undergraduate on a gaming debt in return for a promise from the youth's father to pay. For the bookmaker knows full well that he cannot possibly succeed at law and therefore he is not in fact giving up anything at all. There is no detriment to him in a promise to give up a right which he knows he does not possess.

Nor does it apply if what the promisee surrenders is merely a moral and not a legal claim against the promisor: *Scott* v. *Ricketts* (1967).

If, however, an intending litigant believes in all good faith that he has a claim at law, even though in reality he has not, and such a one promises to renounce his right to sue in return for some consideration from the other party, then this is sufficient to make the contract binding. The test, therefore, appears to be whether the renunciation is of a legal right which is believed to be a valid and *bona fide* cause of action.

The compromise of a disputed claim is therefore always good consideration, provided there is in fact a genuine dispute: *Callisher* v. *Bischoffsheim* (1870).

7.29 Consideration and the performance of existing duties

An area of considerable controversy amongst lawyers is whether there is valuable consideration in a promise to perform a duty which, in one way or another, already rests on the promisor; and whether the actual performance of that duty can be valuable consideration. Lord Denning has said, more than once:

'I have always thought that a promise to perform an existing duty or the performance of it should be regarded as good consideration because it is a benefit to the person to whom it is given': *Williams* v. *Williams* (1957).

But every promise is a benefit to the person to whom it is given – the promisee – and that certainly does not amount to consideration unless the promisee is required to do something for it in exchange. 'Whenever a person promises without benefit arising to the promisor or loss to the promisee, it is considered as a void promise' is the classic definition.

The whole subject however, is involved with two other problems. The first one is public policy. By that is meant the doctrine that there are some otherwise valid contractual obligations which are not enforced because the judges think it is not in the public interest that they should be. But there are cases which appear in the current textbooks where promises were held not to be enforceable for want of consideration, where the real reason was that it was not regarded as being in the public interest that they should be enforced.

The other problem is that of the unilateral contract. If the promise is unilateral, as opposed to synallagmatic, and the promisee does the very thing for which he is to be rewarded, is there any reason why he should not receive the promised remuneration – even though he may already be under an existing duty to do the very thing? A police constable has a duty to arrest criminals. If he arrests one for whose arrest a reward has been offered, is there any reason why he should not claim the reward? Our ancestors thought not, as early as *England* v. *Davidson* (1840). Now, however, statute has intervened regarding police officers and rewards.

The manager of a supermarket is under a duty to promote sales to the full extent of his ability. But is there any reason, if the proprietor offers him £500 bonus if he doubles the sales during the next month why he should not be entitled to claim it? Can the proprietor shrug it off by saying, when the manager has achieved the specified target, 'There was no consideration for my promise of an extra £500 – you were only doing what it was your duty already to do?'

These are two of the problems which have confused discussion of whether there is consideration present when there is an existing duty. It is useful to discuss this topic under four headings:

(i)   Where the existing duty is a moral one, even though it does also constitute an obligation imposed by general law.
(ii) Where the existing duty is purely a legal one.
(iii) Where the existing duty is a contractual obligation to a third party, i.e. neither the promisor nor the promisee.
(iv) Where the existing duty is a contractual obligation to the other contracting party.

7.30 Consideration and existing legal duties

In *Collins* v. *Godefroy* (1831) the plaintiff was served with a subpoena to attend a trial in the King's Bench at Westminster Hall and was promised by the party requiring his attendance one guinea a day for his loss of time. It was held by Lord Tenderden CJ that this was a promise without consideration, for the duty of the plaintiff to attend was one imposed by law. Although expressly based on that ground by the judge, earlier decisions to similar effect seem to have been based on the more rational idea that it was in those days contrary to public policy that witnesses called to give evidence should be paid. Nowadays, of course, we accept that as a commonplace and reasonable requirement.

That decision has bedevilled English law for nearly a century and a half. For it has been taken to mean that if there is a legal obligation on a person to do something and he undertakes to another to do the same thing, in return for a promise of remuneration, then the promisor is not obliged to fulfil his promise because there is no consideration for it.

In 1921 the Glamorgan Police Force were asked to provide 100 police officers to be billeted on the premises of Glasbrook's Colliery near Swansea for fear that striking miners were going to get the safety men 'out', and the mine would therefore be flooded. The proprietors of the mine signed a document that they would not only pay for the services of the officers but also their travelling expenses and provide them with food and sleeping accommodation.

In due course the bill for these services, amounting to £2,200 11s 10d was rendered by the police authority, the Glamorgan County Council. The colliery owners, Glasbrook Bros Ltd, refused to pay the bill, raising the defence that the police were doing no more than was their duty, and therefore there was no consideration for their, Glasbrook's, written promise to pay for the protection they had enjoyed. The case was fought all the way up to the House of Lords, where a bare majority of the Law Lords – three to two – decided that the colliery owners' promise was binding, on the ground that the number of constables provided was in excess of what the local police superintendent thought was necessary and therefore provided consideration over and above the obligation resting on the police to take all steps necessary for protecting property from criminal injury: *Glasbrook Bros Ltd* v. *Glamorgan County Council* (1924).

The case has been a leading authority ever since; so that if you request constables to police a pop festival or guard your wedding presents from light-fingered gentry who may be masquerading as guests, your promise to pay for their services will amount to a contractual obligation.

Had it occurred to their lordships, it would have been a more satisfactory and logical justification for their decision to hold that the obligation to provide the constables was, on a true construction of the contrast, a unilateral obligation. In other words, that the obligation was not in reality mutual; for it can scarcely have been held that if the Chief Constable had withdrawn every single officer from Glasbrook's pit because they were needed to cope with a massive riot in some adjacent town, and the mine had been flooded by the withdrawal of the safety men, that the Police Authority would have been liable for the enormous damages which might well have resulted.

However, as the law stands at the moment the position appears to be that if nothing more is done in return for the promise that is already an existing duty in law, there is no consideration for a promisee to pay, and the promise is not binding; whereas if something more is done, then the promise is binding.

7.31 Consideration and obligations to third parties

Happily, here the law is both simple and clear (though the Law Revision Commission of 1937 thought it wasn't). If Tom is under a contractual obligation to Harry to do a certain thing and Bill chooses to promise Tom further remuneration for doing exactly the same thing, there is consideration for both contracts. As Baron Wilde said as long ago as 1861:

'There is no authority for the proposition that where there has been a promise to one person to do a certain thing, it is not possible to make a valid promise to another to do the same thing.'

In *Scotson* v. *Pegg* (1861) the plaintiff was the owner of a ship which contained a part cargo of coal consigned to the defendants. It was therefore, in any event, the plaintiff's contractual duty to the shipper to deliver the coal to the defendant. The defendant promised the plaintiffs to discharge the cargo of coal at the rate of 49 tons a working day, but failed to do so and when sued for damages set up the defence that since the plaintiff was already under a contractual duty to the shipper to deliver the coal to him, there was no consideration for his promise. The promise was held binding.

In the course of argument Baron Martin put the case

'Suppose a man promised to marry on a certain day and before that day arrived he refused, on the grounds that his income was not sufficient, whereupon the father of the intended wife said to him "If you will marry my daughter, I will allow you a £1,000 a year". Could not that promise be enforced?'

Somewhat similar circumstances arose in a case called *Shadwell* v. *Shadwell* (1860). An uncle wrote to his nephew, a young barrister, 'I am glad to hear of your intended marriage with Ellen Nicholl and as I promised to assist you at starting, I am happy to tell you that I will pay to you one hundred and fifty pounds yearly during my lifetime'. The promise was held to be a contractually binding obligation. There was much discussion about detriment and benefit and whether there was any consideration, since clearly on the facts the young man was not marrying at his uncle's request. The case has been bitterly fought over by academic lawyers ever since, and disapproved of by Lord Justice Salmon. Is it in reality any different than if I were to promise you a wedding present and failed to deliver it? Perhaps the only satisfactory explanation is to construe the letter as a simple unilateral promise to the effect that "if you marry Ellen Nicholl I will pay you £150 a year" and forget all about the benefit to the promisor or detriment to the promisee; though one cannot help wondering whether if the recipient of the promise had been a young doctor instead of a young barrister, the conclusion would have been the same.

7.32 Existing contractual obligations

When a promisee is already under a contractual duty to a promisor, the general rule is that there can be no consideration for a further promise by the promisor, unless the promisee has to do something more than he had originally undertaken.

The cases originally relied upon for this doctrine are those of sailors who have been promised higher wages for doing what they had already contracted to do – working a ship to a port. But, once again, the question whether there was or was not consideration has become confused with the issue of public policy, as to whether such promises should be enforced. In *Harris* v. *Watson* (1791), a seaman was promised an extra five guineas by the captain when the ship was in danger; for he had extra work in navigation to do apart from his normal duties. Chief Lord Justice Kenyon, in dismissing the sailor's claim said:

'If this action was to be supported, it would materially effect the navigation of the United Kingdom ... If in times of danger [sailors] were entitled to insist upon an extra charge on such a promise as this, they would in many cases suffer a ship to sink unless the captain would pay an extravagant demand.'

But that remarkable reasoning was provided with a rather more rational basis by Lord Ellenborough in a case of which there are two conflicting reports. The plaintiff in *Stilk* v. *Myrick* (1809) was a seaman engaged for a voyage from London to the Baltic and back for £5 a month. When two members of the crew deserted in Cronstadt, the captain promised to divide the wages of the deserters amongst the rest of the crew. 'Those who remain', Lord Ellenborough said (according to one report), 'are bound by the terms of their original contract to exert themselves to the utmost to bring the ship in safety to her destined port. Therefore ... (the promise) is void for want of consideration'.

A somewhat similar case, *Hartley* v. *Ponsonby* (1857) where the sailors were held able to recover, is distinguishable because in that case there was an express finding by a jury that because the full complement of thirty-six sailors had been reduced by desertion to a mere nineteen – of whom only four or five of them were Able Seamen – the sailors remaining were discharged from their original contract. The result was that they were free if they chose to make a new contract with their employers, and it was on this new contract that they succeeded.

A modern application of the principle is to be found in *Swain* v. *West (Butchers) Ltd* (1936). A manager of the butchering business had been caught out removing marks of origin from the carcasses of beasts – an infringement of the law which entitled the company which employed him to dismiss him. The Chairman promised not to dismiss him if he disclosed irregularities which had taken place by the Managing Director. He did so, but even so he was dismissed. It was held that there was no consideration for the promise, because the manager was already under a contractual duty to make a full disclosure to the company of all matters concerning their interests.

Presumably, therefore, if the management of a company offers a fortnight's holiday in Bermuda to any salesman who doubles his sales within six months, that promise will not be contractually binding since the salesman is already under an existing duty to use his utmost efforts to promote his employers' interests; but one cannot believe that is what a court would really hold. In that case they would probably say 'this is a unilateral promise and if the salesman performs the act required, that is all the consideration that is necessary'.

7.33 Consideration and the release of debts

If a creditor is owed £100 and promises to accept from the debtor the sum of £80 in full satisfaction, that promise is not binding because there is no consideration for it. He can, therefore, collect the £80 and sue for the balance in spite of his promise.

This grossly immoral rule of the common law is attributed to what is known as *Pinnel's* case (1692). This was an action on a bond under seal by which £8 10s was to be paid on 11 November 1600. The defendant debtor at the plaintiff's request on 1 October 1600 – that is, earlier than the due date – paid £5 12s 2d which the creditor accepted in full satisfaction of the whole sum. In so far as the case itself is concerned, it made no law; the plaintiff, the creditor, won on a technical knockout because of the insufficient particularity of pleading by the defendant. The law was made by Coke's observation in his *Institutes* later, that all the judges of the Court of Common Pleas had agreed 'that payment of a lesser sum on the day in satisfaction of a greater cannot be satisfaction for the whole ... but the gift of a horse, a hawk or a robe etc., in satisfaction is good'. This observation, which of course formed no part of the *ratio decidendi* of Pinnel's case, first saw the light of day in print more than a quarter of a century after the case that is reputed to have given rise to it, and there are reported cases in the interval that refute it. However that may be, it passed into law and in the nineteenth century received the accolade of the House of Lords in another case of dubious logic and even worse law.

In 1875 a Mrs Julia Beer obtained judgment in the High Court against Dr John Foakes for the sum of £2,000 19s. Since Dr Foakes could not pay at once, a document in writing was drawn up between the parties whereby Mrs Beer promised 'not to take any proceedings whatever on the said judgment' provided Dr Foakes paid the money by instalments. This the Doctor did; every penny of it. Mrs Beer then broke her promise by proceeding to enforce the judgment by asking for leave to levy execution for the interest accrued since the judgment – £350. The case wended its way from the High Court to the Queen's Bench Divisional Court to the Court of Appeal until it finally appeared in the year 1884 in the House of Lords. In spite of the fact that Dr Foakes was not seeking to set up a contract, the House of Lords held that the rule in Pinnel's case applied and Mrs Beer was entitled to her £350 – plus costs, of course: *Foakes* v. *Beer* (1884).

The same principle has been applied within recent times in *D & C Builders Ltd* v. *Rees* (1965) where the plaintiffs were owed £482.13s 1d for work done as jobbing builders. Being under financial pressure they accepted £300 in full satisfaction and gave a receipt which read 'Received the sum of £300 from Mr Rees in completion of the account. Paid'. Then they successfully sued for the balance.

Had the receipt been delivered in a deed under seal, the release would have been binding, for such instruments, of course, require no consideration. And, of course, it would have been binding if the plaintiffs had accepted the £300 and a cigarette in discharge of the £482; for then there would have been fresh consideration which would have made the promise binding. But the doctrine is law to date, notwithstanding (as Lord Denning has said) that it was ridiculed by Jessel MR, held to be mistaken by Lord Blackburn and condemned by the Law Revision Committee.

7.34   Release of debts at common law

Happily, this distasteful doctrine regarding the release of debt has been mitigated by certain common law exceptions.

(1) Fresh consideration

As has been suggested already, if there is some fresh consideration – however trifling – since the law will not enter into the adequacy of consideration, the promise to release the rest of the debt will be binding. If the receipt in *D & C Builders* v. *Rees* had read '£300 and a cabbage' the plaintiffs would have failed. Once the mere receipt of payment by cheque – which is of course a negotiable instrument – instead of cash was held to be fresh consideration; but in the *D & C Builders* case, the Court of Appeal held that it was not, reversing a decision which had stood unchallenged for more than sixty years.

(2) Alteration in time or place of payment at the request of the creditor

Fresh consideration is also provided if the lesser sum is at the request of the creditor paid at an earlier date than due or in some other place than that nominated by the original agreement. But if this is done at the request of the debtor, this is not fresh consideration, as an unfortunate Mr Vanbergh discovered. He owed St. Edmund's Properties Ltd a sum of £208 under a court judgment. The solicitor for the company agreed that if Mr Vanbergh paid that sum in cash into a bank at Eastbourne no bankruptcy notice would be served against him. Mr Vanbergh did so – and was then served with a bankruptcy notice. The Court of Appeal held that there was no consideration for the promise not to issue the bankruptcy notice and therefore it was not binding. *Vanbergh* v. *St. Edmund's Properties Ltd* (1933).

(3) Payment of lesser sum by third party

In 1817 a creditor sued a son after having accepted in full and final settlement from his father half the money owed by the son. It was held that the creditor could not succeed: *Welby* v. *Drake* (1825). This principle was extended in *Hirachand* v. *Temple* (1911) where Sir Richard Temple sent a draft for a lesser sum than that owed by his son in full settlement of the debt. Without comment, the draft was cashed and the plaintiff then sued the son for the balance.

This draft having been sent to the plaintiffs and retained and cashed by them, we ought to draw the conclusion that the plaintiffs ... agreed to accept it on the terms on which it was sent', held Vaughan Williams LJ.

A quite astonishing variety of reasons have been advanced for this principle and it is better not to try to submit them to logical analysis but to accept as a rule of law, as Lord Justice Fletcher Moulton put it:

'If a third person steps in and gives a consideration for the discharge of the debtor, it does not matter whether he does it in meal or malt, or what proportion the amount given bears to the amount of the debt ... the debt (is) absolutely extinguished'.

(4) Composition with creditors
If all the creditors of a debtor agree to abate their respective claims or even to forgo them entirely (*West Yorkshire Darracq Agency* v. *Coleridge* (1911)) all these creditors are bound by their promise one to another. Again, it is profitless to seek for the consideration for these promises or the legal principle behind this rule. As the Law Revision Committee itself said 'the problem (is) still unsolved, of discovering the consideration for a debtor's composition with his creditors'.

It would, of course, be presumptuous to suggest what, apparently, no judge has yet done, that the real explanation of both the last two circumstances described is the common law principle of estoppel.

(5) Compromise of dispute as to amount
If in fact there is a genuine dispute as to the amount of the debt, a compromise by the acceptance of a lesser sum than that claimed will amount to fresh consideration.

7.35 Promissory or equitable estoppel

There is now a further restraint upon the doctrine that promises without consideration which are relied upon by the promisee as a release of existing contractual obligations to the promisor may be binding. And just as the law in *Pinnel's* case was made by an *obiter dictum*, so, too, this new doctrine emerged from observations made that were certainly no part of the *ratio decidendi* of the case in which they were expressed.

In 1947, Mr Justice Denning, as he then was, was trying at first instance a case called *Central London Property Trust Ltd* v. *High Trees House* (1956), a case of so little legal importance, apparently, that the *All England Law Reports* did not then consider it worthy of inclusion in their series. The plaintiffs had granted to the defendants by deed the tenancy of a block of flats at a ground rent of £2,500 per annum two years before the Second World War. When the war started the flats became virtually impossible to let and by a simple agreement the plaintiffs and the defendants agreed to reduce the ground rent to half the sum specified in the lease. At the end of the war, the plaintiffs' successors in title then sought to return the ground rent to its original figure. In the course of argument it was pointed out that not only were the plaintiffs not bound by the agreement at the outbreak of the war, but they could, had they so chosen on the basis of *Pinnel's* case, have sued for the whole of the arrears, then amounting to £7,916.

To that proposition – which was not an issue before the court – Mr Justice Denning came up with an answer which was to earn immortality for the *High Trees* case. Where a promise is made 'which was intended to create legal relations and which, to the knowledge of the person making the promise, was going to be acted upon by the person to whom it was made, and which in fact was so acted upon ... the promise must be honoured'. Even if there was no consideration.

'The logical consequence' the judge went on to say 'is that a promise to accept a smaller sum in discharge of a larger sum, if acted upon, is binding notwithstanding the absence of consideration; and if the fusion of law and equity leads to the result, so much the better'.

The principle upon which he was proceeding – and extending – was that set out by Lord Cairns in *Hughes* v. *Metropolitan Rly* (1877):

> 'It is the first principle upon which all courts of equity proceed that if parties who have entered into definite and distinct terms involving certain legal results ... afterwards ... enter upon a course of negotiation which has the effect of leading one of the parties to suppose that the strict rights arising under the contract will not be enforced ... the person who might otherwise have enforced those rights will not be allowed to enforce them where it would have been inequitable ...'

It was a principle that seven years later the same court, the House of Lords, appears to have overlooked in *Foakes* v. *Beer*.

This principle has now come to be described as 'promissory estoppel' or 'equitable estoppel', although these terms are a contradiction. Estoppel only applies where there is a statement of existing fact, never where there is a promise as to future conduct. But whatever it may be called, it is now well established law, making a promise without consideration binding in the following circumstances:

(i)　Equitable estoppel 'affords a defence against the enforcement of otherwise enforceable rights but it cannot create a cause of action'. In other words, 'it is a shield but not a sword'. It applies only to the modification or discharge of existing contractual rights. 'The doctrine of consideration is too firmly fixed to be overthrown by a side wind' said Lord Denning in *Combe* v. *Combe* (1951).

(ii) Except in the case of debt, it applies only to the suspension of existing contractual rights – not to their extinction.

(iii) It is still far from clear whether it is a prerequisite of the application of this equitable doctrine that the promisee must have relied upon the promise to his detriment, in the sense at least that he must have changed his position in consequence of it. Lord Denning in an article in *Modern Law Review* has denied this necessity (1952 15 M.L.R.1) but several cases seem to suggest the opposite.

(iv) It is essentially equitable relief to be denied to those who have not themselves behaved equitably; as in *D and C Builders Ltd* v. *Rees* (1965), where the plaintiffs were intimidated into signing the release accepting £300 in satisfaction of the debt of £482 by the words 'That is all you will get', and with the implied threat that if they didn't accept that they would get nothing at all.

7.36 Consideration must move from the promisee

The basic premise on which the doctrine of consideration rests is that the person to whom the promise is made has to do something for it. It is not enough that consideration has been given. It must be given by the very person to whom the promise is made. As the Law Revision Committee acidly remarked: 'We can see no reason, either of logic or public policy why A who has got what he wanted from B in exchange for his promise should not be compelled by C to carry out that promise, merely because C, a party to the contract, did not furnish the consideration'. But it is still the law. William owed John Price £13, Easton promised William that if he would do some work for him, he would pay John the £13. William did the work but Easton failed to keep his promise to pay John Price. John Price sued Easton – and lost. He, it was held, had given no consideration for the promise: *Price* v. *Easton* (1833). The doctrine appears to have originated with the case of *Bourne* v. *Mason* (1668) where the plaintiff failed because he 'did nothing of trouble to himself or benefit to the defendant but was a mere stranger to the consideration'.

Dunlop sold tyres to a wholesaler called Dew and Co., and as a term of the contract the latter undertook that the tyres should not be sold to the public at less than the manufacturer's retail prices and that this condition would be imposed on any person to whom they resold the tyres. Selfridges bought them from Dew and Co. and specifically covenanted in writing:

'We will not sell any Dunlop tyres to any private customers at prices below those mentioned in the said price list current at the time of sale'. Selfridges then sold the tyres at cut prices, as they had already intended to do at the time when they signed the undertaking not to. Dunlop sued Selfridges and failed. There were two separate contracts; but, more important, the House of Lords held that there was no consideration moving from Selfridges to Dunlop. 'What then did Dunlop do or forbear to do, in a question with Selfridges? The answer must be "Nothing"', said Lord Dunedin. 'To my mind this ends the case': *Dunlop* v. *Selfridges* (1915).

7.37   Mistake and its effects on contractual obligations

What effect does a mistake by one or both of the parties to a synallagmatic contract have on the contract? No subject is more difficult to deal with in the restricted confines of a book like this, not least of all because the law as enunciated by the courts has changed radically within recent years and there is anything but agreement amongst judges and academic lawyers as to what it is.

The first task is to look at and analyse the different types of mistake which may have some bearing on contractual obligations. One of the most popular of such analyses is that of Cheshire, Fifoot and Furmston's *Law of Contract*, which has had some judicial approval. According to this, mistake may be divided into three classes:

(1) unilateral mistake: where one only of the parties is labouring under mistake;
(2) common mistake: where both parties to a contract share the same mistake;
(3) mutual mistake: where the parties misunderstand one another in the process of making the contract.

Unhappily, there is no general agreement on the use of these words and lawyers are as imprecise as was Dickens when he referred to 'our Mutual Friend', when what he really meant was 'our common friend'. *Chitty on Contracts* uses the term 'mutual' for 'common' and in *Magee* v. *Pennine Insurance Co. Ltd* (1969), Denning MR referred to the mistake in question as being 'common'; Winn LJ said it was 'mutual' and nobody suggested that it might have been unilateral. Yet since it is more than possible on the facts that only one of the contracting parties was under a mistake, this seems to be the most apt expression for it.

In fact, whether the mistake is unilateral, common or mutual, whatever this may mean, it is certainly clear that no general principles of English law can be derived from this analysis.

The Romans have been here before us in the same predicament, and it is helpful to look at their analysis of the various kinds of mistakes, so long as we do not assume that our answer should be their answer. Unfortunately, as a result of the influence of Pothier and the consensus theory, judges in the nineteenth century were inclined to do this, and even as recently as 1939 one judge based the whole of his judgment on an extensive quotation from Pothier – and inevitably arrived at the wrong answer, as everybody is now agreed: *Sowler* v. *Potter* (1939).

According to the Romans, the sort of mistakes which might affect a contract were of two classes:

(1) *error in causa*, that is, in the motive or reason for entering into the contract. Such contracts were voidable for fraud (*dolus*) and this corresponds with our law about misrepresentation [5.05].

(2) *error in consensus*: where there appeared to be a mistake in the agreement. This might be due to:

> (a) *error in negotio*: mistake as to the nature of the contract, where the parties are mistaken about the type of the transaction, i.e. A thinks it is a contract of sale and B thinks it is a contract of hire.
>
> (b) *error in corpore*: mistake as to the subject matter of the contract. A sells B a slave, Stichius, A thinking of one Stichius and B of another of the same name.
>
> (c) *error in substantia*: where there is a substantial difference between the thing bargained for and the thing as it is actually – whether the mistake be that of both parties or only of the buyer; and this includes the situation where the subject matter of the contract, unknown to the parties, has ceased to exist at the time when they are making their agreement – in the case of goods, what the Romans termed *res extincta*.
>
> (d) *error in persona*: mistake as to the identity of the other contracting party, where the identity of the other contracting party is material. X thinks he is contracting with Y but in fact he is contracting with Z. There is little authority in Roman law about mistake as to the quality of a person, as distinct from his identity, e.g. where A mistakenly believes B to be rich but knows his true identity. A mistake of this nature appeared to have had no effect on a contract.

This is a helpful analysis and therefore we shall look to see, first, how English common law and, secondly, equity dealt with these problems.

7.38   Mistake as to the nature of the transaction

The most material application of this sort of mistake is where a person executes a legal instrument as the result of a fraudulent misrepresentation by another as to what the contract is all about. In *Lewis* v. *Clay* (1898), Lord Richard Neville induced the defendant who was a friend of his of many years' standing, to put his signature to a document covered by a piece of blotting paper in which four apertures had been cut. Lord Richard falsely represented to his friend that all he was doing was witnessing his signature. In fact the defendant was signing two promisory notes for £11,000 and two letters authorising payments out of the proceeds to his lordship.

On these facts, there was no question but that the document was voidable – that is, it would be set aside for fraud. But until the defendant knew of the fraud and took steps to avoid the obligation by exercising his right to repudiate it, the obligation was good and if any innocent third party acquired rights in it in the meantime, the obligation could not be avoided.

The defendant therefore fell back on the doctrine of *non est factum* ('It is not my act') on the analogy of the case given in Coke's Reports as *Thoroughgood's case* (1584). There an illiterate man had a deed read over to him falsely and to it he then put his seal. He was held not to be bound in any way by it. In other words, the whole transaction was void from the very start, with the result that nobody, not even an innocent party, could acquire any rights under it.

Similarly, in *Foster* v. *MacKinnon* (1869) the defendant who was 'a gentleman advanced in years' was induced to endorse a bill of exchange under the misrepresentation that it was a guarantee. The Court of Common Pleas held that the defendant never intended to endorse a bill of exchange at all, but intended to sign a contract of an entirely different nature.

> 'That being so, it was as if he had written his name ... in a lady's album ... and there had been, without his knowledge, a bill of exchange or a promissory note ... inscribed on the other side of the paper'.

It was not his act and he was in no way liable on it, unless the jury were to find that he was negligent in putting his signature in this fashion on what turned out to be a negotiable instrument.

The doctrine of *non est factum* was considered by the House of Lords *Saunders* v. *Anglia Building Society* (1970) which is the same case as that reported in the Court of Appeal as *Gallie* v. *Lee* (1969), by which name it is more familiarly known to lawyers. In view of that authoritative decision it is profitless to set out the convolutions and controversies that have existed for a century about this part of the law, save to note that many of the existing cases were expressly overruled and some others are highly suspect as a result.

The law as it now exists may be summarised in three propositions:

(i) 'Whenever a man of full age and understanding, who can read and write, signs a legal document ... which is put before him for signature then ... if he signs it ... relying on the word of another as to its character or contents or effect, he cannot be heard to say it is not his document.

(ii) 'By his conduct ... in signing it he has represented to all into whose hands it may come, that it is his document ...' In other words a man is estopped by his signature (though, according to Lord Pearson, it is wrong to use this word in this connection – one should instead say 'precluded from denying') unless he is blind or illiterate. We are back to *Thoroughgood's case*.

(iii) 'If his signature was obtained by fraud – he may be able to avoid it up to a point – but not when it has come into the hands of one who has in all innocence advanced money on the faith of its being his document or otherwise has relied on it as being his document' – per Lord Denning in the Court of Appeal. In other words, it is not void but voidable and the ability to avoid it is lost if an innocent third party acquires rights under it before it has been avoided.

(iv) 'A person who signs a document and parts with it ... has a responsibility ... to take care what he signs, which, if neglected, prevents him from denying his liability under the document according to its tenor' – per Lord Wilberforce in the House of Lords.

So, apparently, even a blind or illiterate person may lose the right to avoid his signature if he has been careless, and a third party has acquired rights. In the case under consideration, the elderly Mrs Gallie intended to make the deed of gift of her leasehold house to her nephew, on condition that she could live there for the rest of her life. She signed a document which she believed to be to this effect. At the time, she had broken her glasses and could not read it, but was told it was a deed of gift to her nephew. It was, in fact, an assignment of the lease to a man called Lee for £3,000, receipt of which she had acknowledged without receiving a penny of it. On the strength of the assignment the Anglia Building Society advanced £2,000 to Lee.

It was held that Mrs Gallie could not set up the defence of *non est factum* or recover the title deeds.

As Lord Reid said in the case:

'The plea of *non est factum* cannot be available to anyone who was content to sign without taking the trouble to find out at least the general effect of the document ... It is for the person who seeks the remedy to show that he should have it.'

This applies equally to a person who signs a document with blanks which he knows the other party will fill in: *United Dominions Trust* v. *Western* (1976).

7.39 Mistake as to the subject matter of the contract

As we have seen [7.37] if the parties are apparently agreed but one is referring to one thing and the other to another, there is no contract. This is not because there is no agreement between them, because the law demands not real agreement – a true meeting of minds – but only the outward appearance of it.

Lord Atkin in the leading case on mistake, *Bell* v. *Lever Bros* (1932) said:

'if mistake operates at all, it operates so as to negative or in some cases nullify consent'.

By negative, he meant the situation where the parties have misunderstood one another in the process of negotiation, so that although there is an appearance of agreement, there is in reality none. But this proposition does not apply to all cases where there is apparent agreement. It only applies where there is latent ambiguity in what the parties have agreed and therefore no contract that the court can find to enforce. If there is apparent agreement which the courts could enforce, one party cannot be heard to say that it does not represent his true intentions.

A man, by telegram, ordered three rifles. In the course of transmission, this became altered to 'the' rifles and, from previous negotiations, was assumed by the recipient of the telegram to be fifty. Fifty rifles were therefore despatched. The court held that there was no contract between the parties, for the excellent reason that although there appeared to be outward agreement on 'the rifles', no court could possibly say whether it was three or fifty: *Falck* v. *Williams* (1900).

And where the parties enter into an agreement when it is known that there is no consensus between them, they are bound by the apparent terms as interpreted by the courts. In *L.C.C.* v. *Henry Boot and Sons Ltd* (1959) the parties disagreed, before they signed a written contract, about the meaning of an 'up and down' clause in it but did nothing to clarify the situation. Later, one party set up that there was no contract, because there was no true agreement between them – an indisputable fact – in spite of the apparent agreement. The House of Lords held that the apparent agreement, as interpreted by the courts, was the only material thing. Subjective intent and the consensus theory play no part in the modern law.

To summarise: *error in corpore* only affects the contractual obligation in English law if there is ambiguity in the apparent agreement, and the courts are unable to decide which contract to enforce: and that only because the promise is too uncertain to enforce.

7.40   Mistake as to existing goods

This subject may be divided into four classes:

(1) *Res extincta* – an agreement made when, unknown to either party, the subject matter of the contract has ceased to exist.

If a chattel, this is dealt with by the Sale of Goods Act 1979, sections 6 and 7:

> 'Section 6. Where there is a contract for the sale of specific goods and goods without the knowledge of the seller have perished at the time when the contract is made, the contract is void.
>
> S. 7. Where there is an agreement to sell specific goods and subsequently the goods, without any fault on the part of the seller or buyer, perish before the risk has passed to the buyer, the agreement is thereby avoided.'

This apparently applies not only to specific goods, but to specifically described goods. In *Howell* v. *Coupland* (1876) where there was a contract to supply 200 tons of potatoes to be grown on a particular farm, the crop failed completely. 'Neither party becomes liable if the performance becomes impossible.' This part of the law really relates to the doctrine of frustration rather than mistake, since the impossibility of performance is subsequent to the formation of the contract. Clearly, where the seller is under the mistaken belief that the specific goods are still in existence when he makes the contract, by this section the contract is void.

The same principle does not apply to non-specific goods. If I have a cellar full of wine, and sell 50 dozen cases of Chateau Quim 1969 in the belief that this quantity is safely in my cellar, but in fact it has all been destroyed by fire, I am not excused performance. I have either to go out on the market to buy 50 dozen cases to fulfil my obligations, or pay damages for non-delivery.

The position is less certain where I sell 50 dozen cases of Chateau Quim 'now in my cellar'. They are not specific until they have been allocated in the contract out of all the other bottles of Chateau Quim, but the better opinion is that the contract is void. As Lord Denning said in *Solle* v. *Butcher* (1949):

> 'In the case where goods have perished at the time of sale ... they are really contracts which are not void for mistake but are void by reason of an implied condition precedent, because the contract proceeded on the basic assumption that it was possible of performance.'

This observation has not received universal approval, but it is good law; it means that if the seller expressly warrants the continued existence of the goods at the time of the contract, the contract is not void but he may be liable to damages. No implied term can be written into a contract where there is an express term covering the same situation. In an Australian case, *McRae* v. *Commonwealth Disposals Commission* (1951), the defendant sold to the plaintiffs a wrecked oil tanker said by them to be stranded on a certain reef off New Guinea. After the defendants had, at considerable expense, equipped an expedition to recover the ship, they discovered that there was no tanker stranded on the reef, not least of all because there was no such reef. The contract was not void but the defendants were liable because they had on the true interpretation of their contract, expressly warranted there was such a ship.

7.41 Mistake as to the ownership of property

A man cannot buy his own property and therefore it has been suggested that all contracts for the sale and purchase of rights that the purchaser in fact already owns, but doesn't know he does, are void. But *Cooper* v. *Phibbs*, the case usually advanced in support of this contention, was an equity action to set aside a lease and the court proceeded on the basis that the contract was not void at common law but voidable in equity on such terms as the court cared to impose.

7.42 Impossibility at the time of making the contract

If there is commercial impossibility at the time of formation of the agreement the contract will not be enforced by the courts. In *Griffiths* v.

Bryner (1903) a contract for the hire of a room overlooking the Coronation procession of Edward VII was held void because at the time of making the contract the procession had already been postponed. This is consistent with the position that if the postponement took place after the contract, the contract was frustrated by supervening impossibility of performance. So, too, where the parties contracted to deliver 50 tons of sisal per month from a particular estate for processing, but the estate was unable to produce 50 tons a month: *Sheikh Bros* v. *Ochsner* (1957).

If I contract to fly you to the moon when that is impossible, the contract is void.

7.43   False contractual assumptions

Contracts entered into under a mistake about a certain fact fall into this class. Both parties may think that a picture is a Constable whereas in fact it is not; both parties may think that a particular prior contract between them is binding, whereas in fact it is not.

In *Bell* v. *Lever Bros* (1932), Bell had entered into a contract with *Lever Bros*, whereby Bell would be employed for a fixed period. In the belief that it was a binding contract, Lever Bros entered into a second contract to discharge the first, and paid him a share of £50,000 to be released from their obligations. Later, they discovered that Bell had been guilty of breaches of the contract which entitled them to terminate the first contract.

The situation may be expressed thus:

Contract 1: A has contract No. 1 with B. A mistakenly believes the contract to be binding on him. Therefore he makes contract No. 2.
Contract 2: A had contract No. 2 with B to relinquish rights under contract No. 1.

In *Magee* v. *Pennine Insurance Company* (1969) Magee made a contract of car insurance with the Pennine Insurance Company whereby they insured his car against third party risk and damage, and under that he paid premiums for a number of years. The car was then involved in an accident, so that it became a total write-off. In the belief that the first contract was binding on them, the insurance company entered into a second contract, one of compromise, whereby they undertook to pay £355. They then discovered that Magee had falsely represented that he held a driving licence, whereas in fact he could not drive and had never had a licence, and therefore they were entitled to repudiate the contract of insurance at any time.

The situation therefore was:

Contract 1: A has contract No. 1 with B. A mistakenly believes the contract to be binding on him. Therefore he makes contract No. 2.
Contract No. 2: A has contract No. 2 with B to relinquish rights under contract No. 1.

In fact, the two cases are logically indistinguishable. In the first case in 1932 the House of Lords refused to grant any relief to Lever Bros. Although all the judges in the House of Lords apparently appear to have accepted the proposition of Lever Bros counsel that:

> 'whenever it is to be inferred from the terms of the contract or its surrounding circumstances that the consensus has been reached on the basis of a particular contractual assumption, and that assumption is not true, the contract is avoided.'

They seem to have decided that this only applied 'where the assumption was fundamentally to the continued validity of the contract or a foundation essential to its existence'.

In the circumstances the mistake was not sufficiently fundamental and to adopt Lord Atkins' words 'the state of the new facts did not destroy the identity of the subject matter as it was in the original state of facts'.

In *Magee* v. *Pennine Insurance Co. Ltd*, however, the Court of Appeal by a majority of 2 to 1, exercised equitable discretion to set aside the contract. Lord Denning said:

> 'a common mistake, even on a most fundamental matter does not make a contract void at [common] law; but it makes it voidable in equity',

and he distinguished Bell and Lever Bros on the ground that the House of Lords had only been dealing with the common law position and had not considered the law of equity. That was in fact untrue, since counsel had cited several Chancery decisions, and Lord Warrington, in his dissenting speech, made it clear that both common law and equity cases had been considered by the House.

There have been no subsequent cases which elucidated this aspect of the law and all that can currently be said is that it is believed that the courts may exercise some equitable jurisdiction to set contracts aside if they were concluded in circumstances where both parties had laboured under a misapprehension as to their legal rights: see *Grist* v. *Bailey* (1966). The whole topic has been a fruitful field for academic controversy and it is regretted that it is impossible to state the law with any degree of certainty.

7.44   Mistake as to the identity of the other contracting party

Here, too, the law has, once again, turned a number of rapid somersaults. In 1873 a gentleman with the name of Alfred Blenkarn hired a third floor room at No. 37, Wood Street, Cheapside, London in which street, at No. 123, was a well-known and reputable firm called William Blenkiron and Sons. Blenkarn ordered goods from Roberts, Lindsay and Co. in Belfast on notepaper carefully printed to resemble that of Blenkiron. In the belief that they were supplying Blenkiron, Roberts, Lindsay and Co. supplied Blenkarn with 25 dozen cambric handkerchiefs on credit, which he promptly sold to Cundy and Co. who re-sold them without delay.

The question was: were these goods, originally the property of Roberts, Lindsay and Co., obtained from them by fraud, so that the property passed from them, though under a contract liable to be avoided; or did the property never pass from the plaintiffs because they had made no contract at all? On the answer to that lay the answer to the question as to which of the two innocent parties should suffer the loss?

The House of Lords decided there was no contract. 'Of [Blenkarn] the plaintiffs had never heard and of him they had never thought. With him they never intended to deal ... as between him and them there was no consensus of mind which could lead to any agreement or any contract whatsoever'. The innocent Cundy and Co. were liable to pay damages to Roberts, Lindsay and Co. for conversion of their goods.

In *King's Norton Metal* v. *Eldridge Merrett and Co.* (1879) the facts were only slightly different. A rogue called Wallis had notepaper printed with the heading 'Hallam and Co., Soho Hackle Pin and Wire Works, Sheffield' with a picture of a large factory with smoking chimneys. On that notepaper he ordered a quantity of brass rivet wire from the King's Norton Metal Co. Ltd. The goods were supplied on credit and rapidly sold to Eldridge Merrett and Co. Ltd. The Court of Appeal decided that there was a contract between the plaintiffs and Wallis, and the mistake only related to the qualities of the latter and not his identity; and therefore the defendant got a good title to his goods.

On that basis apparently there may be no contract if the supplier mistakenly believes he is dealing with a real person, who does in fact exist, but he is dealing with another. Whereas, if he thinks he is dealing with a real person and that person does not exist there is a contract. Not surprisingly, this conclusion has not been without criticism. The Law Reform Committee in 1966 recommended that all contracts entered into under a mistake as to the identity of the other party should be voidable rather than void so far as innocent third parties are concerned.

Where the parties are actually face to face, the courts, after a great deal of vacillation, have come down firmly that there is always a contract, even though the supplier may have been led to believe that the person in front of him is somebody other than he is. In *Lewis* v. *Avery* (1971), a rogue obtained possession of a car by posing as Richard Greene, a television actor, and giving a cheque in that name. The innocent purchaser of the car from the rogue got a good title. The Court of Appeal disapproved of its own previous decision, ten years earlier, in *Ingram* v. *Little* (1903). Even if the seller is mistaken as to the identity of the person before him, he means to sell to that person in front of him 'whoever he may be'.

Chapter 8

Covenants in Law, *alias* Implied Terms

8.01 Gaps in the contract

In addition to the terms which the parties have expressly agreed, whether orally or in writing, the courts may imply other terms into a contract. The matter was admirably explained in an article by Professor Granville Williams in *The Law Quarterly Review* some years ago:

'The courts will generally enforce consequences logically implied in the language of contracts, wills, statutes, and other legal documents and transactions. The point now to be noticed is that the legal doctrine of implied terms goes much farther than this. Judges are accustomed to read into documents and transactions many terms that are not logically implied into them. As an academic matter, non-logical implication may be classified into three kinds:

(i) of terms that the parties (the plural shall throughout include the singular) probably had in mind but did not trouble to express;

(ii) of terms that the parties, whether or not they actually had them in mind, would probably have expressed if the question had been brought to their attention; and

(iii) of terms that the parties, whether or not they had them in mind or would have expressed them if they had foreseen the difficulty, are implied by the court because of the court's view of fairness or policy or in consequence of rules of law.

Of these three kinds of non-logical implication

(i) is an effort to arrive at actual intention;

(ii) is an effort to arrive at hypothetical or conditional intention – the intention that the parties would have had if they had foreseen the difficulty;

(iii) is not concerned with the intention of the parties except to the extent that the term implied by the court may be excluded by an expression of positive intention to the contrary ...

'The view may perhaps be held that this particular process is not very happily called "implication". It is not so much the interpretation of a pre-existing and expressed intent as legislation amending or supplementing the expressed intent. Terms so read into the contract might better be called "constructive" than implied. However, this is simply a question of nomenclature; and in case no fixed nomenclature can be maintained in practice, because terms of classes (i), (ii) and (iii) merge into each other. There is no legal difference between the three classes, and the only practical difference is that the courts are more ready to imply terms of class (i) than of classes (ii) and (iii). Terms of classes (ii) and (iii) are mainly of specified types and are comparatively rarely added to, though it is always open to the court to add to them ...'

Implied terms were formerly termed 'covenants in law', as distinguished from express terms, but this expression has become obsolete.

'Implication means the supplying of what has not been expressed'

said Lord Wilberforce in *Liverpool City Council* v. *Irwin* (1976). Unhappily the law on this subject is still anything but clear and most judgments dealing with the subject are both illogical and trade only in linguistics.

Lord Denning in the Court of Appeal in the case just quoted suggested that the courts should fill any gaps that the parties had left in their contracts if it was reasonable to do so. He got slapped down for his pains, in the House of Lords, where it was said by Lord Salmon that his proposition was 'contrary to all authority' and that only where it could be shown that that it was necessary to imply a term because otherwise the contract would be 'inefficacious, futile and absurd' could it be done.

If ever there was case where there was a necessity of supplying terms in a contract which had not been expressed, it was that one. Tenants of a tower block of flats entered into a document issued by the Housing Department which imposed a massive string of obligations on them, but as Lord Wilberforce said:

'On the landlord's side there was nothing, no signature; no demise; no covenants.'

The question was: what was the obligation of the landlord in respect of those parts of the building which it had reserved to itself – the stairs, the lifts (a necessity since there were fourteen floors), the garbage shoots? Some obligations on their part had to be implied.

Lord Denning made a vigorous response in a subsequent case in the Court of Appeal, *Shell U.K. Ltd* v. *Lostock Garages Ltd* (1977) in which he divided implied terms into two classes. He said:

'The first category comprehends all those relationships which are of common occurrence such as the relationship of seller and buyer, owner and hirer, master and servant, landlord and tenant, carrier by land or by sea, contractor for building works, and so forth.

In all those relationships, the courts have imposed obligations on one party or the other, saying they are implied terms. These obligations are not founded on the intention of the parties, actual or presumed, but on more general considerations.

In such relationships the problem is not solved by asking: what did the parties intend? or, would they have unhesitatingly agreed to it, if asked? It is to be solved by asking: has the law already defined the obligation or the extent of it? If so, let it be followed. If not, look to see what would be reasonable in the general run of such cases ... and then say what the obligation shall be.

In these relationships the parties can exclude or modify the obligation by express words, but unless they do so, the obligation is a legal incident of the relationship which is attached by the law itself and not by reason of any implied term.'

He then went on to discuss the second category, and said:

'These are cases, not of common occurrence, in which from the particular circumstances a term is to be implied. In these cases, the implication is based on an intention imputed to the parties from their actual circumstances.

In such cases a term is not to be implied on the ground that it would be reasonable, but only when it is necessary and can be formulated with a sufficient degree of precision.'

8.02 Types of implied terms

Although Lord Denning divided terms which the courts will imply into only two categories, at least five can logically be distinguished:

(1) Terms implied by statute, such as those contained in the Sale of Goods Act 1979 [8.03, 8.04]. themselves a replica of those contained

in the same statute of 1893, which in turn was a codification of the existing common law, which had in the eighteenth century taken into itself the Law Merchant. The courts have long imposed 'covenants in law' which have nothing whatsoever to do with the actual or presumed intention of the parties. Another statute imposing implied terms is the Defective Premises Act 1972.

(2) Similar conditions written into contracts by the courts on the analogy of the statute to contracts which are not contracts of the sale of goods but contracts of 'work' or 'work and materials': the repair of false teeth; the dyeing of a woman's hair; and building work [8.05].

(3) by the custom of the part of the country [8.08].

(4) by the usage of a particular trade [8.09].

(5) to give commercial effectiveness to a particular contract – *The Moorcock* doctrine [8.10].

It should be noted that all these apply even when the contract is under seal.

8.03 Implied terms under the Sale of Goods Act 1979: as to title

In addition to the express terms of a contract, the Act writes several implied terms into every contract of sale. That is, there are conditions and warranties which are not expressed, but are taken to be a term of the contract.

The first of the implied terms is as to title and quiet possession. There is an implied condition that:

(i)   the seller has a right to sell the goods;
(ii) the buyer shall enjoy quiet possession of them;
(iii) the goods are free from any charge or encumbrance in favour of a third party.

An auctioneer sells a horse that was not intended by the owner to be offered for sale at the auction. The owner cannot, of course, be forced to part with the horse, but the auctioneer is liable in damages to the buyer for breach of the implied condition of section 12(1).

8.04 Implied terms under the Sale of Goods Act 1979: as to quality

In every contract of sale there are three implied conditions.

(1) If the sale is by description that the goods correspond to the description; Section 13.

Every sale where the buyer has not seen the goods is a sale by description. That is self-evident. A contract was made for 3,000 tins of canned fruit from Australia packed in cases containing 30 tins a case. When the goods were delivered they were 3,000 tins certainly, but most were packed in cases containing 24 tins a case. The buyer rejected the lot. It was held that he was entitled to do so, since failure to correspond to the contractual description is the breach of a condition: *In re Moore and Landauer and Co.* (1921).

But it may also be a sale by description where the buyer has seen a sample, in which case the goods delivered must correspond with both the sample and the description.

And it may be a sale by description, even where the seller has seen the goods.

Mr Grant went into a shop and asked for a pair of men's underpants and was sold a pair of underpants in a transparent package. He wore them and contracted dermatitis in the most tender part of his anatomy, as the result of corrosive bleach having been left in the garment. It was held this was a breach of the description 'men's' woollen underpants' and that he was entitled to damages for his injury: *Grant* v. *Australian Knitting Mills Ltd* (1935).

(2) There is a further implied condition where goods are bought from somebody who habitually deals in goods of that type, that the goods shall be of merchantable quality: section 14(2).

It took the courts some eighty years to decide what was meant by 'merchantable quality'. The most approved definition was that put forward by the Australian judge, Mr Justice Dixon, in the *Australian Knitting Mills* case (*supra*).

> 'The condition that goods are to be of merchantable quality requires that they should be in such an actual state that a buyer fully acquainted with the facts and therefore knowing what hidden defects exist ... would buy them without abatement of price obtainable for such goods if in reasonable sound order.'

The 1979 Sale of Goods Act (Section 14(6)) provided a definition of merchantable quality as:

> 'Goods of any kind are of merchantable quality within the meaning of subsection (2) above if they are as fit for the purpose or purposes for which goods of that kind are commonly bought as it is reasonable to

expect having regard to any description applied to them, the price (if relevant) and all the other relevant circumstances.'

It may be doubted whether this has clarified the matter in any way.
(3) There is also an implied term that goods should be reasonably fit for the purpose required (section 14(3)):

'Where the seller sells goods in the course of a business and the buyer, expressly or by implication, makes known

(a) to the seller or
(b) where the purchase price or part of it is payable by instalments, and the goods were previously sold by a credit-broker to the seller, to that credit-broker,

any particular purpose for which the goods are being bought, there is an implied condition that the goods supplied under the contract are reasonably fit for that purpose, whether or not that is a purpose for which such goods are commonly supplied, except where the circumstances show that the buyer does not rely or that it is unreasonable for him to rely, on the skill or judgment of the seller, or credit-broker.'

8.05 Analogous terms imposed by the common law

In 1956, there came before the Court of Appeal the case of *Lynch* v. *Thorne*. The plaintiff had agreed to purchase a partially completed house from a builder and had signed a contract for the completed house with a plan and specification attached to it.

The specification provided only for nine inch thick brick walls which in fact made the house unfit for human habitation because of rain penetration. The County Court judge gave judgment for the plaintiff on the basis that there was a term to be implied in the contract that when completed the house would be fit for human habitation.

Incredibly, the Court of Appeal under Lord Evershed, Master of the Rolls, reversed him. His Lordship said:

'Here there was an express contract as to the way in which the house was to be completed. The express provisions were exactly complied with, and any variation from them [which] would have rendered this wall water-proof would have been a deviation from the express language of the contract.'

Equally incredibly, it still appears in some contract books today as if it were good law.

It did not commend itself to another Court of Appeal, this time under Lord Denning, also Master of the Rolls in the case of *Harbutt's Plasticine* v. *Wayne Tank* (1970). Like the builder in the Lynch case, the defendants were responsible for design and construction work. They designed and constructed a system for keeping molten wax flowing all through the factory. This system consisted of using a plastic 'Durapipe' wrapped round with heating cables. The express provisions of the accepted specifications and plans were complied in all details. Unhappily, the first night the system was switched on, it burnt the whole factory down.

The Court of Appeal held that apart from complying with the plans and specifications, there was an over-riding implied obligation that the whole work would be reasonably fit for the purpose required. In fact, the court held that stainless steel pipes should have been used, although Lord Justice Widgery and Lord Justice Cross both pointed out that this would have constituted a breach of contract.

The case was more noticed for its decision that a limitation of damages clause in the contract where, whatever happened, damages were to be limited to the price of the contract, namely £2,330, was over-ridden by the court on the grounds that there had been a 'fundamental breach' of contract by the defendants which prevented them from relying on that term. A 'fundamental breach' was one that deprived the other party substantially of all the benefit he might expect to receive under the contract, and the effect was to avoid the contract and therefore the defendants could not rely on the exemption clause. As a result, the defendants were liable to pay the entire cost, £151,420, of rebuilding the factory.

This was established law for the next ten years, until the House of Lords repudiated the doctrine in the case of *Photo Production Ltd* v. *Securicor Transport Ltd* (1980). There, the defendants were able to escape liability when one of their employees had burnt down a factory and its stock valued at £615,000, because of an exclusion clause which provided that 'under no circumstances shall the company ... be responsible for any injurious act or default by any employee of the company ...' Lord Wilberforce said 'The case of *Harbutt* must clearly be over-ruled'.

But it was clearly over-ruled on that one point alone: whether a fundamental breach of control prevents a limitation of damages clause or an exclusion clause being relied upon. It in no way impugned the other important point: a design and build contractor is responsible for ensuring that what he produces is reasonably fit for the purpose required.

There are a number of other decisions to that effect.

8.06   Implied terms under the Defective Premises Act 1972

This Act is rarely, if ever, used since the common law has since provided much better remedies. It applies only to dwellings.

Any person who takes on work 'for or in connection with the provision of a dwelling' – and this clearly applies to architects as much as contractors and sub-contractors – owes three duties:

(a) to see that it is done in a workmanlike or professional manner;
(b) with proper materials; so that
(c) the dwelling will be fit for habitation when completed.

These obligations clearly over-rule the express terms of the contract, although there is an exoneration clause in section 1(2), and it is qualified by section 1(3) which is masterly in its ambiguity.

The Act also provides a limitation period quite different from that laid down by the Latent Damages Act 1986.

8.07   Implied terms by custom

Some relics of feudal law remain in the English legal system in that customs of particular parts of the country will be upheld if they are 'certain, reasonable and notorious'. As such they will be incorporated into contracts, including contracts under deeds, unless there is express provision to the contrary.

The leading authority is *Hilton* v. *Warren* (1836) where the issue at stake was the lease of a Norfolk farm, where it was proved to the satisfaction of the court that it was the custom of the country that a tenant who had been given notice to quit was entitled to compensation for seeds and labour on the arable land, although the lease was silent as to this. Baron Parke said:

'It has long been settled that, in commercial transactions, extrinsic evidence of custom and usage is admissible to annex incidents to written contracts, in matters with respect to which they are silent.

The same rule has also been applied to contracts in other transactions of life, in which known usages have been established and prevailed; and this has been done upon the principle or presumption that, in such transactions, the parties did not mean to express in writing the whole of the contract by which they intended to be bound, but contract with reference to those known usages.

Whether such a relaxation of the strictness of the common law was wisely applied, where formal instruments have been entered into, and particularly leases under seal, may well be doubted; but the contrary has been established by such authority, and the relations between landlord and tenant have been so long regulated upon the supposition that all customary obligations, not altered by the contract, are to remain in force, that it is too late to pursue a contrary course; and it would be productive of much inconvenience if this practice were now to be disturbed.'

8.08   Implied terms by trade usage

The most common example of this is, or rather was 'the baker's dozen'. It was well understood that in the trade that if a dozen buns were ordered, the customer got thirteen (although this particular usage has since disappeared).

8.09   Implied terms under *The Moorcock* doctrine

Terms may be implied to give commercial effectiveness to a contract.

This is often called *The Moorcock* doctrine after the case of that name in 1889. A jetty owner entered into an agreement with the owners of *The Moorcock* to discharge her at the berth alongside their jetty. Both parties knew that when the tide ebbed the ship would take the ground. When she did so she suffered damage as the result of settling on a hard ridge. The Court of Appeal held that there was an implied term that the berth was safe for the ship.

This doctrine has only restricted application, as Lord Justice MacKinnon pointed out:

'*Prima facie* that which in any contract is left to be implied and need not be expressed is something so obvious that it goes without saying; so that if, while the parties were making their bargain, an *officious bystander* were to suggest some express provision for it in their agreement they would testily suppress him with a common "Oh, of course".'

In *The Moorcock* case the judge said:

'The question which arises here is whether when a contract is made to let the use of this jetty to a ship which can only use it, as is known by both parties, by taking the ground, there is any implied warranty on the part of the owners of the jetty, and if so, what is the extent of the warranty. Now, an implied warranty, or, as it is called, a covenant in law, as distinguished from an express contract or express warranty, really is in all cases founded on the presumed intention of the parties, and upon reason.

The implication which the law draws from what must obviously have been the intention of the parties, the law draws with the object of giving efficacy to the transaction and preventing such a failure of consideration as cannot have been within the contemplation of either side; and I believe if one were to take all the cases, and they are many, of implied warranties or covenants in law, it will be found that in all of them the law is raising an implication from the presumed intention of the parties with the object of giving to the transaction such efficacy as both parties must have intended that at all events it should have.

In business transactions such as this, what the law desires to effect by the implication is to give such business efficacy to the transaction as must have been intended at all events by both parties who are business men; not to impose on one side all the perils of the transaction, or to emancipate one side from all the chances of failure, but to make each party promise in law as much, at all events, as it must have been in the contemplation of both parties that he should be responsible for in respect of those perils or chances.'

In this type of implied term it is not possible for the courts to imply a term if the parties have considered the position and made express provision for it in the contract. The same is true of implied terms arising out of custom of a trade.

A charterparty provided that the chartering broker's commission should be paid 'on signing this charter (ship lost or not lost)'. This was held to be an express term allowing the broker's commission even though, as happened, the ship was requisitioned by the French Government and never actually sailed under the charterparty. An implied term by custom that the broker should only be entitled to commission if hire was actually earned under the charterparty was therefore rejected as inconsistent with the express term: *Les Affretéurs* v. *Leopald Walford* (1919).

But as has been seen in the case of implied terms imposed by operation of law these may override the express contractual provisions of the parties.

Chapter 9

Interpreting Contractual Documents

9.01   Parol evidence not admissible

One of the strangest but well-established principles of construing a contractual document or a deed is that parol evidence is not admissible to establish what the parties really meant. By 'parol evidence' is meant oral statements and correspondence. This applies to all the negotiations which took place before the document was created.

In *Arrale* v. *Costain Civil Engineering Ltd* (1975) an injured workman had signed a receipt for payment of £490 statutory compensation in the state of Dubai which included the words:

'I accept in full satisfaction and discharge of all claims in respect of personal injury whether now or hereafter to become manifest arising directly or indirectly from an accident which occurred on 3 July 1968. Signed ... '

He subsequently instituted proceedings in England for damage for breach of the employer's common law obligations to him. The trial judge held that the receipt debarred him from any further action, but the Court of Appeal unanimously set this aside.

Lord Denning said:

'The judge placed much reliance on the discussions between the parties. He held that in the discussions it was made clear to the plaintiff that the document was not confined to matters arising out of the ordinance.

Now I do not think the judge was entitled to take the discussions into account. The general rule is that when a contract has been reduced into writing, evidence of previous negotiations is not admissible in order to construe it. That rule was emphatically reaffirmed in *Prenn* v. *Simmonds* (1971).'

Lord Justice Stephenson said:

'I agree that he was not entitled to look as he did, at the evidence of intention and antecedent discussions in order to interpret the document: *Prenn* v. *Simmonds* (1971).'

Lord Justice Geoffrey said:

'What neither side pointed out to the learned judge was that the construction of the written document was a matter of law for the court.

He added:

Now, I think it is quite fixed – and no more wholesome or salutary rule relative to written contracts can be devised – that where parties agree to embody, and do actually embody their contract in a formal written deed, then in determining what the contract really was and really meant, a court must look to the formal deed and to that deed alone.

This is only carrying out the will of the parties.

The only meaning of adjusting a formal contract is, that the formal contract shall supersede all loose and preliminary negotiations – that there shall be no room for misunderstandings which may often arise, and which do constantly arise, in the course of long, and it may be desultory conversations or in the course of correspondence and negotiations during which the parties are often widely at issue as to what they will insist on and what they will concede. The very purpose of a formal contract is to put an end to the disputes which would inevitably arise if the matter were left upon verbal negotiations or upon mixed communings, partly consisting of letters and partly consisting of conversations.

The written contract is that which is to be appealed to by both parties, however different it may be from their previous demands or stipulations, whether contained in letters or in verbal conversation.

There can be no doubt that this is the general rule, and I think the general rule, strictly and with peculiar appropriateness applies to the present case. The deed, which we have to interpret as the contract, consists of the memorandum and specifications and of nothing else.'

9.02 Ambiguity in contractual documents

A standard time charterparty contained a clause:

'Charterers to have the option to redeliver the vessel after 12 months trading subject to giving 3 months notice.'

Otherwise, the period of charter was to be 'for a period of two years 14 days more or less'.

After the vessel had been in service with the charterers for 19 months, they gave three months notice to determine, so that they surrendered the vessel after 22 months and not the full 24 months.

The issue was whether the word 'after' meant that the charterer could be at liberty to deter only on the expiration of the 12 month period or 'at any time after the 12 months'.

Mr Justice Kerr in the Commercial Court found difficulty in interpreting the word 'after' in the charterparty since it has two meanings in English. He therefore agreed to look at the telex messages which had constituted the negotiations before the written contract. He concluded:

'They clearly show that the words "after 12 months trading" were used in an agreed sense. From start to finish the owners wanted maximum duration and certainty whereas the charterers wanted minimum duration and maximum flexibility.

'It is clear that both parties throughout used the word "after" in the sense of "on the expiry of" and not "at any time after the expiry of..."

'... on the basis that the word "after" in cl. 26 is capable of bearing two meanings as a matter of construction, I do not think that there is any authority precluding the Court from examining the pre-charterparty exchanges in order to see whether their owners can make good their contention that the parties were in agreement in using this word in only one of its two senses, and having in effect both given it the same dictionary meaning, to the exclusion of the other meaning. Having then considered the pre-charterparty exchanges on this basis I find that this contention is established. In these circumstances it seems to me that the charterers cannot now depart from this common meaning by asserting that this word has the opposite meaning in the charterparty.'

He justified his admission of the telex messages on this basis:

'If a contract contains words, which, in their context, are fairly capable of bearing more than one meaning, and if it is alleged that the parties have in effect negotiated on an agreed basis that the words bore only one of two possible meanings, then it is permissible for the Court to examine the extrinsic evidence relied upon to see whether the parties have in fact used the words in question in one sense only, so that they have in effect given their own dictionary meaning to the words as the result of their common intention.

In the present case, after some argument about these principles and the limits of the parole evidence rule, I decided to look at the pleaded telex messages, though counsel for the charterers rightly submitted that I could only do so *de bene esse*. He was right about this, because if they did not support the owner's arguments on the lines discussed above, then I would have to put them out of my mind and fall back on my construction as a matter of first impression.'

Note: *de bene esse* means to admit evidence provisionally in order to decide at a later date whether it is relevant or admissible.

9.03 Parol evidence admissible on a plea for rectification

One of the circumstances in which parol evidence is admissible is if one of the parties seeks an order from the court for the rectification of written documents on the ground that they do not correctly represent what the parties in fact agreed should be in them.

Documents which fail to express the true intention of the parties will be rectified – corrected – by the court and this has been done with conveyances, policies of marine insurance and bills of quantities in building contracts, amongst other documents.

The conditions under which the court will rectify a document are:

(i) The error must be of fact and not law.
(ii) The court must be satisfied by 'irrefragable evidence' that there was a mistake in the expression of the contract; that means there must be no doubt whatever about it.
(iii) The mistake must be that of both parties and not merely that of one. In *Higgins* v. *Northampton Corporation* (1927) the Corporation put its seal to a document that correctly expressed their intentions but not that of the plaintiff contractor. There was no power to correct it.
(iv) Until *Joscelyne* v. *Nissen* (1970), it was commonly said that the courts could only rectify a document if there was 'an antecedent binding contract' and not just a common intention to enter a written contract in certain terms. But in that case, the Court of Appeal rejected this view and rectified a written agreement even though there was no previous binding contract but only a common intention to make a contract in certain terms.

Mr Joscelyne had entered into an agreement with his daughter whereby he transferred to her a house and his car hire business on consideration of her paying him a pension for life, and also all his gas, electricity and coal bills. The written document, however, merely recorded an agreement to 'discharge all expenses' of the house, which clearly was not wide enough to include the father's bill for gas, etc. The daughter did in fact pay all such bills until she quarrelled with the father. The court held that it was sufficient that both parties intended to incorporate such a term in the written agreement, in spite of the fact that there was no prior binding contract before the written agreement came into existence. It therefore rectified that document by writing in an obligation to pay the bills named.

In *Thomas Bates & Son Ltd* v. *Wyndham* (1981) a lease had been renewed without the insertion of an arbitration clause which had been in the earlier one. The Court of Appeal held that it could be rectified where the mistake was on the part of one party, if:

(a) he believed that the term was incorporated;
(b) if the other side knew that, due to a mistake, it was not;
(c) if that side failed to notify the other;
(d) if it was inequitable for that party to resist rectification.

But where parol evidence is admitted to support a plea of rectification, the judge must not use it to construe the contract.

9.04 Visible deletions from documents

For a long time the law was that if the parties had deleted a passage from the written document, but that passage was still readable, that deletion could not be used to construe what remained.

In *Inglus* v. *Buttery & Co.* (1878), a shipowner entered into a contract to the enlargement and refurbishment of a steel ship to Lloyds A100 standards. Part of the contract read

'Iron work – the plating of the hull to be carefully overhauled and repaired *but if any new plating is required the same to be paid for extra.*'

The last words had been deleted and initialed by both parties but were still visible.

In the House of Lords, Lord Hatherley said

'Nor can I think, and I believe your Lordships will concur with me in this opinion, that it is legitimate to look at those words which appear upon the face of the agreement with a line drawn through them, and

which are expressly, by the intention of all the parties to the agreement,
deleted, that is to say, done away with, and wholly abolished.

'It is not legitimate to read them and to use them as bearing upon the
meaning of that which has become the real contract between the
parties, namely, the final arrangement of the document which we must
now proceed to construe.'

However, in *Moltram Consultants Ltd* v. *Bernard Sunley & Sons Ltd*
(1975), which concerned a contract to build a supermarket in Zaire, the
standard form conferred a right of set off in favour of the employers. This
had been deleted but was still visible. A number of subcontractors and
material suppliers engaged in the popular African custom of driving a load
of materials through one gate of the site, getting a delivery note signed and
then exiting with the full load through the other gate, no doubt with the
full connivance of the gateman there. They then returned with another
delivery note and the happy circle proceeded.

As a result, the architect's weekly certificates resulted in the payment to
the main contractor of sums in excess of those correctly due and these
amounted to some £33,526. Bernard Sunley, the main contractors, then
sued for five weeks'unpaid certified sums amounting to £44,991.

On an application for summary payment under Order 14 R.S.C. the
employers claimed to be entitled to 'set off'the £33,526 and asked for leave
to defend. Leave was refused and judgment was given for £44,991. A
judge, the Court of Appeal and finally the House of Lords refused to set
aside that judgment. In the House, Lord Cross said:

'Condition 28(d) states that the only sums which can be deducted from
the amount stated to be due in an interim certificate are

(i) retention money and
(ii) any sum previously paid.

'It is, moreover, to be noted that the printed form which the parties
used provided for a third permissible deduction which the parties
deleted. It ran as follows:

"(iii) any amount which the employer or the co-ordinator on his
behalf shall be entitled to deduct from or set off against any money
due from him to the contractor (including any retention money) in
virtue of any provisions of the contract or any breach thereof by the
contractor".

'When the parties use a printed form and delete parts of it one can,
in my opinion, pay regard to what has been deleted as part of the

surrounding circumstances in the light of which one must construe what they have chosen to leave in.

The fact that they deleted (iii) shows that these parties directed their minds (*inter alia*) to the question of deductions under the principle of *Mondel* v. *Steel* (1841) and decided that no such deductions should be allowed.'

'*A fortiori* no deduction could have been allowed for an alleged mistake by the architect in issuing a certificate.

'The claim to reopen the certificate would have had to be dealt with in an arbitration under condition 33.'

The *Mondel* v. *Steel* case was one in which the defendants had contracted to build a ship for the plaintiff for £3,608. The plaintiff paid most of this sum but withheld £220 claiming that the ship had been built defectively and not up to specification. A jury decided this to be so. The Court of Exchequer held that the plaintiff was entitled only to withhold this money as a deduction from the agreed price on the sale of goods 'between the ship as she was and what she ought to have been according to the contract', but was not entitled to withhold monies by way of set off for a claim for damages. He was therefore entitled, having secured an abatement of price, to bring a separate action for damages.

The reference by Lord Cross to 'the question of deductions under the principle of *Mondel* v. *Steel*' is therefore misleading. There is no common law right of set off for unliquidated or unqualified claims for damages. However, the crux of the case is that the courts are entitled to look at deletions from a printed standard form in order to deduce the intentions of the parties.

9.05   Contracts and deeds

One trap that the businessman can easily fall into is the legal doctrine that a binding agreement in writing can be merged into a subsequent deed, and swallowed up by it.

This was expressed by Mr Justice Stamp in *Hisset* v. *Reading Roof Co.* (1968) when he said:

'It is of course the law of England that if two parties to a single contract embody its terms in a deed which they both execute, the simple contract is thereby discharged, just as a simple contract debt is merged in a judgment. You cannot have two agreements covering the same matters at the same time.'

This principle was restated by Lord Russell in *Knight Sugar Co* v. *Alberta Railway Co.* (1938) when he said:

'It is well settled, that, where parties enter into an executory agreement which is to be carried out by deed afterwards to be executed, the real completed contract is to be found in the deed. The contract is merged in the deed.

'The most common instance, perhaps, of this merger is a contract for sale of land followed by conveyance on completion. All the provisions of the contract which the parties intend should be performed by the conveyance are merged in the conveyance, and all the rights of the purchaser in relation thereto are thereby satisfied.'

He did, however, add an important qualification:

'An instance may be found in *Palmer* v. *Johnson* in which it was held that a purchaser could, after conveyance, rely upon a provision of the contract and obtain compensation.

The foundation of this decision was that, upon the construction of the contract, the provision for compensation applied after completion. In other words, the parties did not intend it to be performed by the subsequent deed, and it was therefore not satisfied by, or merged in, that deed.'

In more modern times, the difficulty has been resolved by asking the question whether the parties in fact did intend to incorporate in their later deed all the terms of their original agreement.

In the *International Press Centre* v. *Norwich Union* (1986), the parties had entered into an agreement by which the defendants pre-let, before construction, the Shoe Lane building off Fleet Street. An express term of that agreement was that the Norwich Union warranted that the building would be 'erected in a good and substantial and workmanlike manner and with the best materials of their respective kind obtainable'. When the building was constructed, a lease by deed was entered into between the two parties, whereby the lessees undertook

'From time to time and at all times during the said term to keep the demised premises and the fixtures therein in good and substantial repair, order and condition and where necessary through any cause whatsoever to rebuild, reconstruct or replace the demised premises or any part thereof ...'

The building proved defective in that mosaic cladding had to be replaced by the tenants at a cost of £378,538.

In the subsequent action, it was claimed that the lease by deed had superseded entirely the original agreement pre-letting the premises. It was held that the obligation of the agreement were not on the facts superseded by the subsequent deed.

However, it is clearly very important that any subsequent agreement by a deed or a conveyance should exactly replicate the original agreement or make clear what terms of the original agreement are not superseded by the subsequent deed.

Table of Cases

Note

A photocopy of the full judgments in any of the cases listed below can be obtained from the British Library through any public library.

References are to section numbers.

Table of Statutes

Index

Note: Numbers following entries refer to section numbers.